Handbook of Inflation Indexed Bonds

Edited by

John Brynjolfsson
Vice President and
Fixed Income Portfolio Manager
PIMCO

and

Frank J. Fabozzi, Ph.D., CFA
Adjunct Professor of Finance
School of Management
Yale University

Published by Frank J. Fabozzi Associates

Cover design by Scott C. Riether

ISBN: 1-883249-48-1

Printed in the United States of America

Table of Contents

Contributing Authors

Roger L. Anderson	U.S. Department of the Treasury
Karim Basta	Merrill Lynch
Daniel S. Bernstein	Bridgewater Associates, Inc.
John Brynjolfsson	PIMCO
John Casaudoumecq	Salomon Smith Barney
Michael Chadwick	ABN AMRO Australia Ltd.
Raymond T. Dalio	Bridgewater Associates, Inc.
Mark Deacon	U.K. Debt Management Office
J. Benson Durham	TIAA-CREF
Frank J. Fabozzi	Yale University
Andrew C. Fairbanks	Prudential Securities
Victor A. Gallo	Jackson National Life Insurance Company
P. Brett Hammond	TIAA-CREF
Alan Heuberger	W.H. Gates Foundation
William Kan	Merrill Lynch
Christopher F. Kinney	Brown Brothers Harriman & Co.
Martin Klaponski	Merrill Lynch
David B. LeRoux	Jackson National Life Insurance Company
William T. Lloyd	Barclays Capital
Gerald Lucas	Merrill Lynch & Company
Barbara J. Moore	SEI Investments
Ciaran O'Hagan	CIC
Wesley Phoa	Capital Management Sciences
Timothy Quek	Merrill Lynch & Company
Edward P. Rennie	PIMCO
Andrew Rosen	Salomon Smith Barney
William A. Schneider	DiMeo, Schneider & Associates, L.L.C.
Michael Schumacher	Salomon Smith Barney
Laurence B. Siegel	The Ford Foundation

Foreword

For any of you investors that are befuddled as to where to put your money to work, Uncle Sam has come up with a potential remedy. It's a remedy that comes as close to resembling an investment, with nothing to lose but a lot to gain, as anything I've seen in the investment world and it's sure to put an authentic smiley face on your investment portfolio for years to come. It's called an inflation-indexed bond and I'm extremely bullish on this instrument.

In mid-1996 the Treasury headed by Secretary Robert Rubin announced that the U.S. government would be in the business of selling inflation-indexed bonds — bonds that adjust their total annual yield for changes in the inflation rate. If your primary concern in managing institutional or retail funds is to earn a stable return that exceeds the rate of inflation, then these bonds may be for you. They come as close to an outright "guarantee" that the funds invested will beat inflation as you can get, and for that reason alone they're worthy of any investor's or trustee's consideration whether investing $10,000 or $140 billion like my own firm PIMCO. While these bonds are new to the U.S. financial markets, they are not new instruments. Inflation-indexed bonds have actually been used in Canada and the U.K. for some years now — Canada since 1991 and the U.K. from 1981 — and other countries such as Australia, New Zealand, and Sweden.

Inflation-indexed bonds differ from normal Treasury issues in one dramatic way. When you buy a normal Treasury bond, the coupon or annual interest payment is fixed. It won't change from the time you buy it until the day it matures. That's why bonds are called fixed income investments. These indexed bonds, however, change their annual payment, and ultimate principal value, based upon the changing rate of inflation. If inflation goes up you get paid more. If inflation goes down you get paid less.

Although many of the details of these bonds may seem complex, the fundamentals behind them are quite simple. Each indexed bond whether it has a maturity of 5, 10, or 30 years offers an initial interest rate that should be considered an investor's "real" yield over and above the rate of inflation. For example, in July 1998 the Treasury auctioned $8 billion of a 30-year inflation-indexed bond with a real coupon rate of 3⅝%. That might seem pretty paltry considering you could have earned 5% with Treasury bills at the time and 5⅝% with government bonds, but it's really not. It only seems low because that's the yield before the government adds its annual adjustment for inflation. It's what we call the "real" yield or the yield that's available if inflation never existed in the first place. We all know, however, that inflation has become an almost permanent part of our lives, so the U.S. Treasury will top that real 3⅝% yield off with an annual adjustment for inflation. Let's say inflation's average is 2% over the next year. Well your actual return or yield that the government is going to pay you will be 3⅝% + 2% for inflation or 5⅝%. That 5⅝% now starts to look very attractive when compared to bank CDs, long-term Treasuries, or even common stocks.

This adjustment process for inflation continues year after year until your bond matures, in July 2028, so if you hold that investment until maturity, you're going to be "guaranteed" a yield that's 3⅝% above inflation no matter what. Sounds pretty good doesn't it? Well, it is. London's *Financial Times* praised the bonds as a "risk-free asset" that "deserve warm welcome." *The Wall Street Journal* wrote that "conservative investors who flock to Treasury bonds for safety may soon have even less reason to worry." I think they're right.

But there's a small catch. While you're guaranteed to beat inflation, the price of these bonds will still go up and down in the open market. Not that much, mind you, but enough to make these bonds different from Treasury bills or a money market account. The fact is, that while you're guaranteed a certain "real" yield over and above inflation, the price of the bond itself fluctuates. If you decide to get out before the bond matures, you could have a capital gain or a capital loss that could affect your overall return from the bond.

There's a good deal more to learn about these types of bonds. That's where the *Handbook of Inflation Indexed Bonds* comes in. In this collection of 22 chapters you will find comprehensive coverage of their role in strategic asset allocation, the mechanics of these instruments, their valuation and price volatility characteristics, the experience of several countries that have issued these bonds, and strategies involving these instruments. The book is an indispensable volume for investors contemplating an allocation to inflation-indexed bonds — and given the significant benefits of these bonds, there should be a good number of such investors around.

William H. Gross
PIMCO

Chapter 1

Introduction

John Brynjolfsson
Vice President and Fixed Income Portfolio Manager
PIMCO

Frank J. Fabozzi, Ph.D., CFA
Adjunct Professor of Finance
School of Management
Yale University

This book provides comprehensive coverage of the history, structure, and opportunities of inflation-indexed bonds (IIBs). Our principal objective is to help the reader develop a working knowledge of an important new asset class that offers substantial risk/reducing opportunities.

The U.S. Treasury Department entered the IIB market in January 1997, and in its first 18 months of issuance sold $50 billion of the securities with maturities of 5 to 30 years. The Treasury did this in a time marked by disinflation and IIB underperformance, and significantly, the Treasury did it without much fanfare and with little dealer support. It's no surprise that the Treasury is pleased with the program and has expanded it.

The book's contributors are recognized investment professionals who have advanced the industry's understanding of IIBs. The chapters were selected for their insight and thoroughness, and range in difficulty from topical to complex. Several of the chapters present some rather detailed supporting evidence, but general readers of financial materials should have little trouble grasping the full intent of each argument. Individually, the chapters stand apart in their examination, interpretation, and presentation of historical evidence, markets, and market theory. Together they speak to the strengths and frailties of IIBs, addressing in detail the characteristics we feel demand particular thought and analysis. After a good deal of deliberation the editors decided against editing the chapters for content duplication. Simply stated, we felt doing so would detract more from the intent of the contribution of the author or authors than it would contribute to the flow of the book.

Inflation-protection bonds (IPBs), *Treasury inflation-protection securities* (TIPS), *real bonds*, *Consumer Price Index bonds* (CPI bonds), *Treasury inflation-indexed securities* (TIIS), *Treasury inflation securities* (TIS), *inflation-linked bonds* (ILBs), *inflation-linked securities* (ILS); these are just some of the acronyms and terms used in published works to describe the subject of our book. If the reader is looking for the "correct" term to encompass the entire asset class of inflation-adjusted securities, look elsewhere. Instead of offering absolutes we've opted to publish the chapters as submitted by the contributors, offering the reader redundancies, inconsistencies, contradictions, and even a few arguments that raise more questions than they answer. As editors, we're not trying to make anyone comfortable — IIBs are an investment product and like all investment products, for every thankful buyer, there is a thankful seller. We're trying to advance the understanding of the risk opportunities of IIBs, and by doing so motivate readers to rethink their financial goals and investing assumptions. We recognize this objective is perhaps difficult, but it is a prerequisite to effectively utilizing IIBs.

The book is organized into five sections. Section I covers strategic asset allocation. Section II introduces and defines terms, and discusses methods of analyses and evaluation. The chapters in this section introduce the concepts of real yield, the structure of IIBs, the theory of nominal yields, the risk premium, the interaction between real rates and inflation expectations, and the price volatility (duration) of IIBs. And, there is even comprehensive coverage of the Consumer Price Index (CPI), the index used in for IIBs by the Treasury, reminding us it's an index that has always been up for grabs, not the end-all measure of inflation. The experiences of the U.K., Australia, Canada, the United States, and France with IIBs are documented in Section III. Why sovereigns issue IIBs and the issuance by corporations and agencies in the United States is covered in Section IV. In Section V the use of IIBs by individual and institutional investors is explained.

Our hope is that after reading this book, you will be comfortable with the distinctive characteristics and benefits of IIBs and well on the way to discerning their strategic and tactical value.

Section I:

Strategic Asset Allocation

Chapter 2

Musings About Real Asset Allocation

John Brynjolfsson
Vice President and Fixed Income Portfolio Manager
PIMCO

INTRODUCTION

A purpose of this chapter is to motivate you into action. With that in mind it goes beyond describing inflation-protection bonds (IPBs). Hopefully it serves as a backdrop for the other chapters. But before action, there must be thought — so let me begin there.

THINK OUTSIDE THE BOX

The first concept I introduce here is "Think outside the box." This does not mean that thinking inside the box — subscribing to conventional wisdom — is wrong. *It simply means risk trusting your intellect too.* Oddly enough, investing in IPBs — one of the safest investments ever introduced — demands this type of "risk" taking!

Consider the following quote by Socrates that is a curious example of thinking outside the box: "Know thyself." One of the mistakes that investment managers in general make is spending too much effort knowing "thy-others." We spend our time expecting to stumble upon gifts. We forget that incremental returns are earned by focusing on what we do well.

For a foundation executive, as an example, the questions should be: What are our goals? What are our liabilities? Through introspection, looking at the organization first, thinking about how it differs from other organizations, and how it differs from the broader universe of investors, the executive can add incremental value. So "know thyself."

LIABILITY DETERMINATION FIRST

One translation of modern portfolio theory (MPT) I hear all too often is "diversification is the only free lunch." There is an underlying assumption that must be satisfied before this conclusion applies, however. MPT assumes that economic actors

5

have completed an introspection. They must have eliminated their idiosyncratic risks and addressed their unique operational considerations first. Only then, can we conclude that diversification is their last remaining opportunity for a "free lunch."

If a university has a staircase with ice on it, diversification is not the best way to mitigate that risk. Spreading some salt would be its first free lunch. Turning to idiosyncratic risks of a financial nature, if the university has a goal of delivering goods and services to the community for posterity, then mitigating that risk involves managing endowment assets in the context of the perpetual real liability. This liability is not fixed in dollars and cents. It is fixed in the amount of goods and services which will hopefully be delivered to the community. Once again, before MPT can be applied, the idiosyncratic liabilities need to be addressed.

IMPLEMENTING MODERN PORTFOLIO THEORY

In order to implement MPT, market and investor inputs are required. Market inputs such as returns, volatilities, and correlations for each asset class are in some cases observable, but more typically they are not. Investor inputs, as I alluded to earlier, are just as important and may be more important, than market inputs. Both types of inputs are often subjective. All too frequently in order to arrive at inputs which are less subjective, historical data are relied on heavily. The following discussion explores this tendency.

The Correlation Input Drawn from History

One of the most important inputs for an MPT optimization is a correlation matrix. The correlation between two assets is a quantification of the extent to which the returns of two assets tend to move together (positive correlation), independently (zero correlation) or in mirror images (negative correlation). We can examine how robust typical correlation inputs are by creating a simple simulation that uses known underlying correlations between two assets to generate the more commonly observed correlation figures used by practitioners. The result is startling.

Arbitrarily we can call the two assets "Bonds" and "IPBs." We can fix the underlying the correlations to 0.4 (i.e., 40%) for the first 10 years, and then to zero (as might be the case if there were a structural change in the economy) for the next 10 years. Although we are able to fix the underlying correlation, we will not actually define the asset returns — a randomizer, using the correlations we provide, generates the two sets of simulated monthly asset returns. Unfortunately, real world investors don't get to see the underlying correlation, all they get to see is the outcome.

Exhibit 1 provides a graph of the outcome. The jagged line in the exhibit uses rolling 12-month periods of data to generate each of the points plotted as a correlation. Given such series of points, the investors are supposed to be able to determine the true underlying correlation, which is not observable, but for the convenience of the reader is shown as the dashed line.

Exhibit 1: Correlation Outcome (Simulated)

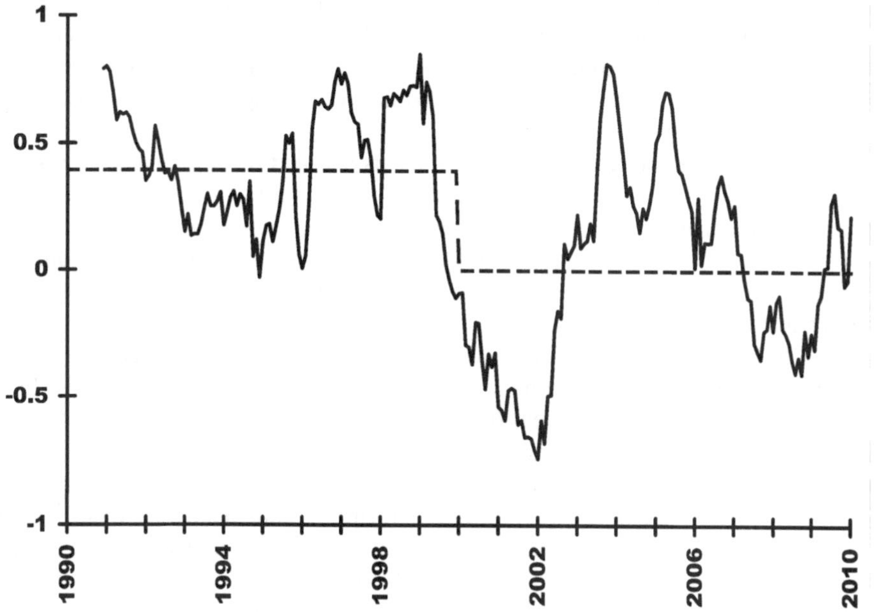

A shrewd analyst might be able to conclude that correlation "kind of" trended down. Others probably wouldn't be so discerning, and therefore would conclude that the correlation seems to be about 0% throughout. The ultra discerning analyst would, of course, have a great explanation for each twist and turn in the graph based on a plethora of "current events."

My point here is that you should not rely too heavily on historical data. Do your homework and understand what it is that is generating the observed correlations or returns, because that will give you a better insight into, or at least another angle on, what the future risks, returns, and correlation will be.

RECOMMENDATIONS FOR IMPLEMENTING A REAL ASSET ALLOCATION POLICY

I have four specific recommendations for implementing a real asset allocation policy. The first is to maximize real returns, not nominal returns. You can look at real returns and real risks for every asset class. In fact, it is easier to look at, and understand the economics of the real returns and real risks for asset classes, since they simply involve inputs (labor and capital), process (productivity), and outputs (goods and services). The economic forces that generated these past real returns are the same forces that will drive real returns in the future. In other words, to a large extent you can ignore all purely monetary phenomena.

My second recommendation is: "Look forward, not backward." This should be obvious, but many practitioners and academics in the interest of being objective ignore this simple reality altogether. When you are doing an asset allocation, you do not want to put your money into a portfolio that has done well in the past, you want to put it into a portfolio that will do well in the future, when you can reap the benefits of owning it.

"Optimize solutions, not constraints" is my next recommendation. I often run optimizations completely unconstrained. This is a technique that will help you avoid the arbitrary nature of the constrained Markowitz approach. In other words, if you have a lot of constraints, and you run a Markowitz optimization, the software will tell you more about the constraints that are binding than the asset classes that are generating value.

Subsequently, once you know which asset classes are generating value for you, it is easy to introduce the constraints. By ignoring constraints at the first stage, you will make a good deal of concrete progress, and have a solid reality check for the somewhat arbitrary solutions that subsequent constrained optimizations generate.

The fourth recommendation is to "identify fundamental classes." There are four fundamental asset classes that I have identified. The equity asset class represents a risk allocation to the real output of the economy. The nominal bond asset class does the opposite, locking in nominal value and nominal growth of capital. The inflation-linked bond asset class, within which I would include more general inflation sensitive assets, locks in real returns based on current prospects. Cash is the fourth asset class. Resist the temptation to include every new investment product as a separate asset class. Such opportunities should be explored at the implementation stage — not asset allocation stage — of your investment process.

EXAMPLE

I implemented these four recommendations and obtained the efficient frontier shown in Exhibit 2. Obviously, I needed inputs. Ignoring my very own recommendation, I started out with historical inputs for equities, bonds, and cash as a base case.[1] Inputs for inflation-linked bonds are also required. There is a nice feature about inflation-linked bonds, which doesn't apply to any of the other asset classes. For inflation-linked bonds, future real returns are contractually guaranteed by the U.S. Treasury.[2]

In terms of risk, I have estimated the risk for inflation-linked bonds as 4.2%. If you were looking at real risk and you had a time frame that coincides

---

[1] I have done this in the interest of clarity. My purpose here is to provide an understandable example, not to justify anyone's particular inputs.
[2] Assuming the securities are held to maturity and coupons are reinvested at the original real internal rate of return.

with the maturity of the inflation-linked bond, in essence, the risk would be zero. However, on a mark-to-market basis, ignoring liabilities, inflation-linked bonds do have some risk. It is substantially less than the risk of nominal bonds, and I would suggest, even less than the risk of cash. To be conservative, I have used a number equal to the real risk of cash.

Incidentally, for long-term investors cash is not a riskless asset in real or nominal terms. The real return on cash, even though it may be known for the next three months, over time, is quite volatile. During the entire decade of the 1970s, cash averaged a negative real return. During the 1980s, because of the budget deficits, trade deficits, and a monetary authority that was crushing inflation, the real return on cash was extremely high, almost 5%.

CONCLUSION

We are now equipped to define "real asset allocation." Certainly this term refers to optimizing real returns and real risks. However, it means more. One should look forward and consider liabilities. Most importantly one should "think outside the box."

Exhibit 2: Real Asset Allocation: The New Efficeint Frontier

Asset	Real Risk (%)	Real Return (%)
Equity	20.6	7.2
Bonds	7.1	2.1
Cash	4.2	0.6
TIPS*	4.2	3.0

* For TIPS the reported real risk is estimated and real returns are contractually guaranteed. Other risks and returns are based on Ibbotson 1926-1995.

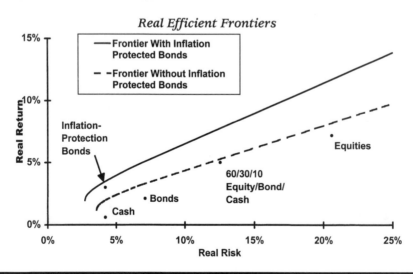

Chapter 3

Shifting the Efficient Frontier with Inflation-Indexed Bonds

Raymond T. Dalio
President/CIO
Bridgewater Associates, Inc.

Daniel S. Bernstein
Director of Research
Bridgewater Associates, Inc.

INTRODUCTION

The recent issuance of U.S. inflation-indexed bonds by the U.S. Treasury is one of the most important developments for U.S. investors to come along in a long time. inflation-indexed bonds provide investors with a new, U.S. dollar denominated asset class that has: (1) a U.S. dollar real return that is known and fixed to maturity; (2) an expected return that is comparable to conventional nominal bonds; (3) a risk which is considerably lower than conventional bonds of the same duration; and, (4) correlations with conventional bonds and stocks that are low or negative (depending on the time horizon).

As a result of these characteristics, inflation-indexed bonds tend to displace conventional bonds and merit a significant allocation in portfolios that seek an optimal amount of return relative to risk. In addition, for investors with inflation sensitive liabilities, they are clearly the lowest risk investment. In these respects, U.S. inflation-indexed bonds will provide investors with greater diversity, an important ingredient required to create balanced portfolios.

Needless to say, we are excited about this development. For a number of years, we have managed global inflation-indexed bond portfolios which, through currency hedging, provided investors with a facsimile of what the Treasury has issued. In the process, we developed a deep appreciation of this asset's characteristics and idiosyncrasies. We also learned how to trade them against each other based on anomalies in their relative pricing. The development of a U.S. inflation-indexed bond market will add depth and liquidity to other inflation-indexed markets.

This chapter discusses the characteristics of inflation-indexed bonds, and through an analysis of their impact on the efficient frontier, how they fit into investor's portfolios.

11

Exhibit 1: Inflation-Linked Yield Estimate and Actual

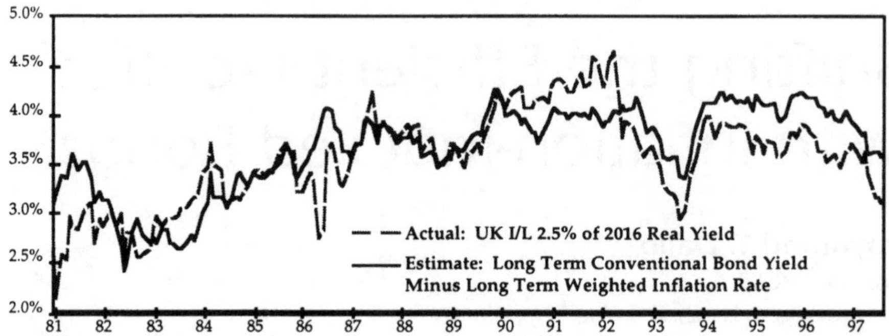

INFLATION-INDEXED BOND KEY CHARACTERISTICS

In order to study the implications of including U.S. inflation-indexed bonds in portfolios, we have estimated how we think they would have behaved over the past 40 years. This was based both on their behavior in other countries, such as in the U.K. after 1981, and the behavior which is implied by their structure.

The pricing and return of an inflation-indexed bond revolves around the real yield, therefore, to estimate how a U.S. inflation-indexed bond would have performed in the past is a matter of estimating real yields in the past. Of course, if we could measure inflation expectations precisely, this would be a simple task — real yields would be roughly equal to the nominal bond yield minus inflation expectations. Not having explicitly stated 10-year inflation expectations to rely on, we used a proxy for them based on the long term, cyclically adjusted, core inflation rate. For example, Exhibit 1 shows where inflation-indexed bond real yields actually traded since they were issued in 1981 in the U.K. Also shown is our estimate of the inflation-indexed real yield based on the conventional bond yield versus this inflation expectation proxy. As the exhibit suggests, our estimate is a fairly good, though certainly not perfect, proxy for how inflation-indexed bond real yields were actually priced by the market. The estimates have worked comparably well in other countries.

In order to estimate what inflation-indexed bond yields would have been in the past in the United States and how U.S. inflation-indexed bond yields would have behaved on a monthly basis, we went through the same process for the United States. While imperfect, the estimates are more than adequate given our purposes and are certainly better than the alternative of assuming no volatility in real bond yields. The derived estimates of past U.S. real bond yields are shown in Exhibit 2. As indicated, we estimate that real bond yields would have averaged about 3.5% over the last 40 years. Assuming that our process in the United States works about as well as it did in the U.K. since 1981, the average error in any one of the estimated points in the exhibit is about 25 bp. Of course, we used the actual real yield on the U.S. inflation-indexed bond ever since January 1997 when that bond was first issued.

With an estimate of where the inflation-indexed real yield would have traded, it is a straightforward calculation to derive the total return of a U.S. inflation-indexed bond. We derived a total return based on a 10-year maturity, roughly 8-year duration (with respect to changes in real yields) U.S. inflation-indexed bond.

The Real Returns and Risks of U.S. Inflation-Indexed Bonds Relative to Fixed Income Bonds and Stocks

In Exhibit 3, we show what the total real return of a U.S. inflation-indexed bond would have looked like given the real yields indicated in Exhibit 2. We were then able to make a comparison to the real returns of 8-year duration conventional government bonds and the S&P 500 over the same time frame. Exhibit 3 shows the cumulative *real* value of a dollar invested in each asset.[1]

Exhibit 2: Estimated U.S. Inflation-Indexed Bond Real Yield

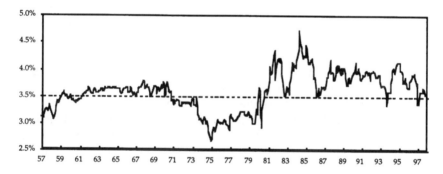

Exhibit 3: Real Value of a Dollar Invested in U.S. Asset Classes

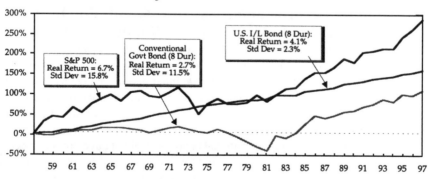

[1] The average real return is slightly higher than the average real yield due to a positively sloped yield curve.

We make several observations about Exhibit 3. The first is that one should not necessarily extrapolate the past returns. For example, many would adjust upward the historical bond return and perhaps downward the historical stock return. But the historical riskiness of assets is probably more representative, particularly in a relative sense. Exhibit 3 indicates that in real terms, the riskiness of traditional stocks and bonds in comparison to that of inflation-indexed bonds is massive. For example, in the numbers over the past 40 years, conventional bonds carried about 5 times the risk of inflation-indexed bonds in real terms, and stocks carried about 7 times the risk in real terms. This is because inflation-indexed bonds are directly linked to inflation and the other assets are not, and the volatility of real yields is considerably less than the volatility of nominal yields.

Why do inflation-indexed bonds have some real return risk? When one buys inflation-indexed bonds, one locks in a known real return over the life of the bond. However, just as year-by-year returns of a conventional bond are driven by movements in the market-determined nominal bond yield, so the year-by-year returns of an inflation-indexed bond are determined by movements of the market determined inflation-indexed real yield. Therefore, interim volatility of inflation-indexed bonds is a function of the volatility of real yields.

Real yields, by definition, are not affected by changes in inflation expectations, and instead are affected by less volatile factors such as fluctuations in real economic growth rates and the tightness of monetary policies. We estimate that about 70% of the historical movements of nominal yields on conventional bonds are driven by changing inflation expectations. The fact that real yields are far more stable than nominal yields can be seen in countries that have issued both inflation-indexed bonds and conventional bonds. All this factored into our estimate of where the U.S. inflation-indexed real bond yield would have traded, which as previously indicated, would have had a range of about 3% to 4.5%, far less than the 3% to 15% range of nominal bond yields over the same period. So in the end, even though inflation-indexed bonds do carry some uncertainty of real return, the stability of their yields has meant that this volatility has been very small relative to other asset classes.

The Nominal Returns and Risks of U.S. Inflation-Indexed Bonds Relative to Fixed Income Bonds and Stocks

In Exhibit 4, we show the cumulative nominal value of a dollar invested in the same assets as above and their returns and risks in nominal terms. Also indicated is the "return" and "risk" of inflation itself. Of course, inflation-indexed bonds have had a higher risk when measured in nominal terms because inflation itself has "risk" in nominal terms. Note that the annual standard deviation of inflation was 3.2% while the standard deviation of inflation-indexed bonds on an annual basis is slightly higher at 3.7%. Even in nominal terms, conventional bonds were about three times as risky as inflation-indexed bonds and stocks were about four times as risky as inflation-indexed bonds. Note also the gradually increasing margin between the inflation-indexed bond nominal return and inflation, which again reflects the stability of real return.

Exhibit 4: Nominal Value of a Dollar Invested in U.S. Asset Classes

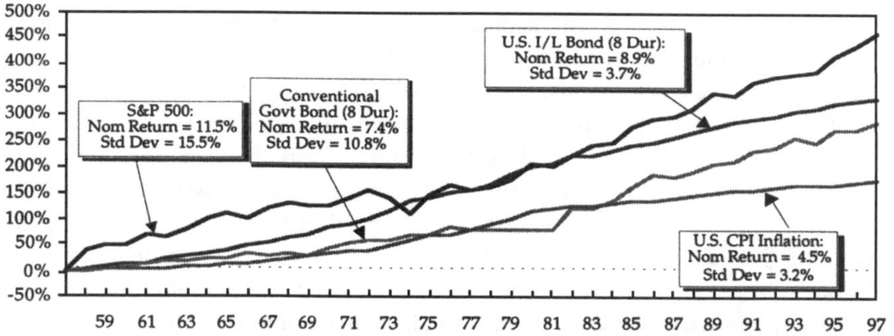

U.S. Inflation-Indexed Bond Correlation to Other U.S. Assets and Inflation

Expected returns, risks, and correlations are the building blocks of modern portfolios. So far, we have looked at the return and risk characteristics of U.S. inflation-indexed bonds and how they compare against traditional stocks and bonds in the United States. We will now examine their correlations to other asset classes.

Before looking at the numbers, you can imagine why U.S. inflation-indexed bonds should have a low correlation with stocks and bonds. Since inflation-indexed bonds are structurally tied to inflation, we know that over longer time horizons inflation-indexed bond returns will have a strong positive correlation with inflation. Conventional bonds, of course, are likely to have a negative correlation with inflation since their returns are generally inversely related to changes in nominal interest rates and inflation. Stocks tend to be positively correlated with nominal bonds. So, we would expect inflation-indexed bonds to be positively correlated with inflation and negatively correlated with bonds and stocks.

This is borne out by the correlations reported in Exhibit 5 which shows the correlations between U.S. inflation-indexed bonds and inflation over everything from 1-month returns up to 10-year returns. Also shown in the exhibit is the correlation between traditional bonds and stocks and inflation over all of these time horizons. The numbers generally confirm what is intuitively obvious. The correlation between inflation-indexed bond returns and inflation is moderately positive over short time frames and very highly positive over long time frames.

The reason why the correlation between inflation-indexed bonds and inflation varies is because of movements in real yields. If, for example, real yields were to move higher in a month when inflation rises, that could make the inflation-indexed bond return fall even though inflation rose. But as we already noted, real yields tend to be fairly stable. Over long time frames, the impact of movements of real yields is small in relation to the changes in the inflation rate, which is why we get long-term correlations that are in excess of 90%. Inflation-indexed bond returns will never be 100% positively correlated with inflation because there is always some change in the real yield. Also note that the correlation between both conventional bonds and stocks and inflation is negative over all time frames reported. Again, this is not a surprise. In the past, it has always been the case that any upward movement in inflation, whether long term or short term, has had a very negative effect on both stocks and bonds. For example, both assets performed poorly during the 1970s as inflation rose and eroded real yields. On the other hand, the disinflationary period of the 1980s brought strong returns for both stocks and bonds.

We also looked at correlations between inflation-indexed bonds and traditional stocks and bonds. These are shown in Exhibit 6. Note that the correlation between inflation-indexed bonds and conventional bonds is high on a very short-term basis. That is because short-term movements in nominal yields and real yields tend to move together, while the impact of changes in monthly CPI inflation tends to be small, because the changes in real yields dominate inflation-indexed bond performance. But as the time frame is extended, the correlation between inflation-indexed bonds and conventional bonds drops precipitously and turns negative. Again, this is because over longer time horizons the inflation impact grows while the volatility of real yields becomes less significant. Negative correlations between inflation-indexed bonds and conventional bonds exist when looking at 3-year returns or longer. The correlation between inflation-indexed bonds and stocks are close to zero over short time frames and also becomes negative as the return time frame was extended and changes in inflation become dominant in inflation-indexed returns.

Exhibit 5: Correlations Between U.S. Asset Classes and U.S. Inflation

	I/L Bond (8 Yr. Dur)	Conventional Bond (8 Yr. Dur)	S&P 500
1 Mo.	48.2%	−10.8%	−16.6%
3 Mo.	56.2%	−16.3%	−20.5%
12 Mo.	77.5%	−25.3%	−24.9%
3 Yr.	93.4%	−27.5%	−25.5%
5 Yr.	94.1%	−20.1%	−24.5%
10 Yr.	96.8%	−8.6%	−19.4%

Exhibit 6: Correlations to U.S. Inflation-Indexed Bonds (8 Year Duration)

	Conventional Bond (8 Yr. Dur)	S&P 500
1 Mo.	77.7%	12.0%
3 Mo.	65.4%	1.8%
12 Mo.	27.8%	−16.5%
3 Yr.	−8.5%	−28.3%
5 Yr.	−2.6%	−27.2%
10 Yr.	−1.3%	−24.4%

The fact that correlations between inflation-indexed bonds and inflation are high, and inflation-indexed bonds and other financial assets are low or negative (depending on the time frame one chooses) confirms what is intuitively obvious: that these securities are a highly effective inflation hedge and an excellent portfolio diversifier.

U.S. INFLATION-INDEXED BONDS IN THE PORTFOLIO: AN EFFICIENT FRONTIER ANALYSIS

Given the characteristics of inflation-indexed bonds, how much should be added to an existing portfolio and at the expense of what? One way to answer this question is through an analysis of the impact of U.S. inflation-indexed bonds on a U.S. efficient frontier. We did this both in real terms and in nominal terms to reflect both of the previously mentioned perspectives.

To calculate an efficient frontier, one obviously needs assumptions of return, risk, and correlation for each asset. To derive ours, we adjusted returns to what we think are reasonable forward-looking expectations. We started with real returns. For the real return of U.S. inflation-indexed bonds, we used 3.5%. This is about where the real yield of the U.S. inflation-indexed bond has been trading since inception and is equal to the long-term average real yield that we came up with in our estimates. For conventional nominal bonds, we also used a real return of 3.5%. This is consistent with our view that the pricing of inflation-indexed bonds has typically been for a roughly similar expected return as conventional bonds. A 3.5% real return on conventional bonds is also consistent with inflation expectations of about 2%, which is about where we think investors are "pricing" inflation as of this analysis. In other words, with bond yields running at about 5.5% and inflation expectations running at about 2%, the implied real yield of conventional bonds is about 3.5%.

For the U.S. stock return, we used the historical real return of 6.7% since 1958. While we think this is at the high end of reasonable prospective returns, we know that many investors use the historical return of stocks as a proxy for their return, so we made no adjustments. For risk, we simply used the historical standard deviations of 1-year returns since 1958. That period encompasses both the non-volatile 1950s and 1960s and the volatile 1970s and 1980s, and therefore seems reasonable to us as a proxy period for risk. We also used the historical correlations since 1958, as we had no reason to believe that correlations would be significantly different going forward.

Exhibit 7 shows the results of our efficient frontier analysis in "real space." The real frontier represents the perspective of an investor with an inflation-sensitive liabilities' perspective. In the exhibit, the solid line indicates what the efficient frontier would look like with only the S&P 500 and 8-year duration conventional bonds. Moving up from the bottom of the solid line, which represents an all-bonds portfolio, one can see that initially risk is reduced and return is raised because of both the diversification and higher return benefits of stocks. Then the risk begins to rise as the portfolio is weighted more toward all stocks because the volatility of stocks overshadows the diversification benefits.

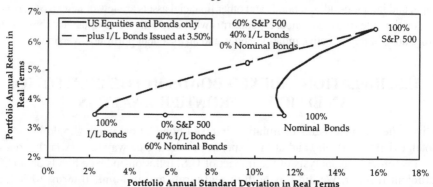

Exhibit 7: Real Efficient Frontiers

The dashed line in the exhibit is the efficient frontier that is the result of adding U.S. inflation-indexed bonds to a portfolio of traditional stocks and bonds. As indicated, the "real risk" of the portfolio was reduced substantially. This is a function of both the low real risk of U.S. inflation-indexed bonds themselves (2.3% annually) and the low/negative correlation between inflation-indexed bonds and the other assets. Efficient frontiers are only as good as the assumptions that go into them and different investors will make different assumptions. Nevertheless, the left-shifted impact on the efficient frontier due to inflation-indexed bonds is not highly sensitive to the assumptions we have made. We would note that the risk of inflation-indexed bonds is so much lower than conventional bonds that it would take dramatically higher risk assumptions and/or lower return assumptions for there to be no left-shifted impact at all.

We also ran the efficient frontier in "nominal space." (See Exhibit 8.) We did this by adding a 2% inflation expectation to all of our real return assumptions noted above. Again, historical risks and correlations were used as is. The picture is not much different. The risk reduction of shifting out of nominal bonds to inflation-indexed bonds is large, though a bit less than in real terms, and the trade-off once again becomes between risk and return. Again, this is a function of both the stability of U.S. inflation-indexed bonds, both in real and nominal terms, and their low/negative correlation with equities.

CONCLUSION

Inflation-indexed bonds have a unique set of return, risk, and correlation characteristics that clearly mark them as a new asset class. As we have noted, investors will form different assumptions about the attributes of these bonds; however, it is difficult to construct a reasonable set of expectations for inflation-indexed bonds that would not have a significant impact on the efficient frontier.

Exhibit 8: Nominal Efficient Frontiers

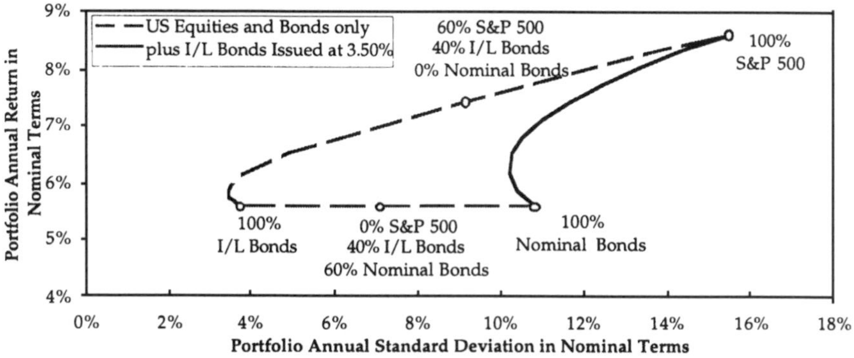

As the efficient frontier analysis indicates, inflation-indexed bonds tend to displace primarily conventional bonds. In low risk portfolios that are dominated by conventional bonds, this risk reduction is large. The efficient frontiers also show that combinations of inflation-indexed bonds and equities are less risky than combinations of conventional bonds and equities. Ultimately, this means that when inflation-indexed bonds are included in the portfolio, more weight can be given to equities without increasing the overall risk of the portfolio. This is even more true for investors that have inflation-sensitive liabilities where the risk reducing impact of inflation-indexed bonds is a certainty.

For these reasons, we expect that inflation-indexed bonds will ultimately significantly alter how investors approach the construction of their portfolios and will occupy a core position in many portfolios.

Chapter 4

Using Inflation-Indexed Securities for Retirement Savings and Income: The TIAA-CREF Experience

P. Brett Hammond
Manager, Corporate Projects
TIAA-CREF

INTRODUCTION

One of the principal potential uses of inflation-indexed securities is for retirement savings and income, but plan sponsors, plan providers, and individual retirement savers in the United States have little or no experience with using these instruments for pensions. TIAA-CREF,[1] the world's largest private pension system and the nation's premier retirement services provider for people who work in education, was an early backer of inflation-indexed bonds and supported enthusiastically the U.S. Treasury's plan to offer them. Once the Treasury took this step, TIAA-CREF introduced an inflation-linked bond variable annuity account to its 2 million participants in May 1997. As of mid-1998, it was the only such variable annuity in the United States.[2]

What are the attractions of inflation-indexed bonds for defined contribution pensions? How can inflation bonds be used to improve pensions? How is TIAA-CREF's experience with establishing an inflation-linked bond account instructive and what else could be done? Most important, what challenges did TIAA-CREF face along the way and how did it address them? TIAA-CREF's experience shows what is possible to do with inflation-indexed bonds to help

---

[1] Teachers Insurance Annuity Association — College Retirement Equities Fund

[2] Three other firms have introduced mutual funds based on inflation-indexed bonds: PIMCO, Brown Brothers Harriman, and American Century

---

The views expressed in this chapter are the author's alone and do not necessarily reflect the position of TIAA-CREF.

retirement savers and annuitants cope with one of the most important sources of risk to retirement income. It shows how far we can get with inflation bonds, but also how far we still need to go to take full advantage of these new instruments.

This chapter first reviews the purposes of using inflation-indexed bonds for pensions by contrasting the short- and long-term perspective on these new instruments. It then examines the issues pension systems face in helping individuals find inflation protection. It then details why TIAA-CREF responded to the advent of inflation-indexed bonds in the way it did. Finally, it addresses inflation-related issues and challenges that still remain for TIAA-CREF and other pension providers and briefly lists some practical options for future consideration.

The purpose of this chapter is to address in a highly practical way the consideration one pension system gave to the problem of inflation. The hope is that other organizations faced with similar challenges may find the responses to them instructive.

THE SHORT AND LONG-TERM CONTEXT FOR THE INFLATION-INDEXED BOND MARKET

The Shorter Run

So far, the U.S. inflation-indexed bond market hasn't behaved in a way that might make it especially attractive to dealers, individuals, and many institutional investors. Since January 1997, when inflation-indexed bonds were introduced, actual inflation rates and future inflation rate expectations have declined steadily. For example, the inflation rate for all of 1997 as measured by the Consumer Price Index (CPI-U) was a little over 1%, while the Producer Price Index declined absolutely.[3] Further, confidence was high that the current anti-inflation monetary policy regime in Washington would continue.

The effect on inflation-indexed bonds wasn't surprising. Leaving aside comparisons among bond durations, the yield (as of mid-1998) on the ordinary 10-year U.S. Treasury was well under 6% and the yield on the inflation-indexed 10-year Treasury was about 170 basis points less.

The list of unattractive features continued:

- Investors experienced significant price fluctuations in the two outstanding inflation-indexed bonds. Since it was issued, the 10-year inflation-indexed bond price return was significantly negative.
- Bid-ask spreads on inflation-indexed bonds were high and turnover low as compared to traditional benchmark Treasuries.
- Few corporations chose to issue inflation-indexed bonds.

---

[3] Calculation based on U.S. Bureau of Labor, monthly CPI-U, and PPI reports for 1997.

- Although the Chicago Board of Trade inaugurated in July 1997, a program of inflation-linked futures and options, three contracts traded the first day and then none for at least nine months.
- After many dealers established separate inflation bond desks, several quickly reduced or consolidated those operations.

All of this suggests that there was little worry that inflation would increase any time in the near or medium term and that dealers and investors did not experience the inflation bond market as an immediate success.

The Longer Run

But there were also some positive signs for the U.S. inflation-indexed bond market:

- The U.S. Treasury demonstrated its commitment to the future of the market by holding a series of 5- and 10-year inflation-indexed bond auctions and introducing a 30-year inflation-indexed bond, thereby establishing a full yield curve for those instruments. It also created the mechanisms for an inflation bond STRIPS market.
- In fiscal year 1997, the Treasury issued about $23 billion in inflation-indexed bonds — more than the total net new Treasury debt issued that year — with plans to issue about $32 billion per year in fiscal years 1998 and 1999.
- Compared to ordinary bonds, inflation-indexed bonds experienced lower yield and return volatility and relatively low correlations. This behavior is to be expected and should continue.

More generally, and most important, the short-run disappointments were predictable for three reasons. First, the inflation bond market was new and needed to develop further. Second, inflation was low, which in turn may have lowered the immediate impetus for many buyers to seek a short-term inflation hedge. Third, the long-term features of inflation-indexed bonds may not have been apparent to many in the market.

The Perspective of the Retirement Saver and Annuitant

In theory, the new inflation hedge offered by inflation bonds is especially applicable to retirement savers and annuitants for two related purposes. First, annuitants and older retirement savers are relatively vulnerable to a *steady erosion* of purchasing power due to many years of persistent inflation. Second, they are also vulnerable to a *sudden loss* of purchasing power, because of an inflationary spike like those of the early and late 1970s.

In the former instance, many younger breadwinners are relatively well protected from persistent inflation because, in the long run, salaries and wages track or exceed inflation. The result, for people whose retirement pay will be set as a percentage of final income (i.e., defined benefit pensions), is a built-in retirement pay escalator during their working lives. A similar escalator effect applies to people who set aside a portion of their income each year as retirement savings or have their employer do so in a defined contribution pension. In contrast to younger breadwinners, retirees' access to this escalator, however, is limited in many cases to Social Security, which is indexed annually to increases in the CPI. Other defined benefit pensions are rarely indexed to inflation and other defined contribution pensions are never indexed to inflation. Therefore, most retirees no longer have access to the automatic escalator effect provided by increases in salary and wages during their working lives.

In the latter instance, a sudden inflationary spike also differentially affects working and retired people. Although such a spike may immediately depress the real value of current income and wealth, including accumulated retirement savings, younger workers may have many years of employment ahead of them to adjust to this loss by saving more, working harder, or taking more risk with invested savings. In contrast, older workers nearing retirement and retirees may not have the luxury of time. Their choices may be limited to delayed retirement or significantly reduced consumption.

In sum, inflation of the persistent or sudden variety can affect older retirement savers and retirees differently than younger workers and their families. Older workers and retirees are more vulnerable to inflation, mainly because they have less access than younger workers to inflation-linked income sources and wealth.

TIAA-CREF EXPERIENCE WITH INFLATION

Over the years, inflation-driven issues such as these have provided a central focus for TIAA-CREF's pension design and protection. In fact, the three inflationary periods that occurred in 20th Century are deeply intertwined with fundamental changes in the TIAA-CREF system, including its creation and most important subsequent transformations.

World War I Inflation

In 1905, U.S. steel magnate Andrew Carnegie provided funds for a $15 million revolving fund — a free pension system — that was used to provide an annual retirement income of $400 plus half salary for the faculty at 96 colleges and universities. Unfortunately, this defined benefit plan quickly failed, because liabilities exceeded assets during a period of rapid salary and price increases and because the plan did not foresee the large number of eligible faculty and their widows.

In response, TIAA was founded in 1918 with a grant of $1 million from the Carnegie Corporation Foundation and chartered to contract with education and research institutions to provide defined contribution pensions to their employees based on a system of individual annuities invested in fixed assets. Other features of the system, many of which were new then but are now in widespread use, included full funding, contractual rights for policyholders, multiple employers and portability (to allow movement by faculty among employers) full and immediate vesting, no cash values prior to retirement, contributions on the part of participants, and low-cost (i.e., no agency) distribution. These elements allowed the company to insure pensions for faculty for more than two decades based on fixed accumulating and payout annuities.

Post World War II Inflation

What led TIAA to consider other pension options was post-World War II inflation, which jumped to an average of over 5% until the 1950s. Fixed annuity rates remained relatively high during the Depression but had declined after the war, and contribution rates for the big wave of newly retired faculty after the war were of course based on many years of low preinflation salaries. As a result, retirement benefits as a proportion of preretirement salary dropped substantially in the late 1940s and early 1950s. Other pension providers were faced with similar circumstances, but in the case of defined-benefit plans, employers rather than employees faced the challenge of meeting the promises they had made with eroding real assets and revenues.

Under William C. Greenough, the TIAA vice president, the company launched studies to discover how an annuity plan could respond more effectively to a variety of investment and inflation conditions. Greenough's 1951 report proposing the variable annuity sought a way to overcome some of the troubles inflicted by inflation.[4] By tracing the performance of common stocks over the previous 70 years, a TIAA study team found the key: a completely new instrument — christened a variable annuity — with a 100% equity investment base. An annuity plan invested in a broad range of common stocks over the period studied, 1880 to 1950, would have provided better returns and better purchasing power than from fixed-income investments:

> This economic study should result in a basic change in planning retirement systems in the future. The factors of inflation and deflation have pretty generally been disregarded in past planning, with unfortunate results. This study shows that common stock would have provided better returns than those available from fixed-income investment in most periods.[5]

The resulting separate legal, actuarial, and investment entity was called the College Retirement Equities Fund, or CREF.

Variable annuities are so common today that it is hard to realize that they were a new invention in 1952. Common stock and mutual fund ownership by indi-

[4] Greenough, *A New Approach to Retirement Income* (New York: TIAA-CREF, 1951), p. 5.
[5] *Ibid*, p. 6.

viduals was not nearly as widespread as it is today, especially in the aftermath of the Depression. This may have prompted some powerful insurance industry interests initially to oppose the concept.

Almost as important an invention as CREF itself was the education initiative that went with it. Meetings with educational associations, college boards of trustees, college administrators, and TIAA participants, all aided substantially in introducing the inflation-fighting purpose of the new variable annuity.

CREF's creation represented a truly significant expansion of investment choice for retirement savers and annuitants. TIAA-CREF was the first to offer to its plan participants the option of choosing how much of their premiums to allocate to the fixed-annuity account and how much to the new variable annuity. And, upon retirement, annuitants faced a similar choice about what proportion of their retirement income they wished to receive from the fixed or variable account. Along with new choices, retirement savers and annuitants also faced new risks, because neither their principal nor their earnings were guaranteed in exchange for the possibility of greater returns on equities purchased through variable annuities.

Was the creation of variable annuities the holy grail of inflation protection? The CREF Stock Account, as it is called, has done very well over the past 45 years, outpacing inflation by over 6% per year.

1970s Inflation

However, although CREF is inflation responsive, it isn't inflation proof. Exhibit 1 shows that CREF Stock Account accumulations failed to keep up with inflation during the 1970s and early 1980s, the 20th Century's third period of high U.S. inflation. The TIAA fixed income account had a similar experience. For retirement savers, this period reduced for a time the expected value of future retirement income based on pension savings and the earnings on those savings (this was mitigated somewhat by opportunities for dollar cost averaging as well as CREF's subsequent performance). For those receiving annuity income, the 1970s had a more directly negative impact. CREF annuity income rates dropped seven times between 1972 and 1982.

Today, TIAA-CREF's communications place more emphasis on the long-term returns to stocks and somewhat less emphasis on CREF as the original holy grail of inflation protection.

Although CREF represented an innovative step forward in the potential for preserving purchasing power, in the early 1980s TIAA reacted to stagflation by devising investment and income policies to improve inflation resistance.

TIAA made changes in its investment policy, which then emphasized corporate bonds held to maturity and mortgages. The company moved to corporate bonds of shorter maturities unless they included equity features that protected longer-term returns. The equity features turned out to be extremely successful in the 1980s although the shorter-maturity strategy missed the chance to lock up very high nominal returns at the beginning of the decade.

Exhibit 1: CREF Accumulation Units Versus Inflation: 1972-1992

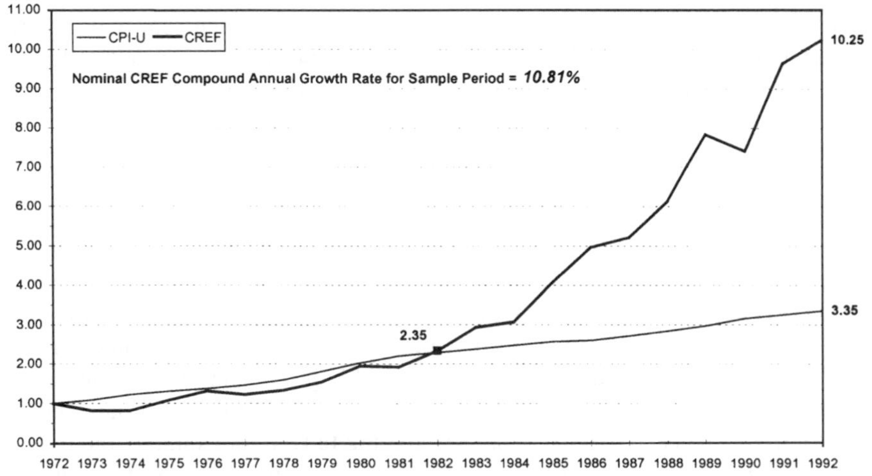

TIAA also focused on ways to tap revenue streams that could improve the mortgage portfolio's ability to hedge against inflation. TIAA developed the concept of participating mortgages where, as the lender on a long-term basis, TIAA received the interest rate on the loan plus a percentage of property income above a threshold amount. Loans without a participating feature were limited to shorter maturities. Participating loans today represent 40% of TIAA's mortgage loan portfolio.

And finally, in the early 1980s the TIAA Account moved into real estate as a major asset class for the benefit of participants, as a hedge against rising property prices.

On the retirement income side, in 1982, TIAA made changes by introducing the *graded benefit payment method* as an alternative to its standard annuity payment calculation method. This new guaranteed annuity option equipped fixed-income annuities to better accommodate inflation.[6] Under the graded method, annuity payments in the first year are based on an interest rate assumption (AIR) of 4% — higher than the TIAA minimum 2.5% guarantee, but lower than the total interest rate used for the TIAA standard method (this has recently been in the neighborhood of 7%).

The graded AIR is lower than the standard TIAA interest rate earned because under the graded method, the annuity dividend based on interest in excess of the 4% AIR is added to the annuity reserve in order to purchase additional annuity income for the following year. The remainder, including the guaranteed income, is paid as current income. The proportional benefit increase each year is close to the difference between a 4% rate and the total interest rate earned.

---

[6] For a more complete description, see Francis King and Michael Heller, "Inflation and the Graded Benefit Payment Method," *Research Dialogues* no. 46, TIAA-CREF (December 1995).

For many annuitants who retired at various times over the past 25 years, the graded payment method would have tracked inflation well as indicated by hypothetical illustrations prior to its introduction and actual experience afterward. However, as under CREF, the amount of income increase each year with a TIAA graded annuity is unlikely to exactly match inflation. But the graded method is excellent at capturing expected inflation as reflected in nominal long-term bond rates. When combined with the inflation-resistant investment policies described earlier, the graded method can also reflect part of unexpected inflation, with a brief lag for inflation results to become integrated into investment returns.

Of course, the *quid pro quo* for steadily increasing annual benefits is that the initial benefit under the graded method has been lower than under the alternative standard method. This poses an interesting menu for new retirees. The choice they face is between (1) higher initial income through the TIAA standard method or (2) a better chance at inflation resistance but lower initial income through CREF or the TIAA graded method. In pursuit of high nominal rates, some people fall prey to a "money illusion" and opt for (1). But as interest rates have moderated somewhat since the 1980s, more are moving to (2). For example, the proportion of TIAA annuitants selecting the graded payment method has grown substantially, from about 2% in 1982 to about 15% in 1997. For people with over $200,000 in annuity assets, the 1997 proportion rises to over 20%.

Another consumer choice is between CREF and TIAA. In the aftermath of the inflationary decade of the 1970s and CREF income's performance then, retirees overwhelmingly preferred TIAA to CREF. Starting about six years ago, however, new retirees have increasingly opted for CREF annuities.

The 1990s

Back on the investment front, TIAA-CREF is still committed to the benefits of long-term stock ownership for retirement savings and income, as indicated by its introduction of several new equities-based variable annuities in the 1990s. In addition, TIAA introduced in 1995 a new variable annuity — the TIAA Real Estate Account — that offered participants a further chance to pace or even outperform inflation. Real estate, in many periods of time, has enjoyed returns that have kept abreast of the increasing cost of living.

For example, since at least 1978, correlations between short-term changes in large-company nominal stock returns as well as short-term changes in nominal intermediate and long-term bonds and changes in inflation are negative (−0.28 and −0.52, respectively). Correlations between short-term changes in comparable real returns are even more strongly negative (−0.47 and −0.75, respectively).

In contrast, unleveraged real estate, as measured by the Russell-NCREIF (National Association of Real Estate Investment Fiduciaries) index starting in 1978, is not highly correlated with stocks and bonds. And, at least since 1978, changes in real estate's nominal returns as measured by this index are correlated positively with inflation (0.53) and its real returns are relatively uncorrelated with inflation (0.01).[7]

TIAA's Real Estate Account, in contrast to real estate investment trusts (REITS), isn't leveraged with mortgages, so that the underlying assets are able to isolate returns to real assets as well as an inflation component. One cloud on this potentially bright future is the history of real estate returns in the early 1990s, which were below inflation rates. This recent experience illustrates the well-known risks of real estate, including fluctuations in the value of property, uncertainty about future income and expenses, and other issues such as environmental compliance. Still, both TIAA and CREF enjoyed good returns during this same period, so a combination strategy could be an effective hedge against future real-estate downturns.

Although many of the aforementioned changes at TIAA-CREF positioned the company to help its retirement savers and retired annuitants do a *better* job of coping with inflation, none provided an asset or a program that explicitly tracked inflation changes. If such an asset were available and TIAA-CREF were able to understand its behavior, it might be an attractive addition to the company's inflation-fighting arsenal.

ASSESSING INFLATION INDEXED BONDS

Thus, the promise of *real*, inflation-indexed bonds raised considerable interest and support at TIAA-CREF. Twice before — in the early 1960s and again in the early 1980s — internal groups of TIAA-CREF managers explored then-nonexistent U.S. inflation-indexed bonds for their possible uses in annuities. Each time, they concluded that the company would have to wait until a major institution such as the federal government made a commitment to creating an inflation-indexed bond market.[8] Then, in the middle 1990s, TIAA-CREF analysts and leaders committed to a continuing search for better inflation protection returned to the issue of inflation-indexed bonds. They turned to the research literature on the theoretical characteristics and potential uses of inflation-indexed bonds.[9] Most important, they sought out lessons from actual experience with inflation-indexed bonds.

Lessons from Foreign Experience with Inflation-Indexed Bonds

With no U.S. domestic inflation-indexed assets to examine, TIAA-CREF turned to other developed countries where inflation-indexed bonds were in use and where information about them was relatively accessible. From their experiences, TIAA-CREF reached nine conclusions:

---

[7] Quarterly data for these correlations are drawn from Jeffrey D. Fisher, "Alternative Measures of Real Estate Performance: Exploring the Russell-NCREIF Data Base," *Real Estate Finance* (January 1995), pp. 79-86 and the CPI-U.

[8] Internal TIAA-CREF memorandums and interviews with current and former TIAA-CREF managers.

Exhibit 2: U.K. Inflation-Indexed Bond Price Volatility
U.K. "Linker" (2.5%, 2013)
Indexed Par Value: High, Low, and Year-End

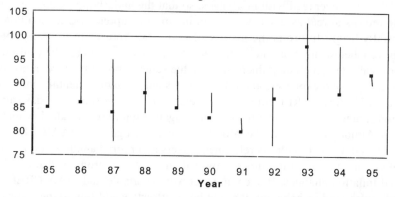

1. *Other countries' early experience with inflation-indexed bonds may not tell us much about these bonds' behavior during periods of increasing or high inflation.* Like the United States in 1997, the United Kingdom (1981), Canada (1991), and Australia (1985), all introduced sovereign inflation-indexed bonds during periods of declining inflation in those countries. Since then, these countries have experience very few periods of increasing inflation (see point 4 below).

2. *After their introduction, inflation-indexed bonds can exhibit significant price volatility.* As Exhibit 2 shows, from 1985 to 1995, the 2013 U.K. "linker" (inflation-indexed bond) price closed as low as 77 and as high as 103. The price return of one U.K. linker (2.5 2001) tracked fairly closely the price of a roughly comparable U.K. "gilt" (nominal or ordinary bond) (9.125 2001), as shown in Exhibit 3.

3. *Inflation-indexed bonds had lower yield volatility than roughly comparable ordinary bonds.* As Exhibit 4 shows, the U.K. 2011 linker had significantly

[9] See Zvi Bodie, "Inflation, Indexed-Linked Bonds and Asset Allocation," *The Journal of Portfolio Management* (Winter 1990), pp. 48-53; Alicia H. Munnell and Joseph P. Grolnic, "Should the U.S. Government Issue Indexed Bonds?" *New England Economic Review*, Federal Reserve Bank of Boston (September/November 1986), pp. 3-21; Zvi Bodie, "An Innovation for Stable Real Retirement Income," *The Journal of Portfolio Management* (Fall 1980), pp. 5-13; Zvi Bodie, "Inflation Risk and Capital Market Equilibrium," *NBER Working Paper No. 373* (July 1979); James Tobin, "An Essay on the Principles of Public Debt Management," in *Macroeconomics, Vol. 1 of Essays in Economics* (Markham Publishing Company, 1971); Robert L. Hetzel, "Indexed Bonds as Aid to Monetary Policy," *Federal Reserve Bank of Richmond 1991 Annual Report* (1991), pp. 4-15; U.S. Congress, House, "Hearings on Inflation-Indexed Treasury Debt as an Aid to Monetary Policy," Commerce, Consumer and Monetary Affairs Subcommittee of the Committee on Government Operations, House of Representatives, 102nd Congress-Second Session (Washington, D.C.: U.S. Government Printing Office, June 16 and 25, 1992), pp. 6-24; Hetzel *op. cit.*; Alan S. Blinder, "A Way to Free Small Savers from Casino Society," *Business Week* (December 8, 1996).

lower yield variation (0.38 standard deviation) than the 2011 nominal bond (1.00 standard deviation). The linker had a better risk-adjusted return as well. Similarly, the Australia 2010 inflation-indexed bond has been less volatile in terms of yield than a similar nominal bond (Exhibit 5).

4. *Inflation-indexed bond returns performed well during periods of increasing inflation and less well when inflation is decreasing.* Exhibit 6 shows relative total and annual returns for nominal and inflation-indexed bonds in the U.K. for five periods from 1986 to 1996. In all but one period inflation was declining or fluctuating, and linkers performed less well than nominal bonds. In the one period when inflation increased, inflation-indexed bonds considerably outperformed nominal bonds.

5. *Inflation-indexed bonds could have been used to diversify portfolios, i.e., to seek higher overall returns and/or lower overall risk.* Exhibit 7 shows the results of a mean-variance analysis using portfolios constructed of U.K. assets, including indexes for equity, nominal bonds ("gilts"), and cash, can shift the efficient investment frontier. Using actual correlations among U.K. asset classes from 1986 to 1996, the analysis shows that linkers, when sold short, could have improved a portfolio holding equities and bonds and another portfolio holding equities, bonds, and cash. The reason for short selling under these circumstances is that inflation-indexed bonds performed poorly in comparison with other equities, so that short positions increase overall portfolio returns.[10]

Exhibit 3: Rolling Yearly Price Return for Nominal and Indexed U.K. Government Debt with Rolling Yearly U.K. Inflation Rates: February 1992-November 1997

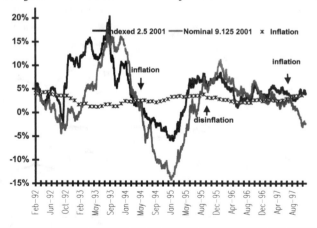

[10] This analysis was performed by the author using inflation-indexed bond, nominal bond, and cash-equivalent return data provided by the Bank of England compared with the U.K. MSCI 12-month rolling annual return data from 1986 to 1996.

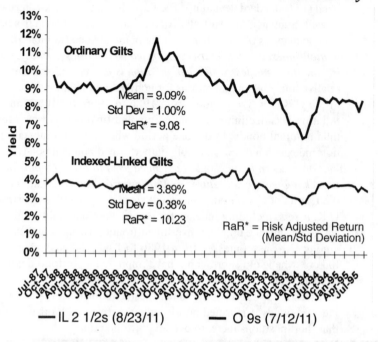

Exhibit 4: U.K. Government Bond Yield Volatility

Ordinary Gilts

Mean = 9.09%
Std Dev = 1.00%
RaR* = 9.08 .

Indexed-Linked Gilts

Mean = 3.89%
Std Dev = 0.38%
RaR* = 10.23

RaR* = Risk Adjusted Return
(Mean/Std Deviation)

— IL 2 1/2s (8/23/11)   — O 9s (7/12/11)

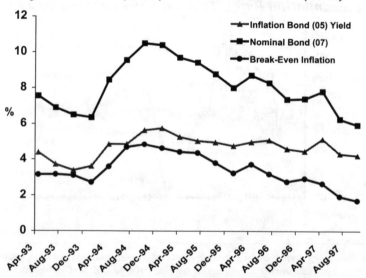

Exhibit 5: Australia: Yield Comparison for
Inflation Bond (2005) and Nominal Bond (2007)

▲ Inflation Bond (05) Yield
■ Nominal Bond (07)
● Break-Even Inflation

Exhibit 6: Relative Return Performance of U.K. Linkers and Nominal Bonds

Period	Inflation	Nominal Bond Real Return		Real Bond Real Return	
		Total	Annual	Total	Annual
A (9 mo)	Decrease	42.1	—	9.7	—
B (21 mo)	Fluctuate	11.4	6.4	9.8	5.5
C (33 mo)	Decrease	20.1	6.9	6.4	2.3
D (24 mo)	Increase	-2.3	-1.2	20.3	9.7
E (18 mo)	Decrease	11.9	7.8	9.7	6.4

Source: SEI Investments

Exhibit 7: U.K. "Linkers" in Portfolios: 1986-1996

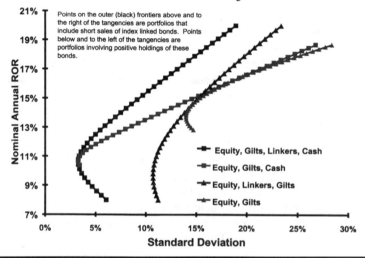

6. *Pension funds found inflation-indexed bonds attractive, especially to match long-term liabilities.* Inflation-indexed bonds represent about 20% of total U.K. public debt, the highest proportion of any developed country. After a period of declining inflation-indexed bond purchases by pension funds in the late 1980s, interest since then increased so that today pension funds hold, on average, about 50% of their fixed-income investments in linkers.[11] This is a relatively high percentage of a relatively low total, since equities represent over 80% of all U.K. pension fund holdings. In addition, U.K. pension funds are more likely than their U.S. counterparts to face future liabilities that are inflation-related. The U.K. has a higher proportion of workers covered primarily by defined benefit plans than the U.S., and a higher proportion of defined benefit pensions

[11] Roger Bootle, *Index-Linked Gilts: A Practical Investment Guide*, second edition (New York: Woodhead-Faulkner, 1991).

is explicitly indexed to inflation. Nevertheless, the U.K. experience suggests that inflation-indexed bonds could also be attractive to U.S. pension funds.

7. *Because of their attractiveness to large, long-term oriented institutional investors, inflation indexed bonds did not experience rapid turnover.* In all of the countries mentioned so far, inflation-indexed bonds are not bought and sold as frequently as comparable ordinary bonds. In the U.K., they turn over about a third as often as nominal bonds,[12] and in all countries bid-ask spreads for inflation-indexed bonds are considerably wider than for nominal bonds. These findings may simply be another way of saying that they are attractive as buy-and-hold assets for pension funds and other institutions with long-term asset-liability matching challenges.

8. *Relatively few private inflation-indexed bond issuers have emerged.* Although several public entities (in addition to the central government) have offered inflation-indexed bonds to the public in the U.K., Canada, and especially Australia, relatively few corporations have followed suit. The inflation-indexed bond market in those countries is dominated by government and agency securities.

9. *Arbitrage opportunities have existed among various sovereign inflation-indexed bonds.* U.S. purchasers of foreign inflation-indexed bonds will face two potential problems: (1) they will face currency risk and (2) foreign securities will only more or less track U.S. inflation, because they are explicitly tied to the issuing country's inflation indicators and not the U.S. CPI-U. On the other hand, U.S. purchasers of foreign inflation-indexed bonds may benefit from diversifying their investments abroad through various other country or region-based effects on interest rates, economic growth, and other factors. Further, pension fund managers can take advantage of price and yield differences among countries to improve overall portfolio performance. Exhibit 8 illustrates, at the end of October 1997, the yield curves for the four English-speaking countries that have issued inflation-indexed bonds.

In sum, foreign inflation-indexed bond markets have developed slowly, but are now important and different components of other developed countries' overall fixed-income markets. These bonds have emerged about as one might expect as long-term, buy-and-hold assets useful for institutions and individuals with future income needs that are vulnerable to an inflationary spike or steady inflationary erosion. These signals were very important to TIAA-CREF as it developed its own approach to supporting the initial creation of this new asset class and then the subsequent development of an inflation-linked bond account.

---

[12] Calculations based on data supplied by the Bank of England for the period 1982 to 1996.

Exhibit 8: International Real Yield Curve Analysis: October 31, 1997

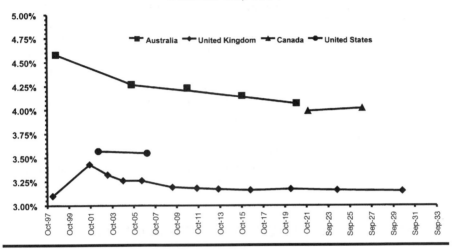

THE U.S. TREASURY DECISION TO ISSUE INFLATION-LINKED BONDS

Although the foreign experience with inflation-indexed bonds was instructive, it could hardly take the place of actual U.S. inflation-linked assets. In 1994, when TIAA-CREF learned that there was renewed interest within federal financial policymaking circles in inflation-indexed bonds, it began working on its own analyses of these bonds as well as offering to support their issuance by the U.S. Treasury. As part of these activities, company researchers analyzed the existence and size of the inflation risk premium, or the return people are willing to give up in order to gain the benefit of inflation protection. To put it another way, the inflation risk premium is the amount the federal government can save by issuing inflation-indexed bonds instead of ordinary bonds.[13] TIAA-CREF, in partnership with Stanford University's Center for Economic Policy Research, also sponsored an April 1995, Washington conference on inflation-indexed bonds that was attended by Treasury officials, academics, and Wall Street analysts and researchers.[14] Finally, TIAA-CREF CEO John Biggs publicly supported the idea of U.S. Treasury inflation-indexed bonds as attractive candidates for purchase by retirement savers and retired annuitants.[15]

---

[13] P. Brett Hammond and Andrew Fairbanks, "The Inflation Risk Premium," paper presented at the Washington Press Club conference on inflation-indexed bonds, April 21, 1995. Also see Chapter 11.

[14] "Should the Federal Government Issue Inflation-Indexed Bonds?" Washington Press Club conference (April 21, 1995).

[15] John Biggs, "The Demand for Inflation-Indexed Bonds," paper presented at the Washington Press Club conference on inflation-indexed bonds, April 21, 1995.

With analytical and political support from a range of similar-minded economists and financial leaders (at the U.S. Treasury, the Council of Economic Advisers, the World Bank, the Securities Exchange Commission, the Office of Management and Budget, and elsewhere), Treasury Secretary Robert Rubin was persuaded by Deputy Secretary Lawrence Summers to announce, in May 1996, a program to issue inflation-indexed bonds beginning in 1997. The rationale for doing so was largely based on the opportunity for the Treasury, over the long run, to save an amount equal to the inflation risk premium. The Treasury spent the balance of 1996 selecting a design for inflation-indexed Treasuries and soliciting comments from the public that could aid in choosing a final design. The design of these instruments is often known as a Canadian-style principal adjustment approach linked to the CPI-U with a three-month lookback. Equally important to retirement savers, tax treatment of inflation-indexed bonds favors their use in pensions and other tax deferred accounts.[16]

TIAA-CREF'S INFLATION-LINKED BOND ACCOUNT

Designing the Account

As the Treasury prepared to issue inflation-indexed bonds, TIAA-CREF prepared to take advantage of their appearance. The company formed a team of internal managers and experts to design and implement an inflation-linked bond account that would open for business as soon as possible after the first auction of U.S. inflation-indexed securities.

Drawing on foreign experience as well as the company's own experience with pension products intended to resist inflation, TIAA-CREF made a number of basic decisions about the account. First, the team set a goal for the account of providing to TIAA-CREF participants a total return in excess of inflation. Second, it was decided that the account would be a CREF variable annuity. Like other CREF accounts, it would be marked-to-market, so that it would aim to meet its overall goal, but would not provide a guarantee of future growth. Third, it would offer retirement savers as well as retired annuitants the option of placing a portion of their funds in the account. And fourth, the account would be able to purchase a variety of assets, including inflation-indexed bonds issued by the Treasury and other government agencies, U.S. corporations, foreign governments and corporations. It would, at the discretion of the account manager, also be able to purchase nominal bonds and money market securities.

In addition to designing the overall features of the account, the inflation-linked bond account team also designed new systems to support the special inflation indexing features associated with the individual assets held in the account

---

[16] The Treasury has ruled that inflation-indexed bonds will be treated for tax purposes like nominal zero-coupon bonds. Any inside increase — in this case the increase in the principal due to monthly inflation adjustments — will be taxed in the year it accrues, even though it won't be paid out until maturity.

and sought SEC approval for the first-ever variable annuity based on inflation-indexed bonds. The team also polled TIAA-CREF's 6,000 participating institutions for permission to offer the new account.

Perhaps the most critical element in preparing to launch a new Inflation-Linked Bond Account was individual education. TIAA-CREF prepared new educational materials for two million individual participants introducing them to the concept of inflation indexation and to the details of the new account. It also sponsored educational programs for the company's counseling staff so they could knowledgeably assist participants in learning how the new account worked and how it fit into the TIAA-CREF variable annuity family. And the team worked with representatives of a broader effort underway at TIAA-CREF to develop retirement contributions and asset allocation advice. The result was that the inflation-linked bond account was one of several options used in software that could help participants match their self-reported risk profiles and other needs to retirement savings investment allocation decisions.

Inaugurating the Account

In January 1997, the U.S. Treasury announced the first auction of $8 billion in 10-year Treasury inflation-indexed notes. TIAA-CREF proceeded to seed its Inflation-Linked Bond Account on January 29 with $50 million on loan from TIAA and it participated in the first auction that same day. Subsequently, account manager Steven Traum took advantage of a small wave of corporate and agency issuers to purchase a small amount of a J.P. Morgan 4% inflation-indexed note (2012). And, as prices returned to earth following the first-ever auction, account managers began to purchase additional amounts of the 10-year Treasury and the subsequently auctioned 5-year Treasury notes.

The Inflation-Linked Bond Account opened for business on May 1, 1997, as one of the ten investment options offered by TIAA-CREF to its participants. By the end of the year, the Inflation-Linked Bond Account was the largest account in the country focused on inflation-indexed bonds.

Inflation-Linked Bond Account Participants

By the end of 1997, over 1,800 TIAA-CREF retirement savers and annuitants had chosen to participate in the Inflation-Linked Bond Account. In its educational materials TIAA-CREF targeted the account for people who believe they have some of the following characteristics:

- a limited ability to replace retirement savings or income lost to inflation spikes or steady erosion
- relatively few assets outside their retirement accounts
- are concerned about the future of Social Security

In other words, the Account may be an option for people who face their own individual asset-liability matching challenge where their individual future liabilities (i.e., consumption needs) could be affected by inflation so that their future assets (i.e., sources of income) should be at least partially protected from inflation. Therefore, portfolios including CREF equities, the TIAA fixed-income account, and the inflation-indexed bond account could be appropriate for some people nearing or in retirement.

However, two major cautions are in order. The first caution has to do with the effects of daily price changes on a marked-to-market account as opposed to an individual bond held to maturity. Recall that the CREF Inflation-Linked Bond Account, like any variable annuity or mutual fund, is marked-to-market each business day. An inflation-indexed bond bought and held to maturity will provide a book value that rises in step with inflation, but a similar bond that is marked-to-market will be priced each day. Also recall that although inflation-indexed bond yields and total returns are likely to be more stable than their nominal bond counterparts, experience from other countries indicates that inflation-indexed bond prices are likely to vary considerably. Price changes for individual securities in the account will, in turn, affect the daily unit value of the account. Therefore, *no marked-to-market fund can guarantee to outpace inflation.*

For example, one dynamic that can produce inflation-indexed bond price changes is unexpected inflation. That's because unexpected inflation (or unexpected deflation for that matter) can affect the demand for an individual inflation-indexed security relative to other inflation-indexed and nominal securities, hence the relative prices of those securities. For a bondholder only interested in holding an inflation-indexed bond to maturity, unexpected inflation that leads to demand-driven price changes is unimportant. For such a bondholder, unexpected inflation won't affect the bond's real cash flows, since with inflation indexation the nominal cash flows will increase (or decrease) in step with inflation. But for a marked-to-market variable annuity account or mutual fund holder, anything that leads to inflation-indexed bond price changes will affect the account's daily unit value, which in turn will affect the ability of the account to track inflation.

The second caution concerns retirement annuities. *A retirement income based on an inflation-linked bond variable annuity will be unlikely to keep up with inflation.* Like most variable annuities, CREF sets the initial payout rate for retirees based on a standard assumed interest rate, or AIR. The second year's payout rate is increased or decreased depending on whether the underlying assets chosen by the annuitant increased more or less than 4% in the first year. In CREF's case, the AIR is a conservative 4%, which means that a retiree's second-year income often increases, since on average, CREF's stock and bond accounts increase more than 4% per annum.

However, since currently available U.S. Treasury inflation-indexed bonds and other U.S. inflation-indexed bonds pay coupons of less than 4%, an annuity based on them will see a decrease in real income in the second year. This shortfall can be illustrated if we assume a real rate of return of 3.3% and account expenses of 0.3% to go along with the AIR of 4%. The result is that the second and subsequent years' annuity income will always trail inflation by 1%.

If inflation rises by 3% in the first year, then in the second year the nominal payout will rise by 2% (i.e., 3.3% real return plus 3% inflation return minus 0.3% expenses minus the original AIR equals a 2% payout increaase), which is a decrease in real income of 1% (i.e., 3% inflation increase minus the 2% payout increase). Using these assumptions for a $100,000 annuity, first-year income would be $4,000. The first-year effect of inflation on that income would be $120, but the second-year payout would increase by only $80. When inflation is at 12%, an 11% increase under these assumptions might not seem so bad to a retiree, but when inflation is 2%, a 1% increase seems like a lot to give up. And if instead of 30 basis points, account expenses are more like the industry average of 2.0% for variable annuities, future income would always trail inflation by 2.7%.

The only way to assure that an inflation-linked bond account will be able to assist retirees in keeping up with inflation is to find assets that offer a total return in excess of 4% after expenses. That may be possible as the U.S. corporate market for inflation-indexed products matures and as American managers become more familiar with foreign inflation-indexed securities.

FUTURE DEVELOPMENTS TO SUPPORT INFLATION PROTECTION FOR PENSIONS

U.S. inflation-indexed bonds represent a major step in the search for the holy grail of inflation protection for retirement savings and income. But as the preceding example shows, marked-to-market inflation-linked annuities or mutual funds may not provide perfect inflation protection. Other developments are needed to support pension products that guarantee inflation protection.

Real-Return Fixed Annuities

A real-return fixed annuity would be an excellent complement for an inflation-linked bond variable annuity. Ideally, a fixed annuity based on inflation-indexed bonds held to maturity would have several advantages, including the ability to guarantee a return that always exceeds inflation.[17] Since expected returns on such an account are likely to be lower than for other bond and stock accounts during periods of declining or low inflation, a variation on such a product would be an equity-linked real return annuity. Such an annuity would, on top of guaranteed inflation protection for any premiums placed in the account, pay a portion of the increase in the stock market each year.

The inflation protection advantages of products such as these are obvious, but there are several obstacles to overcome. One is lack of flexibility. The easiest way to provide an inflation guarantee is for the account to purchase and hold infla-

---

[17] At least one company has begun to offer such an annuity for retirement savings accumulations but not for retirement income.

tion-indexed bonds whose maturities coincide with the mortality or desired hold-ing periods of account participants in order to avoid reinvestment risk. But such an account would be available to a wide variety of people whose future mortality and intentions are difficult to predict. The account might need to restrict entry to sev-eral times a year, for example. Handling exit-related issues may be more difficult.

These challenges are magnified for an equity-linked real return annuity. Such an annuity would purchase inflation-linked bonds to cover the guarantee of principal (this might take $75 or more of every $100 in premiums or contributions and use it to purchase STRIPS). It and would use the remaining balance to pur-chase long-term stock options (say S&P options) that would pay a percentage of the gain each year in the market (the exact percentage would depend on the price of the option at the time of purchase).

Market-related developments required to support such an annuity include strengthening the U.S. inflation-indexed bond market through increasing the liquidity and size of the government and private sectors. They also include devel-opment of a robust long-term stock option market that could support the equity-linked portion of the annuity and a lively inflation-indexed bond STRIPs market so that principal STRIPs could be used for accumulating annuities and coupon STRIPs could be used for payout annuities. Annuity design developments include design of a cost-effective retirement payout annuity offering the aforementioned guarantees and regulatory evolution so that insurers and the SEC become fully comfortable with retirement products that contain options as an integral feature. If some of these developments are successful, TIAA-CREF and other annuity pro-viders might be able to come close to the holy grail of inflation protection for retirement: a product that would guarantee inflation protection, provide for some participation in additional returns, and offer payin and payout flexibility.

CONCLUSIONS

TIAA-CREF's experience with inflation protection and inflation-indexed bonds supports the following conclusions:

- TIAA-CREF's creative responses to three periods of significant 20th Cen-tury inflation (WWI; post WWII; 1970s) profoundly shaped the company and prompted innovations that are widely used today throughout the pen-sion industry.
- Inflation-indexed bonds are an important step along the road toward true inflation protection for pensions, because of their ability to ameliorate one of the most debilitating forces that threaten the adequacy of pensions.
- Most important, individual defined-benefit pension participants have a completely new individual asset-liability matching tool that is unlikely to be correlated in the long run with other assets.

- More can and should be done with inflation-indexed bonds for pensions, including the development of market infrastructure, regulations, and design features needed to support guaranteed real-return annuities, possibly with an equity link.

TIAA-CREF has a long history of commitment to finding better ways of helping retirement savers and annuitants cope with inflation. It remains committed to this goal and will continue to seek and support improved practical approaches.

Chapter 5

Recognizing and Achieving Strategic Investment Goals

Barbara J. Moore
Managing Director
SEI Investments

INTRODUCTION

Everyone has a bogey. Institutional investors have intimate knowledge of the number of basis points by which actual investment returns exceeded or fell short of that bogey. Individual investors may have a more vague sense of their achievements versus a goal that may be less well-defined. Whether vague or exact, virtually all goals in the United States are still defined in nominal terms, i.e., before the impact of inflation.

Investors are typically unaware of the real (i.e., inflation-adjusted) returns their assets have generated and the real nature of the liabilities that they are attempting to fund. A better understanding of both sides of this asset/liability equation will lead to simpler and lower-cost investment strategies for institutional and individual investors alike.

This chapter seeks to educate institutional investors as to the inflation sensitivity of their liabilities and the unpredictable real returns from both the core assets in their portfolios — stocks, bonds, and cash — and from two principal assets which investors believe to be particularly inflation-sensitive — real estate and commodities.

Lest investors believe they don't need to move into inflation-indexed instruments in the inflation environment as of this writing, but instead can now "manage" their nominal assets armed with a new awareness of their real liabilities, we'll examine the ability of professionals and amateurs alike to forecast inflation for the short- or long-term: it's a dismal record.

The solution is simple and has been adopted by institutional investors, particularly pension funds, wherever inflation-indexed ("real") bonds are a significant presence in the capital markets. In the U.K. and Canada, roughly 50% of pension funds' fixed income holdings are allocated to real bonds. Beyond real bonds'

43

asset/liability matching properties, their low to negative correlation with nominal assets makes them a superior portfolio anchor while their higher predictability of real return versus nominal assets can lower pension fund funding costs and the variability of that cost. All of these attributes are rendered even more attractive to investors by real bonds' low expense profile: a buy-and-hold strategy adopted by many funds around the world minimizes trading costs and "natural" real bonds are replacing many of the expensive derivative-based inflation hedging strategies of recent years.

UBIQUITOUS REAL LIABILITIES

Investors of all stripes have objectives for their investment portfolios, but are they properly defined? The key to an individual's successful retirement or college funding, a plan sponsor's successful provision of benefits to participants, a foundation's ability to provide grants or an endowment's ability to meet spending targets is recognizing the true nature of each investor's liability. An objective defined in terms unrelated to the essence of the liability growth will make an individual or institutional investor program more expensive and less efficient.

Many investors are not currently aware of the real nature of their liabilities, having learned and lived in a world in which return targets are defined in nominal terms. Even though actuarial practice requires a calculation of the real rate of growth of the liabilities of a pension plan, which is then added to an inflation forecast to derive a nominal return target, the product of this practice is accepted as the "bogey," frequently without thought to the derivation of the bogey. The underlying target is the real rate of growth, making the liability a real liability, rather than a nominal one.

Once pension plans, endowments, foundations, and individual investors fully acknowledge the real nature of significant portions of their liabilities, and recognize the inability of nominal assets to consistently deliver acceptable real rates of return, these strategic purchasers of inflation-indexed bonds will dramatically change perceptions of value in this market.

Defined Benefit Plan Return Objectives

While other nominal return objectives are effectively the combination of real returns and inflation forecasts, none is calculated so explicitly as that of the defined benefit plan's derivation of its estimated future obligations (the Projected Benefit Obligation or PBO) from its current obligation if the plan were terminated today (the Accumulated Benefit Obligation or ABO). In addition to the active lives liabilities, most post-retirement benefits (or retired lives liabilities) are at least partially adjusted for cost-of-living increases.

Exhibit 1: Asset/Liability Matching

LIABILITY   ASSET

INCREASE DUE TO INFLATION		INCREASE DUE TO INFLATION
	Uncertain Today	
INCREASE DUE TO CHANGES IN ACTUARIAL ASSUMPTIONS INTERNAL TO THE FIRM ASSUMING CONSTANT WAGES		INCREASE DUE TO REAL RETURN
	Known Today	
FUTURE LIABILITY IF PLAN WERE TERMINATED TODAY		INVESTMENT TODAY

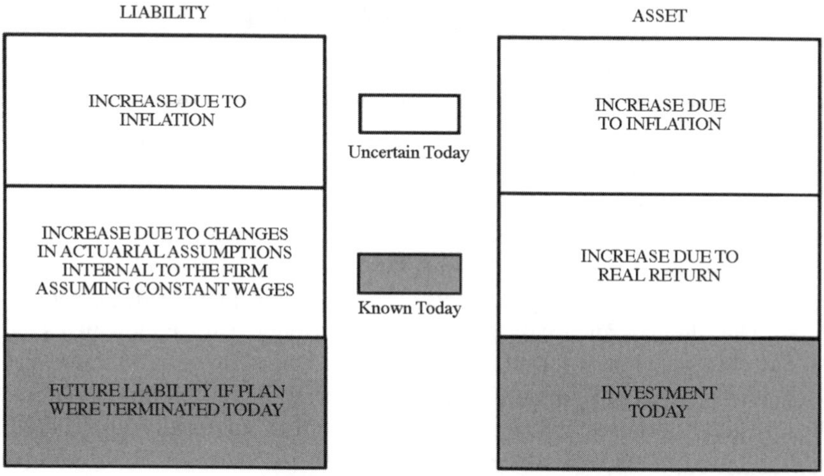

Exhibit 1 illustrates the simplification of the asset/liability matching process made possible by the ability to invest on a real yield-to-maturity basis. The lower left box of the exhibit represents the ABO while the middle and upper left boxes represent the actuarial calculations necessary to arrive at the PBO. Hence, the active lives return objective is to generate a real return to meet the middle box increase. This is often restated as a nominal objective — actuaries pick an inflation forecast to add to real return objectives contained in the middle box, including the company's real growth and that of its industry. The nominal objective is then usually taken as the target and asset allocation decisions using nominal assets are made to attempt to match this nominal objective.

The significant drawback to this process is the well-demonstrated inability of anyone to forecast inflation. The data presented later in this chapter illustrate the dismal track record. This inability to forecast leads to frequent changes in the nominal liability structure and, consequently, in the nominal return objectives. Frequent change creates increased trading costs — this is a very inefficient and expensive PBO derivation and matching process. The introduction of inflation-indexed bonds into the U.S. capital markets and their adoption by pension plans will simplify and render less expensive the asset/liability matching process.

Endowment Return Objectives

Endowments have real objectives for grant and scholarship commitments, with a desire to preserve the corpus and still deliver comparable aid in purchasing power terms over the years to come. Endowments may also have the real liabilities of future building plans. Until the U.S. Treasury has expanded its inflation-indexed issuance sufficiently to foster an active STRIPS market, a real term structure can be created by intermediaries to match these building plans.

Exhibit 2: Standard Deviation of Nominal Returns

	Since 1926	Since 1946	Since 1973	Since 1980
Equities	20.3%	16.5%	17.0%	13.4%
US Long Bonds	9.2%	10.4%	12.8%	13.9%

For short- to medium-term capital spending commitments, endowments currently remove specified amounts from asset classes thought to be more volatile and set these amounts aside in nominal bonds. Volatility trends in the capital markets have been such that nominal bonds require an extra amount, a margin of safety, to be set aside. A quick glimpse at these trends as shown in Exhibit 2 shows the increasing unpredictability of assets historically considered safer harbors.

The choices for a safe harbor for funds tagged for endowments' near-term building plans increasingly fall in the "stable value" area of cash equivalents, the lower real and nominal returns of which increase the amount necessary to be invested to generate the targeted future spending amounts. With the application of inflation-indexed bonds generating a real return of 3%-4%, the amount to be invested can be smaller and calculated far more precisely than with either nominal bonds or cash. The CPI-U will track construction and materials price increases better than any non-indexed asset.

Foundation Return Objectives

In the case of foundations, the real return objective is explicitly stated and is dictated by their 5% annual spending requirements. While a 5% real bond would be the ideal investment for a foundation satisfied with maintaining the real value of its current corpus, in its absence a portion of the portfolio invested in 3%+ real bonds will preserve the corpus more predictably than any nominal asset class could, at least as indicated by historical volatility and real return figures. A real bond anchor will be particularly valuable during uniformly negative real return periods for these other asset classes, which we will see have occurred with surprising frequency.

This real bond anchor will allow the balance of the portfolio to be placed in higher volatility assets such as equities which should generate higher real returns, allowing foundations to achieve 5% real returns for the portfolio over the longer term.

Defined Contribution Return Objectives

As individuals contemplate choices among options provided by their plan administrators, the introduction of an inflation-indexed product will need to be accompanied by educational materials designed to focus the participant's attention on the real nature of their savings and retirement objectives and the effects of inflation on the numbers provided in their monthly portfolio statements. This educational program will mirror that of the insurance companies' product offerings discussed below and can already be found among the materials provided by such institutions as the Teachers Insurance and Annuity Association-College Retirement Equities Fund (TIAA-CREF).

Insurance Company New Product Offerings

Many insurance companies think of their investment operations as essentially spread lending. Several leading companies realize that they now have another spread to create: a real one. We expect to see the introduction of real GICs, real annuities and other creative inflation index-linked investment products offered by the insurance community in the United States.

The literature is full of analyses of the demographic trends that portend enormous growth in financial planning services and investment products over the next 20 to 30 years. Approximately $10 trillion will be transferred to baby boomers from their parents over this period. As the boomers approach retirement, they will shift a portion of their investment assets toward more conservative investments, and this portion will increase steadily over time. As this shift occurs, sensitivity to the effects of inflation on "stable value" investments will increase.

This sensitivity is already surfacing in the surveys of critical retiree topics, which show that retirees are increasingly concerned about the "new" risk of retirement, that is, the risk of outliving their savings. Looked at in real terms, this risk can be seen as the risk of loss of future purchasing power. Future purchasing power is a direct function of accumulated real returns. Since real bonds and any real GIC or annuity products produced by the insurance community will be contractual, real-yielding assets, the case for including inflation-indexed bonds in retiree portfolios will be compelling.

The ultimate goal of retirees, whether it is phrased as such or even thought of as such by the boomers and the current generation of retirees, is to achieve planned (or hoped-for) levels of real retirement purchasing power. The erosion of nest eggs by inflation could clearly thwart that goal.

The education process for retirees needs to include the historical real return generation capability of nominal assets — that is, the returns left after the erosion of inflation. The education process also needs to include the diversification benefits of real products: the low correlation of real bonds with nominal assets will permit retirement portfolios to stay more heavily invested in equities than a nominal bond anchor would allow, creating higher expected real returns without a commensurate increase in volatility.

The insurance and mutual fund industries will need to embark on this education program as they introduce their offerings, further fueling the demand for inflation-indexed products.

NOMINAL ASSETS IN THE REAL WORLD

Stocks, Bonds, and Cash

If we appreciated that we had real liabilities, but either didn't have real assets in which to invest or had not taken the plunge into the new U.S. Treasury inflation-indexed bonds, how would the familiar nominal asset classes look as real return generators?

Exhibit 3: Annual Real Return and Standard Deviation

	Since 1926	Since 1973
Equities		
Real Return	7.5%	8.3%
Standard Deviation	20.5%	17.6%
U.S. Long Bond		
Real Return	1.9%	4.0%
Standard Deviation	10.5%	14.0%
30-Day Treasury Bills		
Real Return	0.6%	1.6%
Standard Deviation	4.2%	2.8%

Exhibit 4: Negative Annual Real Returns

	Incidence since	
	1926	1973
Equities	32%	28%
U.S. Long Bond	40%	44%
30-Day Treasury Bills	35%	26%

Exhibit 3 summarizes the annual real return and standard deviation figures for the three principal asset classes since the beginning of the Ibbotson data (1926) and since the beginning of the floating regime post Bretton Woods (1973, allowing for an adjustment period and for the exit from the comprehensive Wage and Price Controls of 1971 and 1972).

While the risk-adjusted returns for equities clearly win the contest here, many investors desire an "anchor" for short-term and medium-term performance, given the volatility of equities. Nominal bonds have traditionally filled this role, but their relatively high correlation with equities and other nominal assets, especially in times of distress, and the relatively low historical real return performance of these and other nominal assets points up the need for a truly diversifying anchor when times are tough, which is still capable of generating respectable real and nominal returns in happier times. This need is compounded by the volatility of nominal bonds and equities converging. As seen in Exhibit 2, with 13.9% volatility since 1980, it is difficult to view nominal bonds as an "anchor" for a portfolio of equities with 13.4% volatility!

Whether we are aware of the real nature of our liabilities, or just need an inflation hedge, we need to understand the frequency and magnitude of unpleasant real return surprises from nominal assets.

Exhibit 4 examines the frequency with which the realized annual change in CPI-U exceeded the total nominal return for that year for the asset class in question. With equities and T-bills, the total nominal return was more than erased by inflation at very similar levels. Nominal bonds fared worse, which is to be expected given their more negative correlation with inflation. We note in particular that, for every year but one since 1973, when real returns from equities were negative, real returns from long-term bonds were also negative. This fact alone substantiates the critical role of an inflation-resistant diversifier in a portfolio of nominal assets.

Exhibit 5: Average Magnitude of Losses

	Since 1926	Since 1973
Equities	−13.4%	−13.5%
U.S. Long Bond	−7.0%	−8.6%
30-Day Treasury Bills	−3.2%	−1.9%

Exhibit 6: Annual Real Returns Below 3%

	Incidence since	
	1926	1973
Equities	39%	36%
U.S. Long Bond	57%	52%
30-Day Treasury Bills	81%	72%

An examination of the average magnitude of the loss for those years in which real returns were negative shows the volatility of equities manifesting itself clearly.

Exhibit 5 demonstrates that when it hurts, it really hurts, with both equities and, to a lesser extent, nominal bonds. T-bills, due to their lower volatility, don't tend to reach these depths.

Raising the bar from a 0% real return to a level that most investors expect to see as a minimum from the U.S. Treasury's inflation-indexed bond (that is, 3%), we see in Exhibit 6 that equities managed to beat 3% real about 60% of the time, while nominal bonds lose the inflation bet more often than not. We should note that purchasers of the real bonds in the auctions through January 1998 have received clearing real rates of between 3.45% and 3.73%.

Equities have delivered higher real returns commensurate with their additional volatility and have consequently been awarded large percentages of the institutional investor's portfolio. In countries where real bonds already play a significant role, the allocation to equities is generally higher than in the United States. Outside the United States, the funds for investment in inflation-indexed bonds have typically been reallocated from nominal bonds. Over 50% of U.K. pension fund fixed income holdings are invested in indexed-linked gilts and 50% is the targeted asset allocation for inflation-indexed bonds in Canadian pension fund fixed income portfolios. The allocation of investment dollars to inflation-indexed bonds may come from nominal bonds in the United States, but allocations from real estate, cash, and commodities are being considered as well. Focusing on the most obvious competitor for real bond investment dollars within the three asset classes already examined — nominal bonds — their historical real returns have been extremely volatile.

The imbedded real rate of return in nominal debt securities is both unknown and highly uncertain. Issuers and investors "bet" on inflation with nominal bonds: if realized inflation is unexpectedly low, the nominal bond investor "wins"; if realized inflation is unexpectedly high, the nominal bond investor "loses". Analyses of investor returns depicted in Exhibit 7 strongly suggest little or no ability to predict future inflation. The realized real returns shown here range from −15% to +35%. It is highly unlikely that any investor purchased a bond intending to receive negative real returns 40% of the time and real returns of less than 3% between 50% and 60% of the time.

Smoothing the volatility of realized real returns by examining rolling 15-year periods since 1926 does not improve the odds: 58% of the 15-year realized real returns shown in Exhibit 8 were negative.

Exhibit 7: Annual Real Returns from Long-Term U.S. Government Bonds Since 1926

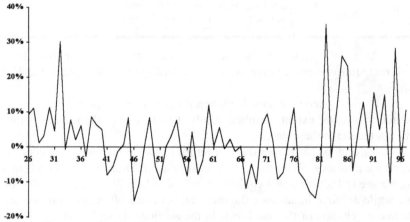

Exhibit 8: Trailing 15-Year Period Real Returns for Long-Term U.S. Government Bonds and CPI Since 1926

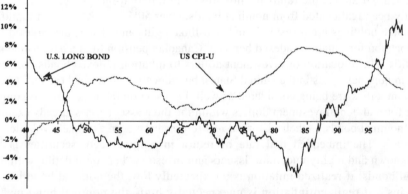

Exhibit 9: Probabilities of Achieving Specified Annual Average Real Returns over Various Investment Horizons Using Corporate Bonds

Compound Annual Return of	Number of Years of Investment Horizon								
	1	3	5	10	15	20	25	30	40
6% or more	0.35	0.25	0.20	0.11	0.07	0.04	0.03	0.02	0.01
5% or more	0.39	0.31	0.27	0.19	0.14	0.10	0.08	0.06	0.04
4% or more	0.43	0.38	0.35	0.29	0.25	0.22	0.19	0.17	0.13
3% or more	0.47	0.45	0.44	0.41	0.39	0.38	0.36	0.35	0.33
2% or more	0.52	0.53	0.53	0.55	0.56	0.57	0.57	0.58	0.59
1% or more	0.56	0.60	0.63	0.68	0.71	0.74	0.76	0.79	0.82
0% or more	0.60	0.67	0.71	0.79	0.84	0.87	0.90	0.92	0.95
−1% or more	0.64	0.74	0.79	0.87	0.92	0.95	0.97	0.98	0.99
−2% or more	0.72	0.85	0.91	0.97	0.99	0.99	1.00	1.00	1.00

Source: Charles P. Jones, J.C. Poindexter, and Jack W. Wilson, "Probable Bond Returns: The Lessons of History," *The Journal of Investing* (Fall 1996). Based on 1926 to 1994 historical performance of corporate bonds.

Even with the addition of a premium return being achieved over a risk-free Treasury return due to corporate credit spreads and using the most favorable investment horizon for forecasting (i.e., the shortest period — one year), a 3% real bond would still have been a superior investment solely from a return standpoint 53% of the time, as seen in Exhibit 9. As time horizons increase to periods at which most investors should be aiming, the odds in favor of real bonds improve dramatically.

Seeking to match real liabilities with nominal assets is clearly risky business. If one can stomach the volatility of 100% equities, they are obviously the best long-term real return generator. As soon as an anchor is contemplated, the inferior historical real return generation capability of nominal bonds and cash, coupled with the tendency of nominal bonds to correlate highly with equities in times of distress, leads one to real assets.

Real Estate and Commodities

A quick comparison of real estate as a real-return generating alternative to real bonds leans fairly compellingly in the direction of real bonds. While the theoretically low correlation of real estate with other asset classes has been a draw for investors historically, the vagaries of supply and demand imbalance have demonstrated how unreliable real estate can be as an inflation hedge and real return generator. The inflation protection of real bonds is contractual, while that of real estate is partial and asset-specific. Annual returns are more predictable with real bonds than with real estate, a useful benefit for contributions-conscious plan sponsors and for managers measured on short-term performance standards. Finally, the total return on real estate is a function of appreciation, which relies on local and national market economies, and exit strategy, which has been improved by the popularity of public market real estate securities but can still be problematic with non-public real estate holdings. By contrast, the total return of a real bond held to maturity is formulaic: a safer bet, although one that is capped at the stated real return.

Looking at commodities as real return generators, commodities deliver returns which are inferior to equities on both a nominal and a real basis with significantly higher volatility. Indices A and B in Exhibit 10 are tradable, widely-followed commodity indices.

Certain investors willingly assume the additional volatility of commodities since they are a good portfolio diversifier, enjoying low correlations with most other asset classes. Other investors, however, are seeking an inflation hedge and would only take the additional volatility of commodities if commodities provided a superior inflation hedge to equities. Unfortunately, they do not deliver a statistically significant improvement on inflation correlation over equities, as seen in Exhibit 11.

An examination of the volatility of commodities' correlation with the CPI-U as seen in Exhibit 12 supports the conclusion that commodities are not a reliable inflation hedge.

For investors seeking diversification and willing to accept the accompanying volatility, both commodities and real estate can add significant portfolio value. For investors requiring an inflation hedge, neither commodities nor real estate will provide the protection that real bonds afford.

Exhibit 10: Annual Real Return and Standard Deviation

	Return		Standard Deviation	
	Nominal Since 1976	Real Since 1976	Nominal Since 1976	Real Since 1976
Equities	14.7%	9.5%	13.7%	14.0%
U.S. Long Bond	9.3%	4.3%	13.2%	14.4%
30-Day Treasury Bills	6.9%	2.0%	3.0%	2.6%
Index A	13.7%	8.5%	30.7%	26.2%
Index B	10.2%	5.2%	17.8%	16.3%
CPI-U	4.7%	N/A	3.2%	N/A

Exhibit 11: Correlation with CPI Since 1976: Rolling 36-Month Periods

	Equities	Index A	Index B
Minimum	−0.607	−0.307	−0.365
Average	−0.172	0.072	−0.020
Maximum	0.209	0.501	0.454
Standard Deviation	0.198	0.165	0.186

Exhibit 12: Correlation of Commodities and CPI: Rolling 36-Month Periods Since 1976

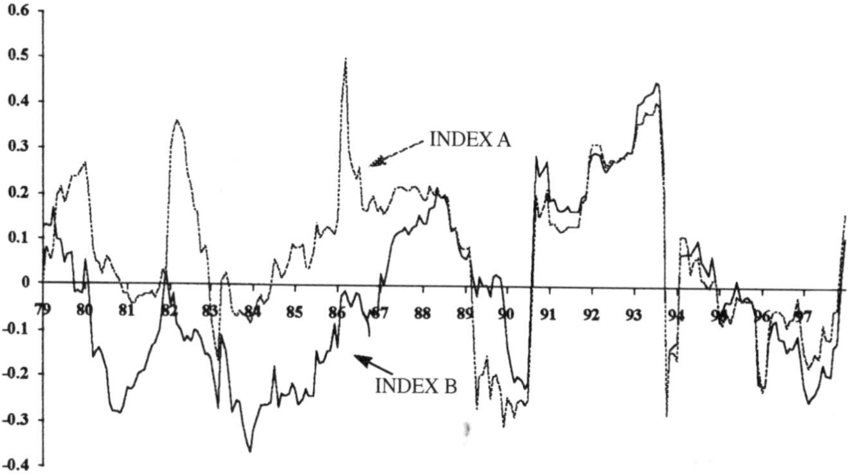

PREDICTABLE PREDICTIONS: SURPRISING SURPRISES

With heightened sensitivity to both the real nature of at least portions of their liabilities and the historical inability of nominal assets to deliver consistently positive and meaningful real returns, many investors might be tempted to acknowledge their exposure to inflation but delay implementing hedging strategies, including inflation-indexed bonds, in the low-inflation environment as of this writing.

Comfortable with the behavior of familiar nominal assets, expressed through correlation and volatility assumptions, many investors may choose to sit on the sidelines while real bonds gradually enter the market — content to delay participation.

How predictable is inflation? How predictable is the correlation among familiar asset classes and between these asset classes and inflation? How volatile is volatility? How much do investors need an inflation hedge, given the inflation experience through 1997?

Inflation Forecasting

The vigilance of most investors against the corrosive effects of inflation on nominal assets has decreased significantly, with globalization of supply, an ardent Federal Reserve chairman, deflationary threats in foreign economies, and other factors cited as evidence of a new regime. The back-of-the-envelope estimate of long-term inflation used most frequently is the most recent 12-month figure. An examination of the short trading history of real bonds in the United States to January 1998 versus this historical 12-month figure shows this estimation process at work as the yield differential between 10-year nominal and real bonds tracks rolling historical 12-month inflation fairly well. (See Exhibit 13.)

Unfortunately, this short-hand approach is highly inaccurate. Looking at the predictive abilities of recent history, Exhibit 14 examines the errors created by using previous 12-month inflation to forecast subsequent 10-year inflation. The period examined, since 1973, happens to include surprises on the high side in the 1970s and on the low side in the 1980s and 1990s.

Exhibit 13: Yield Spread: 10-Year U.S. Treasury Yield Less 10-Year TIPS Yield with 12-Month Rolling CPI

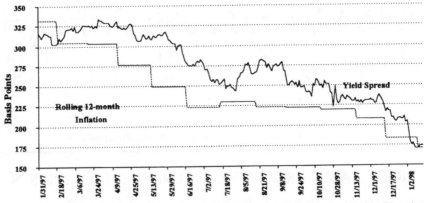

Source: U.S. Department of Labor, SEI Investments, and Bloomberg L.P. (Data provided by Bloomberg Financial Markets ©1998 Bloomberg L.P. All rights reserved.)

Exhibit 14: Prediction Error Using Previous 12-Month CPI to Forecast Next 10-Year Realized Inflation

Source: U.S. Department of Labor and SEI Investments.

Exhibit 15: Prediction Error Using Previous 12-Month CPI to Forecast Next 12-Month CPI Since 1950

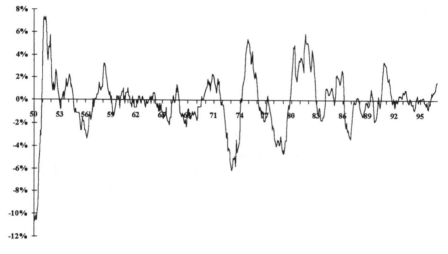

Source: U.S. Department of Labor and SEI Investments.

Investors who retain faith in their ability to forecast inflation may accept the inability of short-term recent inflation to forecast long-term future inflation but believe that their ability to derive a good estimate of near-term inflation is far superior. A glance at history should relieve these investors of their complacency. Looking at the ability of previous 12-month CPI to forecast subsequent 12-month CPI since 1950, Exhibit 15 demonstrates how poor a predictor that practice is. The magnitude of the surprises shown in this exhibit range from –6% to +7%. That is, a +7% error could occur when inflation had been 2% the previous year and was 9% the following year.

Looking back before mid-century, the volatility and errors increase: the surprises on Exhibit 16 range from –17% to +40%.

Investors and economists are equally ill-equipped to forecast inflation. As a final check on forecasting accuracy, a comparison of the Federal Reserve's quarterly Survey of Professional Forecasters' record in forecasting 12-month inflation with the "forecasting ability" of previous 12-month inflation yields a victory for historical data: 62% of the time, the previous 12-month figure was more accurate than the professional forecasters' figure (see Exhibit 17.)

Within the realm of predictions, many investors determine their asset allocations through modelling based on several critical assumptions: return, volatility, and correlation being among the most important. We have seen the highly unpredictable nature of real returns from nominal assets and the volatility of volatility shown in Exhibit 2: how stable are the correlation assumptions employed?

Exhibit 16: Prediction Error Using Previous 12-Month CPI to Forecast Next 12-Month CPI from 1913 to 1950

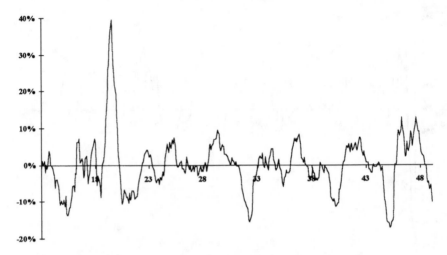

Source: U.S. Department of Labor and SEI Investments.

Exhibit 17: Inflation Prediction Error

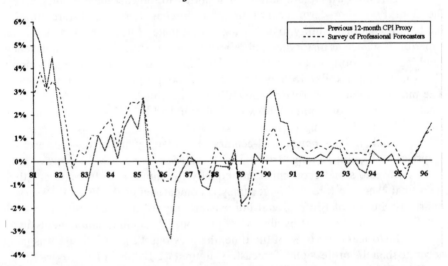

Source: U.S. Department of Labor, Federal Reserve (Philadelphia), and SEI Investments.

Exhibit 18: Correlation of Long-Term Bonds and Equities: Rolling 36-Month Periods Since 1926

Source: SEI Investments and Ibbotson Associates, Inc. Used with permission. [Certain portions of this work were derived from copyrighted works of Roger G. Ibbotson and Rex Sinquefield.]

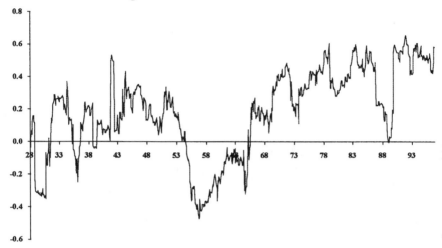

Exhibit 19: Correlation of Long-Term Bonds and Equities: Rolling 36-Month Periods

	Since 1926	Since 1973
Minimum	–0.474	–0.006
Average	0.180	0.407
Maximum	0.654	0.654
Standard Deviation	0.264	0.145

Volatility of Correlation

An initial glance at the correlation of long-term bonds and equities reported in Exhibit 18 answers the question.

Even with the smoothing effect of examining 36-month periods, the range of values hardly demonstrates a constant relationship: –0.5 to +0.7. The data in the first column of Exhibit 19 provide the breakdown of the graph in Exhibit 18. The last column in Exhibit 19 looks at the volatility of the correlation over a more recent period, since 1973. While the standard deviation halved and the range narrowed considerably, there is still a significant disparity between the outlying points and meaningful volatility.

While over the long term equities have been a highly satisfactory inflation hedge, the volatility of the correlation between equities and inflation in the short and medium term demonstrated in Exhibit 20 points up the need for an inflation hedge even for those investors who are 100% invested in equities but who have portions of their real liabilities which are less than long-term.

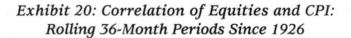

Exhibit 20: Correlation of Equities and CPI: Rolling 36-Month Periods Since 1926

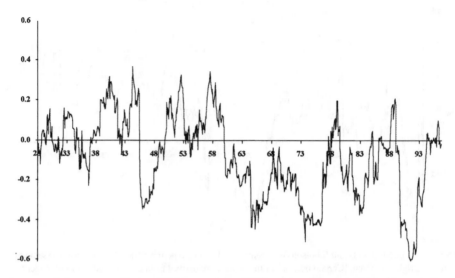

We can reasonably expect real bonds to have a more stable relationship with inflation than that pictured in Exhibit 20 and one which is more predominantly positive. The correlation of inflation with nominal bonds illustrated in Exhibit 21 is also highly volatile and, like equities, predominantly negative in the last several decades.

Exhibit 22 shows that even 30-day Treasury bills have a volatile relationship with inflation, although a stronger and more positive one than the relationships of nominal bonds and equities with inflation.

With knowledge of the volatility in the relationships among nominal asset classes and between nominal asset classes and inflation, the challenge of matching real liabilities with nominal assets becomes obvious. Particularly in periods of unexpectedly low or high inflation, the behavior of real assets will diverge spectacularly from the behavior of nominal assets: correlations could approach −1.0 during extreme economic surprises, such as commodity price shocks.

Looking to the U.K. experience, we see evidence of this divergence by parsing the data into periods of increasing, decreasing or fluctuating inflation. In the one period shown in Exhibit 23 with increasing inflation (Period D), real bonds performed superlatively, while providing consistently respectable real rates of return during periods of decreasing or fluctuating inflation.

Exhibit 21: Correlation of Long-Term Bonds and CPI: Rolling 36-Month Periods Since 1926

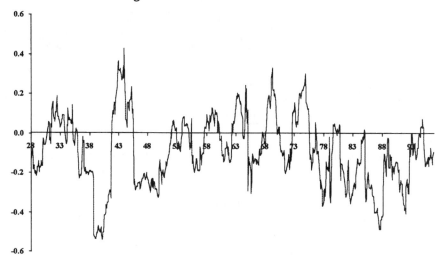

Source: U.S. Department of Labor, SEI Investments, and Ibbotson Associates, Inc. Used with permission. ©1998 Ibbotson Associates, Inc. All rights reserved. [Certain portions of this work were derived from copyrighted works of Roger G. Ibbotson and Rex Sinquefield.]

Exhibit 22: Correlation of 30-Day T-Bills and CPI: Rolling 36-Month Periods Since 1926

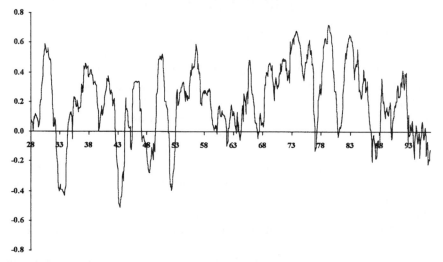

Source: U.S. Department of Labor, SEI Investments, and Ibbotson Associates, Inc. Used with permission. ©1998 Ibbotson Associates, Inc. All rights reserved. [Certain portions of this work were derived from copyrighted works of Roger G. Ibbotson and Rex Sinquefield.]

Exhibit 23: Real Returns of U.K. Nominal and Real Bonds In Various Inflationary Environments

Period	Inflation	Nominal Bond Real Return		Real Bond Real Return	
		Total	Annualized	Total	Annualized
A (0.75 yrs)	Decreasing	42.1%	—	9.7%	—
B (1.75 yrs)	Fluctuating	11.4%	6.4%	9.8%	5.5%
C (2.75 yrs)	Decreasing	20.1%	6.9%	6.4%	2.3%
D (2.00 yrs)	Increasing	−2.3%	−1.2%	20.3%	9.7%
E (1.50 yrs)	Decreasing	11.9%	7.8%	9.7%	6.4%

Based on all of the correlation data presented above, and especially for an investor with real liabilities, we can draw several conclusions:

- nominal assets are ill-suited to hedge inflation risk
- nominal assets are unpredictable in their behavior due to the volatility of both correlation and volatility
- nominal assets are unreliable in delivering consistent real returns
- no investor can forecast inflation

Given these conclusions, many capital markets outside the United States have embraced a simple solution: match real liabilities with inflation-indexed bonds.

A SIMPLE SOLUTION

As we've seen, virtually all investors have at least a portion of their liabilities exposed to the effects of inflation. These real liabilities can best be matched by real assets. Given the volatility of realized real returns provided above, no combination of nominal assets, however cleverly hedged, can match the growth in the liabilities as well as an asset which is specifically linked to inflation. While debates will continue for decades over the optimum measure of inflation for a particular set of liabilities, any broad measure of inflation will always be a better match for a real liability than a non-indexed (i.e., nominal) asset.

Due to the high level of variability of realized real returns from nominal securities, defined benefit plan sponsors must periodically increase contributions to the plan when assets underperform. Because the inclusion of real bonds in a portfolio results in improved matching of assets and liabilities, both the present value of future contributions and the variability of the expected cost can be significantly reduced, as shown in Exhibit 24.

While real bonds are unique in their ability to reduce the volatility of the matching process for defined benefit plans, for any institutional or individual investor with a goal of volatility reduction, real bonds are particularly powerful.

The analysis presented in Exhibit 25 is in nominal space and examines combinations of real and nominal bonds ranging from 100% nominal to 100% real over various time periods.

The optimal combination for volatility reduction with a 1-year horizon falls at roughly 50%, which is the actual or targeted asset allocation for the U.K. and Canadian pension plan real bond holdings, but can be applied to any investor seeking volatility reduction through diversification.

Exhibit 24: Pension Plan Expected Cost versus Cost Variability (50% Indexing of Retired Lives)

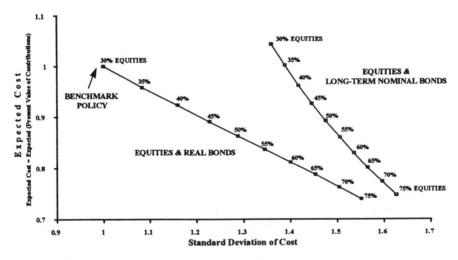

Source: SEI Investments

Exhibit 25: Nominal Return Volatility (1, 3, and 5 Year Time Horizons)

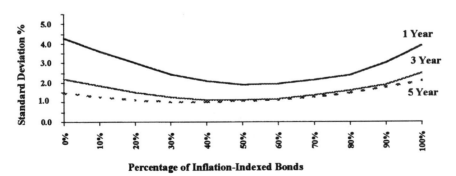

Source: SEI Investments

SUMMARY

Investor goals recede rapidly in the presence of high inflation — virtually no nominal asset class does well in an inflationary environment. Investors in the United States have been desensitized to inflation due to the recent economic environment, but the data presented above demonstrate that recent history is a poor predictor of either the short- or long-term path of inflation.

Whether or not higher inflation returns to the United States, real assets will always be superior matching investments for real liabilities than the predominantly nominal asset classes favored by U.S. investors. Educational efforts by inflation-indexed security issuers and the intermediaries repackaging these securities will address the real nature of substantial portions of all investors' liabilities and heighten awareness of the mismatch of real liabilities with nominal assets.

Coupled with this new awareness, broader knowledge of the low to negative correlation of real bonds with nominal assets will enable investors to appreciate the superior portfolio anchor characteristics of real bonds over conventional anchors, with respect to both performance and expense profile.

The size of the U.S. market should eventually dwarf other nation's issuances. Index-linked gilts in the U.K. account for approximately 20% of the total gilt market. Were the United States to issue at these levels, the U.S. inflation-indexed bond market could exceed $750 billion. This would represent only 30% of U.S. pension funds' fixed income assets, a much lower ratio than the U.K. and Canadian 50% shares.

While equities will probably remain the asset of choice for long-term real return generation, the short- to medium-term predictability of real return generation provided by inflation-indexed bonds will lower pension plan funding costs and provide peace of mind for retirees concerned with maintaining consistent purchasing power. As the boomer generation settles into retirement and receives its $10 trillion asset transfer, demand for investment solutions that address their needs for dependable retirement income and asset protection will elevate inflation-indexed bonds to a position of prominence in the U.S. capital markets.

Chapter 6

Inflation Hedging in a Low-Inflation World: The Plan Sponsor's Rationale

Laurence B. Siegel
Director, Investment Policy Research
The Ford Foundation

INTRODUCTION

Disinflation has been a prominent feature of the economic landscape around the world for almost two decades — that is, for as long as most people now active in the investment business can remember. Why, in this context, should investors concern themselves with inflation-linked bonds and other securities that hedge against inflation?

The reason is that some degree of inflation — low, high, or hyper — has been characteristic of the entire history of the fiat-money standard. (Later, we will compare the fiat-money standard to a gold standard.) Governments which have arranged the monetary system so that they have the mechanism to inflate are possessors of an option. They will not always use the option, but they surely will from time to time. When a government wishes to raise revenues that cannot be obtained from current taxation, or reduce the real value of its debt, inflation will result.

Because many people misunderstand the connection between government budgets, the money supply, and inflation, a brief review of monetary theory is in order. Inflation comes not from greedy businessmen or workers but from a rate in the growth of the money supply that exceeds the rate of growth in the stock of goods that money can buy. Because the money supply is controlled by the central bank, an agency of the government, it is more or less correct to say that only governments can cause a generalized inflation.[1] Of course, in a free economy, governments don't actually set prices, but if the monetary authorities allow the money supply to grow faster than the goods supply, businesses can raise prices successfully and inflation occurs; otherwise some prices rise as others fall, and the general level of prices remains unchanged.

---

[1] A very large supply shock that is not caused by the domestic government, such as the OPEC oil price increases in the 1970s, can cause a one-time rise in the general price level (that is, of goods other than oil) but not a persistent inflation.

Today's Federal Reserve, under the leadership of Alan Greenspan, has been remarkably well focused on restraining inflation, and on expanding the money supply only when the private sector seems to require a stimulus. Central banks should not always be counted on to behave this well. In general, there are two ways that governments can finance expenditures beyond the level supported by current taxation: borrowing and money creation. Rational investors should expect governments to use both tools from time to time. Moreover, from the government's point of view, borrowing and monetary expansion work well in tandem: if the borrower can arrange an unexpected inflation (one that is not incorporated into the yield on the debt), the real cost of borrowing is lowered.[2]

To sum up, governments can obtain financing (that is, defer taxation) through inflationary money supply growth. Moreover, a government has an additional incentive to inflate if it is a net debtor. Finally, governments that are answerable to voters tend to become debtors because voters demand more in services than they are willing to pay for in taxes. The inevitable conclusion is that, in the long run, inflation is more likely than deflation under a fiat-money standard.

A BIT OF HISTORY

Exhibit 1 shows the price level in England (the United Kingdom had not yet been founded) from the year 1260 to 1976. For the first 250 years, the price level was trendless, with inflation and deflation tending to balance each other out. The amount of price change during a "run" in either direction could be substantial, but prices ended the period roughly where they began. In the sixteenth century prices gradually rose, but from 1600 to about 1932 prices were once again trendless. From 1932 to 1976, however, prices rocketed upward with barely a pause. The exhibit is a little out of date, but almost everyone knows what happened after 1976: prices continued upward at varying rates. Consumer prices in England will end the twentieth century at about 40 times their 1932 level.

Obviously the currency slipped a mooring sometime around 1932. But what was the mooring? Over almost the entire period up to 1932, the British government was committed to converting its currency into silver or gold at a fixed rate: a commodity-money standard. On September 21, 1931, however, the British Parliament enacted the Gold Standard Amendment Act, which amended the standard out of existence. Freed from the constraint of keeping the market price of an ounce of gold at the centuries-old standard of 3 pounds, 17 shillings, and 10.5 pence (Lord knows how this figure was originally arrived at), the British government was able to provide liquidity at a rapid rate appropriate to the extraordinary circumstances of the Great Depression. Consumer prices, however, never looked back, and the greatest bear market in the history of the nominal bond market had begun.

---

[2] The economic principle known as *Ricardian equivalence*, named for the early nineteenth century economist David Ricardo, says that there is no difference between current taxation, borrowing, and inflation in terms of their eventual impact on taxpayers. Government spending consumes real resources, and it is the quantity of resources that counts, not the way they are financed.

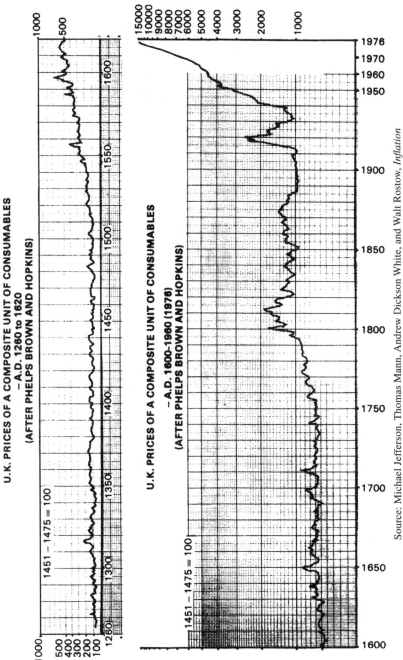

Exhibit 1: Inflation in England from 1260 to 1976

U.K. PRICES OF A COMPOSITE UNIT OF CONSUMABLES
— A.D. 1260 to 1620
(AFTER PHELPS BROWN AND HOPKINS)

1451 – 1475 = 100

U.K. PRICES OF A COMPOSITE UNIT OF CONSUMABLES
— A.D. 1600–1960 (1976)
(AFTER PHELPS BROWN AND HOPKINS)

1451 – 1475 = 100

Source: Michael Jefferson, Thomas Mann, Andrew Dickson White, and Walt Rostow, *Inflation* (New York: Riverrun Press, 1978), pp. 75. Reprinted with permission.

Today, a return to a gold standard would be a disaster, and we do not advocate it in the least. The attempt by the U.S. and British governments to defend their currencies under the gold standard in the 1930s is one of the most widely agreed-upon causes of the Depression. Yet if we are going to live under a fiat-money standard for the foreseeable future, we will have to get used to persistent inflation. Today's inflation rates are probably atypically low, and reflect a confluence of factors: cheap commodities, central-bank restraint, and a surge of technological innovation. In the long run — say, more than five years — the likelihood of renewed inflation is much greater than the likelihood of persistent deflation, and inflation-linked bonds provide a timely defense against this eventuality.

The use of British instead of U.S. history to illustrate these concepts is largely arbitrary. It is fun to be able to show a seven-century price chart, and the modern low point of the price chart lines up in a particularly nice way with the date the gold standard was abandoned in Britain. Data from the United States show similar patterns, but compressed into a shorter time frame. The principle of price stability in a commodity-money standard and inflation in a fiat-money standard is the same everywhere.

INFLATION IS WORSE THAN DEFLATION FOR FINANCIAL ASSETS

For investors in financial assets, persistent inflation is not only more likely than persistent deflation, it is worse for the wallet. Holders of nominal bonds profit from unexpected deflation because nominal yields fall, causing bond prices to rise; moreover, the bondholder is being paid back in dollars that are more valuable in terms of consumer goods. For the same reasons in reverse, unexpected inflation is disastrous for nominal bondholders.[3]

The idea that stocks might benefit (or at least not get hurt) in a deflation is more surprising, because most people's knowledge of deflation comes from the Great Depression, when stocks crashed. More recently, many analysts have been concerned about the prospect of deflation because it might impair the corporate earnings growth on which today's high stock valuations depend. Historically, however, stocks have thrived in deflationary environments. Exhibit 2 shows the record of the U.S. stock market under various inflation and deflation scenarios as measured over 1790 to 1985 by Roger Ibbotson and Gary Brinson,[4] which we have updated to 1997. (Ibbotson and Brinson went back to 1790 to capture deflationary cycles other than the Great Depression of the 1930s; pre-Civil War data should be regarded as approximate.) Notably, the correlation between real stock returns and inflation rates is negative. Stock market returns, after adjustment for

---

[3] Note we said "unexpected." If the inflation is fully expected and incorporated in bond yields, this effect is negated. The realization of an expected change in the price level has no effect on a bondholder's real wealth.

[4] Roger G. Ibbotson and Gary P. Brinson, *Investment Markets* (New York: McGraw-Hill, 1987), p. 89.

inflation, were very good under deflationary, stable-price, and moderately inflationary conditions, but poor when inflation exceeded 4% and sharply negative
when inflation exceeded 8%. Clearly deflation is no bar to strong stock markets.

Some market observers would go further. The investment manager Charles
Gave describes the history of capitalism as "the history of falling prices," in which
economic growth enables the same goods to be produced with fewer resources. This
observation would suggest that increasing prosperity is reflected in declining nominal
prices of goods such as food and shelter, and is correct over the gold-standard period.
(Exhibit 1, which shows gradually rising prices over this period, appears to measure
an expanding basket of goods, overstating inflation in much the same way that
today's Consumer Price Index does.) Under a fiat-money system, the same principle
applies in real but not nominal terms, so that increasing prosperity is reflected in falling real prices of consumer goods; that is, it takes less and less effort to earn a loaf of
bread. (It is said that in 1815, the typical German worker spent 85% of his income on
food. Today's situation is better.) Because of monetary expansion, however, this
decline in real prices takes place behind a backdrop of rising nominal prices.

In conclusion, inflation risk is greater than deflation risk because inflation is not only more likely than deflation — it is more harmful to the real value
of invested assets. Thus inflation-linked bonds and other inflation-hedging securities are a valuable resource to the plan sponsor. To invest in inflation hedges, however, it is not enough that inflation present a risk to real asset values in general.
The plan sponsor is concerned with matching assets to liabilities.

LIABILITIES AND INFLATION

Most new plan assets are defined-contribution assets. Although these assets are allocated by the employee, employers have influence over the allocation and may con-
ceivably face adverse consequences in the future if investment results turn out poorly.
For these reasons we consider defined-contribution asset allocation to be part of the
plan sponsor's purview. We also cover endowments and foundations, which are notably inflation-sensitive, in addition to traditional defined-benefit pension plans.

*Exhibit 2: Real Annual Total Returns on U.S. Stocks under
Different Inflation and Deflation Environments, 1790-1997*

Inflation Rate	Number of Years	Average Annual Real Return on Stocks (%)
Below −4%	32	11.3
−4% to −1%	24	12.9
−1% to +1%	35	12.5
+1% to +4%	63	11.2
+4% to +8%	30	4.2
Above +8%	24	−5.7

Defined Contribution Retirement Plans and Individual Savings

While defined-contribution retirement plans and individual savings have no contractual liability, they exist to fund consumption in the future and thus have a conceptual liability consisting of consumer goods. (More precisely, asset owners can be expected to draw down their fund balances in amounts sufficient to purchase the goods they need and want.) A plausible model of this liability is, therefore, the inflation rate itself. One may modify the Consumer Price Index to account for differential inflation in health care and other consumer goods that are desired by retirees, but such modification does not change the basic principle: the liability moves one-to-one with inflation.

Given such a liability, the natural question is not why one should buy inflation-linked bonds, but why one should buy anything else. The reason, of course, is that the return on inflation-linked bonds is too low to provide a reasonable level of income to retirees at any realistic savings rate. For investors such as retirees who have long time horizons, inflation-linked bonds are the riskless asset and as such earn the riskless rate of return. Stocks, which have had annual returns some 7% higher than fixed-income assets over the past three-quarter century, are the only asset class that offers such an upside. Of course, future stock returns may be much lower — there is no guarantee of earning at an annual pace of 7% above the riskless rate over any time period, even a long one — but investors must take this risk (with some of their money) in order to have any chance of meeting their goals.

The fixed-income portion of a defined-contribution portfolio should be much more heavily weighted toward inflation-linked bonds than current practice suggests. Current practice (virtually nothing in inflation-linked bonds) derives from the fact that these instruments are brand new in the United States, and issuance as a proportion of the overall fixed-income market is minuscule. As issuance grows, the role of inflation-linked bonds in defined-contribution and individual-savings portfolios should rise disproportionately, for these are the investors who can benefit the most from "linkers."

The broad question of how much to allocate to stocks and how much to fixed income is beyond the scope of this chapter. However, it should be noted that the inflation-hedging properties of linked bonds will tend to steal some of the stock market's thunder in terms of the latter's ability to keep even with inflation. To the extent that some conservative investors buy stocks for their inflation protection, they may wish to switch some of these funds to inflation-linked bonds. However, investors who buy stocks to participate in the real growth of the economy should stay with stocks.

Endowments and Foundations

Like individuals, endowed institutions such as universities and charitable foundations have real "liabilities" (again, we use the term in its conceptual, not contractual, sense) because professors' salaries and other costs of education, the needs of foundation grantees, and operating expenses all tend to rise one-for-one with inflation. In fact, many foundations face an IRS requirement that they pay out 5% of the market value of assets to grantees annually. If the real value of principal is to be preserved, this payout requirement ties foundation expenses to inflation, and the investment objective of such foundations is typically to earn 5% (plus an allowance for certain expenses) plus the inflation rate annually. With inflation-linked bonds yielding a real rate of 3.7% as of this writing, the goal is almost — but not quite — achievable with just this asset.

The asset allocation dilemma for endowed institutions resembles that for individuals. In order to meet investment goals or payout requirements, the institution must take more risk than that represented by inflation-linked bonds, because the yield on "linkers" is inadequate to these goals and requirements. Stocks, nominal bonds (including high-yielding corporates), real estate, private equity, and even hedge funds constitute significant portions of many endowed institutions' portfolios. Because these institutions typically regard themselves as leaders in investment innovation, they have been early investors in inflation-linked bonds, as they have been with some of these other asset classes. Some institutions regard inflation-linked bonds as simply another category of Treasuries and classify them with their general fixed-income investments, while others classify them with other inflation hedges.

Defined Benefit Pension Plans

The case for inflation-linked bonds in defined-benefit pension plans is less clear than it is for the other classes of funds we have covered, because at least traditionally the defined benefit plan is relatively insensitive to inflation. This is because traditional plans pay to the retiree a fixed percentage of "final" pay, with no cost of living adjustment (COLA) after retirement. (Final pay may be in fact calculated as the average of the last few years' pay.) Such a formula incorporates inflation from the present through the time the employee retires, but not thereafter. Thus the expected future payout to the retiree moves up with inflation, but less than one-for-one. These expected cash flows are then discounted to calculate a present value of expected future liabilities, using an interest or discount rate that does tend to rise one-for-one with increases in expected inflation.[5] The net of these two effects is a present value of liabilities that declines as expected inflation rises, much like the price of a nominal bond.

In a 1986 study, Laurie Goodman and William Marshall found that for final-pay plans without COLAs, the present value of the pension liability (specifically of the projected benefit obligation, or PBO) fell 6.5% for each 1% rise in the expected inflation rate.[6] A nominal bond portfolio with an "inflation duration" of

---

[5] By "expected inflation" (it should be clear from the context) we mean the inflation rate that is expected over the entire term of the asset or liability being valued.

[6] Laurie S. Goodman and William J. Marshall, "Inflation, Interest Rates, and Pension Liabilities," in Robert D. Arnott and Frank J. Fabozzi (eds.), *Asset Allocation* (Chicago: Probus Publishing, 1988). This conclusion holds if only the expected rate of inflation is varied and all other conditions, including the current price level and expected real interest rates, are held constant. The authors assume that the yield curve is flat and that it undergoes parallel, one-for-one shifts in response to changes in expected inflation. The representative active member of the pension plan being modeled has 10 years to retirement, and expects to collect benefits for 17 years thereafter. Goodman and Marshall indicate while the representative member in this example is older than the average member of most plans, their assumption is realistic because many pension plans are weighted by years of service, so that older employees have a disproportionate claim on assets. We thank Barton Waring of Barclays Global Investors for bringing this work to our attention.

6.5 years has the same attribute and would immunize this particular liability against changes in expected inflation.[7] Inflation-linked bonds will not help much in constructing such a portfolio.

For the pension plan modeled by Goodman and Marshall, inflation-linked bonds also don't help much if the manager diversifies and buy stocks as well as bonds. Stocks, which are real assets, should be presumed for this type of planning to have a duration of zero.[8] If the portfolio is 60% in stocks and 40% in bonds, the bonds would have to have a duration in excess of 15 years in order to bring the weighted-average duration of the fund up to 6.5 years. The only role of "linkers" in this case is as an equity substitute, and the case for that is less than compelling.

As Goodman and Marshall indicate, however, when post-retirement COLAs are introduced into the equation the whole picture changes. If every cash flow in the plan is fully indexed to inflation, the inflation-duration of the plan is zero. (We are back to the problem faced by the individual saver.) To immunize a fully inflation-indexed pension plan, one should hold a portfolio with a zero inflation-duration. While nominal assets may have some role in such a portfolio, it should be composed chiefly of real assets, including stocks, cash, and inflation-linked bonds.

Whether inflation-linked bonds are a plausible investment for defined-benefit pension plans, then, depends on the inflation sensitivity of the plan. The more fully the plan payouts are indexed to inflation, the more an inflation hedge is needed on the asset side.

A COMPARISON OF INFLATION-HEDGING ASSETS

Given the need for investment assets that hedge inflation (that is, that have an inflation-duration somewhere near zero), which ones can be counted on to do so? Let us briefly review each candidate.

Stocks

Stocks represent ownership of real assets: factories, labor contracts, patents, consumer franchises, bandwidth. As such they should rise with inflation, but this can

---

[7] By "inflation duration" we mean the percentage decrease in the present value of an asset (or liability) for each percentage-point increase in the rate of inflation that is expected over the life of that asset. By "interest-rate duration" we mean the effective duration. To construct a bond portfolio with an inflation duration of 6.5 years, one needs to buy bonds with an interest-rate duration that is somewhat longer, with the difference depending on the extent of real-interest-rate risk. Goodman and Marshall calculate, based on historical data covering 1959-1986, that a bond portfolio with an interest-rate duration of 9.0 years would immunize a pension liability with an inflation duration of 6.5 years. This proportion, 9.0/6.5, can be thought of as the hedge ratio between nominal bonds and pension liabilities.

[8] In practice, stocks have a positive duration because companies, due to limitations on their ability to contract in real terms, cannot pass all inflation through to customers. Martin L. Leibowitz and Stanley Kogelman, in "Resolving the Equity Duration Paradox," *Financial Analysts Journal* (January-February 1993), provide a structure in which to understand the empirical fact that stocks behave to some extent like nominal bonds.

be counted on only in the extreme long run. The longest period in modern U.S. history over which consumer prices outran total returns on stocks was the 19 years from mid-1963 to mid-1982 — long by any standard. While we have assumed that stocks have an inflation-duration of zero and thus hedge inflation, plan sponsors hoping to keep their jobs had better have some other arrows in their quiver if inflation picks up.

Cash

The original inflation hedge, cash returns have a high correlation with inflation rates. The only problem is cash's low yield. Cash underperformed inflation over 1972-1981 and then just broke even with inflation in 1992-1994.

Real Estate

Real estate did very well in the inflation of the 1970s and early 1980s, providing leveraged returns that beat inflation rates by a large margin. In the unlikely event that inflation on that scale returned, real estate would probably provide a repeat performance. Like stocks, however, real estate has its own boom-and-bust cycle and its inflation-hedging properties are mostly long run. An institution that made direct investments in commercial real estate (represented by the NCREIF real estate total return index) who bought at the mid-1990 high would not have broken even until late 1995, and would have had returns lower than the inflation rate through mid-1997.[9] Today, most institutions invest in real estate through REITs, which are exposed to the inflation risk of stocks as well as to that of real estate.

Commodities

While commodities are certainly real assets, the commodities that are traded in liquid markets make such a small fraction of total inputs that holding them may or may not hedge inflation well. In addition, commodity prices are many times more volatile than consumer prices. For example, collateralized (unleveraged) futures on the Goldman Sachs Commodity Index (GSCI),[10] which soared in the 1970s, had mixed results in the disinflationary 1980s and 1990s with annual returns ranging from −23% in 1981 to 38% in 1989, while annual inflation was never out of the range of 1% to 9%. Steve Strongin and Melanie Petsch, while noting that commodities are a good inflation hedge for portfolios of stocks and bonds, indicate that "the instability of the relationship between commodity returns and the level of inflation makes commodities a poor protector if the asset being protected

[9] These data represent total returns on the NCREIF real estate index.
[10] GSCI collateralized futures returns are based on a backtest; the index was not introduced until 1991. Data are from Paul D. Kaplan and Scott L. Lummer, "GSCI Collateralized Futures as a Hedging and Diversification Tool for Institutional Portfolios: An Update," forthcoming in the *Journal of Investing* and available on the World Wide Web at http://www.ibbotson.com/Research/gsci/page0000.asp. An earlier version that is currently available in print is Scott L. Lummer and Laurence B. Siegel, "GSCI Collateralized Futures: A Hedging and Diversification Tool for Institutional Investors," *Journal of Investing* (Summer 1993).

is a real income stream."[11] Moreover, the GSCI collateralized futures returns include a substantial "roll yield" or risk-premium component that would have been earned over the backtest period but that may not be repeatable.[12]

Direct natural resource investments are basically additional forms of real estate, except that the land yields its rent in oil, gas, crops, minerals, or trees instead of cash. Because these goods are generally marketable for cash, our comments on real estate apply here as well, except that the cycles in these assets are not particularly correlated with commercial real estate cycles, so holding both may provide some additional inflation protection.

Hedge Funds

The term "hedge funds" originally referred to equity funds that hedge market risk by taking offsetting long and short positions. Those hedge funds that actually hedge to a market-neutral position — and one needs to be careful in identifying them — should produce returns that deviate from Treasury bill returns according to the amount of skill the manager has. Conceptually, at least, such a return pattern should be at least as good an inflation hedge as cash. In practice, one's mileage may vary widely, with a few hedge funds outperforming even the best long-only stock portfolios, and a few hedge funds causing total loss of the investor's capital.

Inflation-Linked Bonds

When real yields are stable, inflation-linked bonds track inflation almost perfectly, and investors who desire inflation protection should hold them. However, neither inflation-linked bonds nor any other investment are a magic bullet for an investor concerned about inflation. They have essentially no upside, and volatility in real yields could cause unexpected (albeit small) capital losses for investors who sell before maturity.[13]

CONCLUSION

Investors should not disregard the threat of inflation simply because they cannot currently identify a reason why it will re-emerge. Moreover, as we pointed out in

---

[11] Steve Strongin and Melanie Petsch, "Protecting a Portfolio Against Inflation Risk," *Investment Policy* (July-August 1997).

[12] The roll yield is earned by closing out futures positions before they expire and buying longer-dated ones. On average this strategy has added return, and its success is attributable to the presence of a risk premium paid by corporate hedgers (who are short in futures) to investors (who are long, and who in this context are sometimes called speculators).

[13] An additional difficulty is caused by the absence of "linkers" from the leading fixed income benchmarks such as the Salomon BIG (broad investment grade) index. Because inflation-linked bonds are expected to underperform otherwise-comparable Treasuries by the amount of the inflation risk premium (that is one reason why the Treasury issues them) "linkers" will be a slight drag on performance. This problem may be rectified by constructing a custom benchmark that includes inflation-linked bonds in the weights in which they are expected to be held.

the first section, there is a structural bias toward inflation in the long run. The essence of risk is that the unexpected may happen. After it does, one can no longer hedge against it as effectively as before, if at all. Inflation-linked bonds are only one of many assets that provide the investor with inflation protection, but they are the most reliable source of that protection, although they are limited in other ways.

On a more timely note, people who are concerned that the primary risk to markets today is a deflationary recession are most likely talking about a blip — a few quarters (or at worst a few years) of declining real GDP in Asia. It is entirely appropriate to hedge against inflation while believing the short-run trend of consumer prices will be downward.

A very different concern, but likewise relevant to investors taking a position in inflation hedges, is the "long boom" theory (sometimes parodied as New Age thinking) in which deflationary growth is the most likely scenario.[14] However, investors should not be terribly concerned about growth causing deflation. Futurists who believe that sustained real economic growth is leading to an era of relative abundance and declining prices may well be right about the real economy, but they are forgetting that the general level of prices is the one economic variable that is primarily monetary. As we said earlier, a sustained decline in real prices (wherein it takes less and less human effort to acquire a given good or service) can take place against a backdrop of rising nominal prices, and that is the economic scenario we are expecting.

---

[14] The "long boom" scenario is articulated in Peter Schwartz and Peter Leyden, "The Long Boom: A History of the Future, 1980-2020," *Wired* (July 1997), also available on the World Wide Web at http://www.wired.com/wired/5.07/longboom.html. Although the article does not specifically forecast deflation, it asserts that technology will greatly lessen inflationary pressures that are traditionally associated with high rates of economic growth.

Chapter 7

Asset Allocation with TIPS

John Brynjolfsson
Vice President and Fixed Income Portfolio Manager
PIMCO

Edward P. Rennie
Senior Vice President & Regional Manager
PIMCO

INTRODUCTION

In Chapter 2, a radical reorganization of how asset allocation is typically performed was recommended. We realize that radical change is not always possible, and that even when it is, context may be helpful. In this chapter we simply incorporate inflation-indexed bonds into a more traditional global asset allocation framework.

TRADITIONAL ASSET ALLOCATION PRACTICAL RESULTS

In the scenarios below we explore a strategic allocation to inflation-protection bonds (IPBs) and address two questions. First, what reallocation do we find most efficient? Second, how does such a reallocation impact portfolio risk and return?

Here are the answers to these two questions. First, assuming the existing allocation includes some cash equivalents, the most dramatic efficiency gains are obtained by reallocating a percentage of cash equivalents into IPBs. The initial incremental allocation generates the greatest gains, but subsequent allocations generate additional efficiency gains. Second, the effect of the reallocation is to increase expected return with little increase in expected risk. Smaller reallocations out of equities and bonds into IPBs generate additional efficiency gains, mainly through risk reduction.

Methodology

The methodology for the analysisis as follows:

- The optimizations employ four distinct sets of scenario inputs. The historical scenario is presented first and provides context. Forward-looking scenarios are then presented to incorporate our base case scenario as well as low inflation and high inflation stress tests.

- The base case scenario is constructed to be consistent with *ex ante* efficiency of a 40/40/20 (equities/bonds/cash) allocation. The focus of the analysis is the introduction of IPBs, not more general asset allocation questions.
- The frontiers and allocations are generated using unconstrained optimizations. Such optimizations are free of distortions and are intuitive. For example, an unconstrained optimization would highlight negative allocation weights if the scenario inputs warrant them.
- The unconstrained frontier is used to determine the best efficiency gaining, *incremental* reallocation. The incremental allocation, identified as *Portfolio B* throughout, represents a 1/10 move toward the "ultimate" frontier allocation. The ultimate allocation, generally, would not be appropriate as first (or last) steps, since constraints would likely bind, and the scenario inputs are not immutable.

HISTORICAL (1987-1996) SCENARIO

Construction of Input Series

Our process starts with a 10-year historical return series for the existing global asset classes: equity, bonds, and cash. We then turn to IPBs, which require special treatment. In particular, during this historical period IPBs did not exist as a "global" asset class. There were only a miscellany of local IPB markets in various stages of development. But we were able to combine the observable local market dynamics of IPBs with parameters describing the global macroeconomic environment. In this way we were able to generate a synthetic global IPB "historical" return index. This synthetic index was then appropriately compared to the other global historical indices, including U.S. cash, from the same period.

Asset Class Performance

The period from 1987 to 1996 was a period of disinflation. Financial asset returns were high and IPB returns were modest. Since volatility of inflation was relatively low, the cash flows and returns of IPBs paralleled the cash flows and returns of nominal bonds. As one would expect, correlations between IPBs and nominal bonds were also high. From an asset allocation perspective, all of these factors were hostile to IPBs.

This episode was not the worst case scenario, but it was close. It is therefore somewhat surprising that IPBs show up with a strongly positive allocation. The inherent structural advantages of IPBs, low risk and a substantial real yield cushion, offset the environmental negatives.

These "near worst case" historical scenarios examined in Exhibits 1, 2, and 3. These scenarios provide a good historical backdrop for the forward-looking analysis presented in subsequent sections.

Exhibit 1: Historical (1987-1996) Inputs

Asset Class	Return	Risk	Correlations				Output
			MS Wrld Eqty	SB Wrld Bond	US T-Bill 30	IPBs (Synth.)	Portfolio B
MS Wrld Eqty	11.19	13.28	100				38.21
SB Wrld Bond	9.70	6.53	20	100			41.77
US T-Bill 30	5.46	1.75	-12	-1	100		4.71
IPBs (Synth.)	6.19	2.21	-11	30	71	100	15.30

Exhibit 2: Frontiers Using Historical (1987-1996) Inputs
Efficient Frontiers

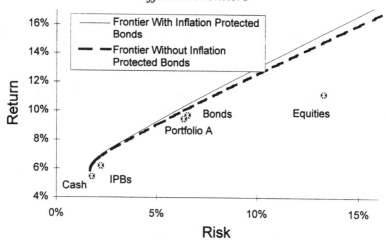

Exhibit 3: Optimized Reallocations Using Historical (1987-1996) Inputs
Efficient Frontiers

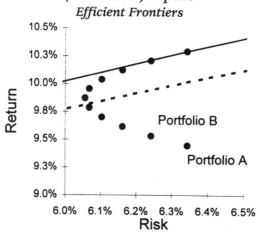

Exhibit 4: Base Case Inputs

Asset Class	Return	Risk	MS Wrld Eqty	SB Wrld Bond	Cash Equivalent	IPBs (Synth.)	Portfolio B
			Correlations				Output
MS Wrld Eqty	8.50%	12.00%	100%				38.72%
SB Wrld Bond	7.00%	6.00%	50%	100%			39.25%
Cash Equivalent	6.00%	1.00%	0%	0%	100%		11.13%
IPBs	6.50%	3.00%	35%	25%	50%	100%	10.90%

Optimizations Using Historical Data

Exhibit 1 shows the inputs used for these optimizations. In Exhibit 2, we plot this input data graphically and then with the help of an optimizer, generate the unconstrained frontiers. The current 40/40/20/0 allocation is labeled Portfolio A. In Exhibit 3, we focus on the frontier around the existing allocation. This allows us to compare the existing allocation and the allocations closer to the frontier.

Exhibit 3 shows Portfolio A as well as a series of allocations, starting with Portfolio B, that lead to the frontier. For reference we also present the Portfolio B allocation in Exhibit 1. There we have labeled it "Output Portfolio B."

We would have had great difficulty implementing any of these more efficient allocations 10 years ago. In particular, perfect foresight and access to a global IPB market would have been needed. For these and other reasons, the analysis based on the 10-year historical scenario is best considered as context for the forward-looking scenarios explored in subsequent sections.

BASE CASE SCENARIO

In this section we employ a forward-looking perspective. We start with our secular forecast for asset class returns, risks, and correlations. Since our desire is to isolate the asset allocation implications of the introduction of IPBs, we need to create a neutral starting point. This is done by adjusting our secular forecast so that we arrive at inputs that make the 40/40/20 allocation *ex ante* efficient. (This simply insures that the optimizer, run without IPBs, generates the 40/40/20 as an optimum. It turns out the main change to our return forecast that is implied by *ex ante* efficiency is a 0.5% increase for equity returns.) From this neutral starting point, we then examine the introduction of IPBs.

Exhibit 4 shows the relatively conservative base case inputs. For example, we ignore our tactical outlook that suggests falling IPB yields are likely to generate capital gains over the next three years. Rather we assume that in the base case scenario IPBs will underperform nominal bonds on average by 0.5% that represents a theoretical risk premium earned by nominal bonds — but not IPBs. The correlation with nominal bonds is also conservative; it is positive but slightly lower than IPB and equity correlations.

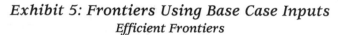

Exhibit 5: Frontiers Using Base Case Inputs
Efficient Frontiers

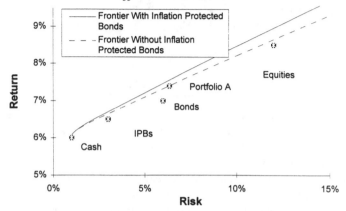

Exhibit 6: Optimized Reallocation Using Base Case Inputs
Efficient Frontiers

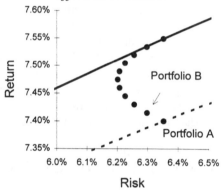

More succinctly, we have used our best judgment to isolate an appropriate set of inputs to use as our base case scenario.

Optimizations Using Base Case Inputs

Just as with the historical inputs, we generate efficient frontiers. There are two notable features of the efficient frontiers shown in Exhibit 5. First, the result reflects the much lower return environment for all asset classes that we forecast for the coming years. Second, by construction, Portfolio A lies precisely on the efficient frontier.

Exhibit 6, where we zoom in on Portfolio A, shows this even more clearly. This plot also includes the 10 incremental reallocations, again starting with Portfolio B. Recall that Portfolio A simply represents the original 40/40/20 allocation. As is shown by the solid line in the exhibit, the addition of IPBs to the optimization expands the opportunity set, moving the frontier to the left and upward.

Exhibit 7: Low Inflation Inputs

Asset Class	Return	Risk	MS Wrld Eqty	SB Wrld Bond	Cash Equivalent	IPBs (Synth.)	Portfolio B
			Correlations				Output
MS Wrld Eqty	10.50%	12.00%	100%				39.52%
SB Wrld Bond	8.00%	6.00%	50%	100%			41.79%
Cash Equivalent	5.50%	1.00%	0%	0%	100%		26.40%
IPBs	5.50%	3.00%	30%	15%	50%	100%	-7.71%

The major reallocation required to arrive at Portfolio B is a reallocation out of traditional cash into IPBs. The optimizer will also reallocate smaller percentages out of equities and bonds into IPBs. The precise allocation is shown in the last column of Exhibit 4.

There is no requirement that the reallocation stop with Portfolio B. The subsequent allocations in the series of 10 allocations shown in Exhibit 6 simply involve the same incremental reallocations, eventually ending with a somewhat levered, unconstrained efficient frontier portfolio. This is not so surprising — the leverage is highlighting the disparity between IPB and cash returns.

Do we feel that such unconstrained portfolios represent the ultimate allocation? No. We present the 1/10 allocation as an appropriate incremental step. Subsequent steps can then be taken, but they may need to incorporate constraints and other considerations, not necessary for the first incremental step.

The optimization process also generates various ancillary results which are not included in the analysis presented in this chapter, but which are available. An example is the optimal separating vector of portfolio weights. This is the re-balancing vector that moves allocations along the efficient frontier in a parallel direction.

BREAKING OUT LOW AND HIGH INFLATION SCENARIOS

The base case scenario is really an amalgamation of scenarios. It is helpful to separate these scenarios to explore more intensively their characteristics and implications. Below we define representative low and high inflation scenarios.

Low Inflation Scenario

We use the base case scenario as a starting point to construct the low inflation scenario. In a lower inflation environment, however, we expect both equities and bonds to enjoy capital gains, and therefore we have adjusted their expected returns up from the base case by +2% and +1%, respectively.

In contrast, because cash rates will likely fall and lower accrual rates will likely adversely impact IPBs, we adjust these returns down by −1/2% and −1%, respectively. In addition, the scenario impacts correlations as shown in Exhibit 7. In this exhibit, because nominal bond and IPB returns tend to diverge, we show a significantly reduced correlation between bonds and IPBs.

Exhibit 8: Frontiers Using Low Inflation Inputs
Efficient Frontiers

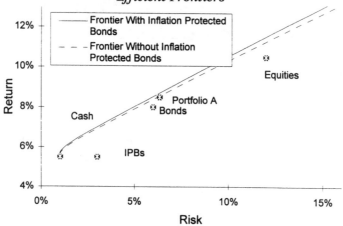

Exhibit 9: Optimized Reallocation Low Inflation Inputs
Efficient Frontiers

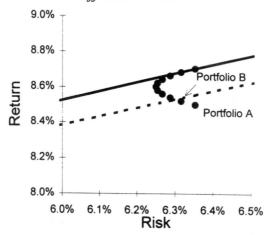

The resulting efficient frontier, shown in Exhibit 8, reflects these relative changes, as do the portfolio reallocations shown in Exhibit 9. Exhibit 7 shows Portfolio B. The IPBs are shown with a negative allocation. This is not surprising. The inputs reflect the observation that lower inflation accruals hurt IPBs. However, there is a caveat: the validity of the result is dependent upon the accuracy of the inputs. Again, we have attempted to err on the side of conservatism. In particular, the past 10-year historical scenario suggests that even in a low inflation scenario IPBs offer opportunities, particularly if real interest rates fall.

Exhibit 10: High Inflation Inputs

Asset Class	Return	Risk	Correlations MS Wrld Eqty	SB Wrld Bond	Cash Equivalent	IPBs (Synth.)	Output Portfolio B
MS Wrld Eqty	6.50%	12.00%	100%				34.95%
SB Wrld Bond	6.00%	6.00%	50%	100%			33.84%
Cash Equivalent	6.50%	1.00%	0%	0%	100%		7.70%
IPBs (Synth.)	7.50%	3.00%	30%	15%	50%	100%	23.51%

Exhibit 11: Optimized Reallocation High Inflation
Efficient Frontiers

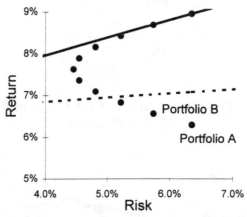

High Inflation Scenario

The *high inflation scenario* is simply the mirror image of the low inflation scenario. In such an environment we expect both equities and bonds to suffer, so we adjust their returns down by −2% and −1%, respectively. In contrast, cash rates are likely to increase in this scenario, and higher accrual rates will positively impact IPBs. To account for this, we adjust their returns up by +½% and +1%, respectively. Correlations, however, will likely respond similarly to those in the low inflation scenario. In particular, we expect nominal bond returns and IPB returns to diverge, and their correlations to fall.

The output column of Exhibit 10 shows the allocation corresponding to Portfolio B. Not surprisingly given this scenario, the optimizer generates a large allocation to IPBs. Again, there is a caveat: the result is dependent on the inputs. Just as the returns for IPBs in a low inflation scenario may be too pessimistic, these may be too optimistic. If monetary authorities rapidly respond to the inflation with tightening, then IPB returns may fall short of the high inflation scenario inputs.

Just as for the previous scenarios, we have graphed the resulting frontiers in Exhibit 11 and zoomed in on the optimized reallocations in Exhibit 12.

Exhibit 12: Frontiers Using High Inflation
Efficient Frontiers

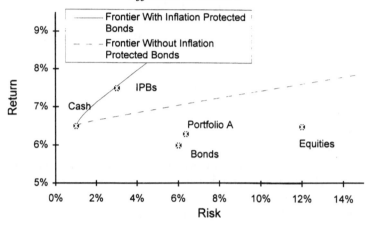

Exhibit 13: Composite H/L/B Averages

Asset Class	Return	Risk	Correlations				Output Avg.
			MS Wrld Eqty	SB Wrld Bond	Cash Equivalent	IPBs (Synth.)	Portfolio B
MS Wrld Eqty	8.50%	12.00%	100%				37.73%
SB Wrld Bond	7.00%	6.00%	50%	100%			38.29%
Cash Equivalent	6.00%	1.00%	0%	0%	100%		15.08%
IPBs (Synth.)	6.50%	3.00%	32%	18%	50%	100%	8.90%

RECOMBINING PARTITIONED SCENARIOS

We can form a composite allocation by averaging the allocations we obtained from the high inflation, low inflation, and base case scenarios. This composite result differs from the base case result as shown in Exhibit 13. In particular, the swings in equity, bond, and IPB returns across the scenarios result in cash being relatively advantaged by this multiple scenario process.

IMPLEMENTING A STRATEGIC ALLOCATION

Benefits of Utilizing a Global Benchmark

There are three major benefits to benchmarking the IPB asset class using a global index. The first relates to diversification. The real returns earned in any single local IPB market will be somewhat buffetted by local dynamics involving currency movements, short-term interest rates, transient inflation, and changes in long-term real yields. Over longer timeframes the real yield contractually guaranteed by the local instruments will be delivered. But still, utilizing a capitalization weighted, global index will tend to diversify much of this short-term volatility.

The second major benefit is the added liquidity provided by the larger market. The United Kingdom and United States make up the majority of the global index. Any single market alone has substantially smaller market capitalization and less liquidity than the index as a whole.

Third, employing a global index facilitates greater flexibility. This is particularly true with respect to taking advantage of global relative value opportunties.

In addition, there is a fundamental reason that a global index is an appropriate benchmark. IPBs represent a pure claim on the expected real return to global capital. The asset class is fundamentally a "global" asset class. Expected real returns on capital are largely independent of the currency in which they are denominated. As globalization of capital markets evolve, capital will flow even more freely. Most likely this will furthur equalize the cross border real returns on capital.

There is a caveat for strategic investors who are focused on substituting IPBs for nominal assets. The broader global diversification does introduce some currency induced volatility. This is discussed next.

Managing Foreign Currency Exposure

Investors in any foreign currency denominated instrument or global index have embedded foreign currency exposure. The investor in foreign IPBs must decide whether to assume this exposure or to hedge the exposure into the home currency. Typically this would be accomplished by offsetting the embedded exposure through a delayed settlement sale of the currency in the forward market. While it is quite clear that partial hedging of conventional bonds into the investor's home currency makes sense, the logic is far less mechanical for IPBs.

Foreign IPBs are "real" assets that expose holders to fluctuations in *real* exchange rates. However, they protect holders from fluctuations in exchange rates caused by inflation. This immunization is accomplished through the inflation indexation of coupon and principal payments. Empirically (particularly over long time horizons), appreciating currencies are associated with low inflationary regimes, while depreciating currencies are symptomatic of high inflation. These observations are consistent with classical purchasing power parity theories.

The implication is that unhedged IPBs seem to make sense in the long run. However, the foreign exchange markets are subject to short-term volatility that is not explained by the classical purchasing power parity logic. In other words, inflation differentials are only one force driving changes in exchange rates. Fluctuations in "real exchange" rates are also important. In the case of highly industrialized countries, for which inflation is relatively muted, volatility in real exchange rates accounts for most of the currency volatility. The implication, in direct contradiction to the classical "unhedged" paradigm described above, is that currency movements are often independent of inflation differentials and thus independent of coupon and principal accretion on IPBs.

The conclusion we draw regarding currency hedging is that the hedge that results in the maximum risk reduction will depend on what fraction of the currency volatility is caused by fluctuations in real exchange rates. The practical answer will therefore depend on which countries are involved, and what time horizons the investor is targeting.

Goals and Restrictions for an
Investment Management Mandate

The fundamental parameters that determine any investment manager's investment goals are the client's benchmark and tracking risk tolerance. Of these two, the more important is the benchmark since it defines what role the manager fills within a client's asset allocation In the current context, the second parameter, tracking risk tolerance, does not express how risky the asset class is. Rather it expresses how far from the benchmark a manager can appropriately deviate from the benchmark to add value. Tracking risk tolerance can also be qualitatively defined as "conservative," "assertive," or "aggressive" management. Given a benchmark and tracking risk, a manager is able to first determine what the "passive" underlying position should be. Second the manager is able to determine how aggressively the active view should be overlaid. While low tracking risk is desirable, potential value-added is generally proportional to tracking risk.

Benchmark, Country Composition and Hedging

The global IPB market currently exceeds US$100 billion in capitalization. It is already a rather substantial and liquid market. The major sovereign issuers have embarked on issuance programs that we anticipate will further increase the IPB market's size and liquidity. Although there are a dozens of issuers, the bonds issued by the United Kingdom, United States, Australia, Canada, and Sweden form the largest markets. These five liquid high quality markets together form Barclays Inflation-Linked Bond Index. The index is available in unhedged, hedged, and local currency versions.

CONCLUSION

The purpose of our exploration in this chapter was to isolate the strategic asset allocation implication of the introduction of IPBs. To accomplish this we performed optimizations with four distinct sets of inputs. We used a historical scenario to provide context. We then turned to forward-looking scenarios starting with our base case. The asset allocation methodology we employed was quite traditional and standard, except of course, that it included IPBs as an asset class. A more radical approach, involving re-examining the purpose and approach to asset allocation methodology, was proposed and explored in Chapter 2.

Section II:

Mechanics, Valuation, and Risk Monitoring

Chapter 8

Quantitative Approaches to Inflation-Indexed Bonds

Wesley Phoa, Ph.D.
Vice President, Research
Capital Management Sciences

INTRODUCTION

Inflation-indexed bonds exist in Australia, Canada, Israel, the Netherlands, New Zealand, Sweden, the United Kingdom, and the United States. In Israel, they have been issued since the 1950s, and have often dominated the bond market there. There are significant differences between these markets: a wide variety of bond structures and tax regimes exist, issuance volumes and the breadth of the investor base vary widely from country to country, and liquidity varies from tolerable to nonexistent.

There has been some disagreement about the degree to which inflation-indexed bonds are "risk-free" and the role which they should play in a portfolio. In particular, it has not been universally appreciated that these bonds can have volatile mark-to-market returns. This chapter examines the factors which determine returns on these bonds, hopefully clearing up some misconceptions, and draws some conclusions about portfolio risk management and asset allocation. It also explains how market real yields can be used to derive implied market inflation forecasts (i.e., a term structure of inflation expectations). This makes them an interesting policy tool, and also has implications for macroeconomic portfolio strategy. The analysis, which is a little more subtle than one might expect, also has potential practical applications for liability management and the valuation of revenue streams in, for example, project finance. As we shall see, it is also useful for forecasting after-tax real returns.

BOND STRUCTURES AND THE CONCEPT OF REAL YIELD

U.S. Government inflation-indexed bonds — called "Treasury inflation-indexed securities," or "TIPS" — are quite new to the U.S. bond markets. Since many investors may still be unfamiliar with how these bonds work, we quickly review the structure in Exhibit 1.

Exhibit 1: TIPS Bond Structure

TIPS pay interest semiannually. Interest payments are based on a fixed coupon rate. However, the underlying principal amount of the bonds is indexed to inflation; this inflation-adjusted principal amount is used to calculate the coupon payments, which therefore also rise with inflation. At maturity, the redemption value of the bonds is equal to their inflation-adjusted principal amount, rather than their original par amount.

The inflation-adjusted principal amount is equal to the original par amount multiplied by an Index Ratio, which is based on inflation and which is recalculated every day. The Index Ratio is simply the Reference CPI on the relevant date divided by the Reference CPI on the issue date.

The Reference CPI for the first day of any month is defined to be the non-seasonally adjusted CPI-U for the third preceding calendar month, while the Reference CPI for any subsequent day in that month is determined by linearly interpolating the Reference CPI for the first of the month and the Reference CPI for the first day of the next month.

Price-yield calculations are as follows. Compute the "real price" of the bond from the quoted real yield via the standard bond pricing formula, using an actual/actual day count basis, round to three decimal places (in $100); then multiply the real price by the Index Ratio to obtain the inflation-adjusted price. Accrued interest is computed in exactly the same way, except that no rounding is carried out.

For example, in order to determine the purchase price of the 3.375% 1/15/2007 TIPS at the original auction, for settlement on 2/6/1997, one had to carry out the following calculations.

- the Reference CPI for 1/1/1997 was 158.3 (the CPI-U for 10/96)
- the Reference CPI for 2/1/1997 was 158.6 (the CPI-U for 11/96)
- the Reference CPI for 1/15/1997 was $158.3 + (158.6 - 158.3)^{14}\!/_{31} = 158.43548$
- the Reference CPI for 2/6/1997 was 158.6 (since the CPI-U for 12/96 was 158.6)
- the Index Ratio for 2/6/1997 was 158.6/158.43548 = 1.00104
- for a real yield of 3.449%, the real price of the bond was $99.378686
- the inflation-adjusted price was $99.379 × 1.00104 = $99.482354

An attractive feature of the TIPS structure is that inflation indexation occurs with no substantial lag. In the U.K., there is an eight month lag in the inflation adjustment of index-linked gilts; in Australia and New Zealand, there is a three to six month lag. The lag means that real returns from these inflation-indexed bonds are subject to short-term inflation risk, and considerably complicates the analysis of the bonds.

The obvious question, of course, is: Where does the real yield come from, and how much can it change? To investors used to thinking of bond yields as being driven by inflation expectations, it is not obvious that real yields should be volatile at all — except perhaps because of temporary imbalances in supply and demand, or changes in liquidity. After all, there are respectable economic theories which suggest that real interest rates should be constant. But in practice, there are various economic reasons why real yields do in fact fluctuate. The following discussion of risk factors expands on the account given by Carmody and Mason.[1]

Causes of Real Yield Volatility

The real yield may be defined as the long-term cost of risk-free capital (net of inflation). That is, since TIPS are competing with other investments, real yields on TIPS will move with the cost of capital in the economy as a whole. Of course, other factors affect real yields: for example, index-linked gilts in the U.K. have had artificially low real yields because of their favorable tax treatment. However, in this chapter we will focus on economic and market factors. Broadly speaking, the two main economic factors which affect real yields are:

1. *Long-term expected growth in real GDP:* Strong growth generally drives up real interest rates, since the demand for capital tends to rise, and borrowers — expecting higher real returns — are prepared to shoulder higher real borrowing costs.

2. *Long-term expected changes in the current account deficit:* Demand for capital is by definition higher in countries with a large current account deficit, driving up domestic interest rates in order to attract required international investment.

Note that short-term trends in real GDP and the current account deficit can have a strong influence on real yields, because they tend to influence the long-term expectations of investors.[2] (Roll has also argued, based on an analysis of tax effects, that real yields should also rise when expected inflation rises; this argument is outlined later in the chapter. For the moment we ignore tax effects.[3])

Real yields on inflation-linked bonds are also influenced by relative demand for these bonds, when compared with competing investments which may offer investors some protection — albeit imperfect — against inflation. The balance between competing investments constantly shifts, depending on subjective factors such as investor aversion to different kinds of risk. Relevant investments include:

1. *Money market investments:* If investors are confident that short-term interest rates will move broadly in line with inflation — which has been the case for monetary policy since the early 1980s, but not before then — then real returns on money market instruments will be relatively stable over the long term.

[1] S. Carmody and R. Mason, *Analysis of Australian Index-Linked Securities*, Deutsche Morgan Grenfell (Sydney) research report (June 1996).

[2] See Chapter 12 in J. M. Keynes, *The General Theory of Employment, Interest and Money* (London: MacMillan, 1936).

[3] R. Roll, "US Treasury Inflation-Indexed Bonds: The Design of a New Security," *Journal of Fixed Income* (December 1996).

2. *Equities:* When profit margins are stable, corporate profits, and hence dividends and dividend growth rates, tend to rise with the price level; thus, it is reasonable to regard equities as an inflation hedge in the long term (remembering that equity investors are exposed to additional risks in comparison to holders of inflation-indexed bonds). Therefore when the equity market is strong, real yields will tend to be high, while a weakening in the equity market will tend to trigger a fall in real yields.

3. *Corporate bonds:* As with equities, corporate bonds performance is partly linked to inflation: rising price levels drive up corporate revenues and reduce the real value of existing fixed-rate debt, and both these factors can cause yield spreads to tighten.

4. *Commodities:* A basket of commodities also provides a partial hedge against inflation, but in practice this investment alternative is not as important as the previous three.

To summarize: real yields are far from stable and the behavior of real yields is just as complex as the behavior of nominal yields. Real yields are influenced by both economic fundamentals and market supply/demand factors across asset classes. It is not at all obvious that inflation-linked bonds should be "among the least risky of all assets." Indeed, in the Australian market these securities are regarded as highly risky in comparison to nominal bonds — though this is partly because of their relative illiquidity.

In all countries where inflation-linked bonds are actively traded, real yields have, historically, been quite volatile. For example:

- In the U.K., real yields on long index-linked gilts fluctuated between 2% and 4.5% in the period 1981–1993.[4] In the period 1984–1994, real yields on short index-linked gilts fluctuated between 1.5% and 5.75%, partly reflecting instability in monetary policy.[5]
- In Israel from 1984–1993, long dated real yields fluctuated between −1.5% and 3.3%; however, they more typically trade in the range ±1%.[6]
- In Australia, real yields have varied from a high of 5.75% in 1986 and 1994, to a low of 3.25% in 1993.[7]

Thus, like nominal yields, market real yields trade in ranges of hundreds of basis points. This translates into very significant price volatility, which is sometimes experienced over a very short period — e.g., Australia, moving from 1993 to 1994. (Of course, the existence of real yield volatility should be no surprise, since real bond returns have always been volatile.)

---

[4] P. Eichholtz, P. Naber, and V. Petri, "Index-Linked Bonds in a Liability Framework," *Journal of Fixed Income* (December 1993).

[5] R. Brown and S. Schaefer, "Ten Years of the Real Term Structure: 1984–1994," *Journal of Fixed Income* (March 1996).

[6] Eichholtz, Naber, and Petri, "Index-Linked Bonds in a Liability Framework."

[7] Carmody and Mason, *Analysis of Australian Index-Linked Securities.*

Exhibit 2: U.S. 10-Year Real Yield, Estimated from Consensus Long-Term CPI Forecasts

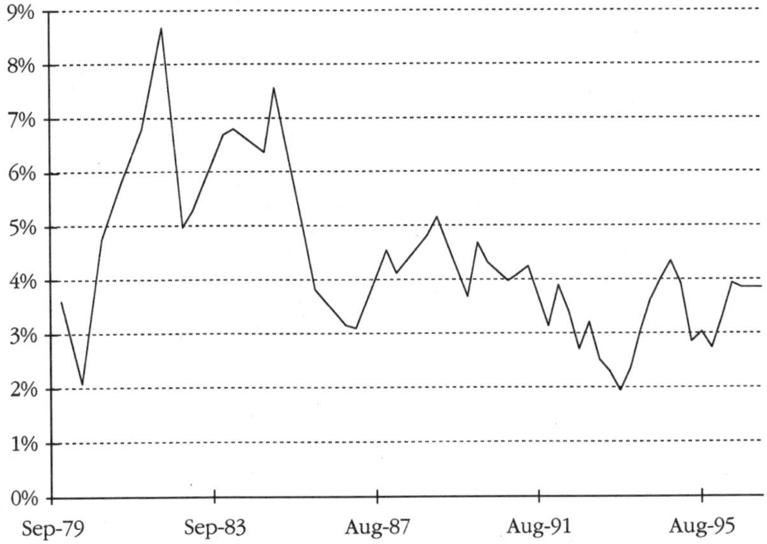

Since there was no U.S. market in inflation-indexed bonds before 1997, it is not possible to observe a long history of market real yields. Real yields are often estimated by subtracting current inflation from current nominal bond yields; but this procedure is obviously illogical, as it assumes that expected inflation is equal to current inflation. One can get a better idea of what market real yields would have been by taking nominal yields and subtracting a consensus inflation forecast. Exhibit 2 shows the 10-year nominal Treasury yield minus the 10-year consensus CPI forecast, as reported in the Philadelphia Fed's Survey of Professional Forecasters. This measures investors' expectations of real returns on 10-year Treasury bonds, and is therefore a reasonable estimate of the 10-year real yield.

Even though using consensus data has a number of drawbacks — as explained at the end of this chapter — this rough analysis yields some useful results. Exhibit 2 shows clearly how long-dated real yields soared in the early 1980s, due to the extreme instability in monetary policy. They stabilized after 1985, once monetarism was discarded and a more stable approach to monetary policy was instituted. Since then they have fluctuated between 5% (in the overheated economy of the late 1980s) and 2% (in the depths of the recession). Note the apparent link during this latest period between long-term real yields and current GDP growth.

Although the U.S. inflation-indexed bond market is extremely young, the extant history of TIPS real yields already displays some interesting phenomena. Exhibit 3 shows TIPS real yields since issuance. During this 6-month period, market real yields traded in a 50 bp range. TIPS yield volatility was 10.3%, compared to 11.6% for 10-year nominal bonds.

Exhibit 3: TIPS Real Yield History and Spread to Nominal Yield Curve

Exhibit 3 also shows the yield spread between the 10-year TIPS and the 10-year CMT nominal yield. This may be regarded as a rough measure of the market's inflation expectations over the next ten years. We will describe more accurate ways to measure this implied market inflation forecast later in the chapter.

This brief history already illustrates some important points. For example, in the early part of February both real yields and inflation expectations fell. From the beginning of March, however, concerns about inflation caused nominal yields to rise. Note that long-term inflation expectations remained capped at around 3.2%, while real yields continued to rise; this reflects the market's view that if inflation were to rise much above 3%, the Fed would act to lower it by raising real interest rates.

In early April, both real yields and inflation expectations were stable. At the end of April, the employment cost index was released and was significantly lower than market forecasts. This caused market participants to revise their inflation forecasts downwards and inflation expectations to fall to around 3%. However, real yields remained stable since the market did not anticipate that this new economic data would result in any change to Fed policy.

Existence of an Inflation Risk Premium

It is often asserted that real yields on inflation-linked bonds should reflect an inflation risk premium, since investors are not exposed to inflation risk as they are with nominal bonds. Note that if future inflation were known — not necessarily zero — there would be no inflation risk premium; it is uncertainty about inflation that creates a risk premium. The more volatile inflation is expected to be, the higher the inflation risk premium on nominal bonds should be, and the lower real yields should be in relation to nominal yields.

It is important to note that it is uncertainty about future inflation which should determine the risk premium, not the historical volatility of inflation. For example, the inflationary episode of the 1970s is not relevant unless investors think it may be repeated. Investors' expectations about the future volatility of inflation are not directly observable (although, see below), but it may be helpful to look at economists' estimates. It is also useful to compare expected inflation volatility with expected volatility in real interest rates, since both factors are relevant to the risk/return opportunities offered by inflation-indexed bonds.

Note that if the inflation risk premium exists, one would not expect it to be unvarying. Since it is related to market expectations about potential uncertainty in inflation, it is comparable to option implied volatility. One would thus expect the inflation risk premium to depend on bond maturity, and also to vary over time; for example, if the market lost confidence in the Fed's ability to control inflation, the inflation risk premium would rise, causing nominal yields to rise relative to real yields. However, since the inflation risk premium is determined by inflation uncertainty over a long period (ten years for the 10-year TIPS), sudden changes would be unusual. The inflation risk premium should experience moderate fluctuations, like long-dated swaption implied volatilities, and not sharp ones, like short-dated exchange-traded option implied volatilities.

In the absence of an inflation-linked derivatives market, the inflation risk premium is not directly observable. Naive attempts to measure it can lead to grossly overstated estimates. A number of proposed methods for measuring it turn out to be spurious. For example, it has been asserted that the differential between money market and bond yields arises because of an inflation risk premium, which can thus be estimated by looking at the long-term average spread between the Fed funds rate and the 2-year bond yield (about 70 bp in the period since deregulation). This argument has a grain of truth, but the conclusion is incorrect as it stands. There are other reasons why money market yields are usually lower than bond yields: liquidity preference and the impact of capital charges both have important effects. Furthermore, if the spread between money market and bond yields reflects a risk premium, this is not just an inflation risk premium but a real rate risk premium as well.

Also, the argument that the difference between the Fed funds rate and the 2-year bond yield equals the inflation risk premium implies that the yields of money market securities reflect no inflation risk premium, while this risk premium is fully priced into 2-year bond yields. This would only be plausible if money market securities were not (perceived to be) subject to inflation risk, and this is far from obvious, particularly since real money market returns were frequently negative during the 1970s.

Thus we must look for more valid ways of estimating what the inflation risk premium should be. One approach, which we describe later in this chapter, is based on an analysis of historical real and nominal yields. It suggests that the market inflation risk premium on a 10-year nominal bond is somewhere between −15 bp and 25 bp.

A second approach is sometimes possible. If there were an efficient market in both conventional and index-linked bonds with a range of maturities stretching from 10 years to 30 years, one could in principle determine the market's long-term expectations about nominal and real yield volatility as reflected in the observed convexity bias, and hence to deduce the market's long-term expectations about inflation volatility.[8] A reasonably long yield history would be required to obtain reliable results. At the moment this procedure would only be practicable in the U.K., and the applicability of this procedure to yields on index-linked gilts is questionable because of their favorable tax treatment. In the United States, once the 30-year TIPS has been actively traded for some time, it will be possible to carry out this analysis.

A third approach is to try to observe inflation uncertainty directly. Exhibit 4 shows the probabilities attached by economists to various GDP growth and inflation scenarios; it is taken from the Survey of Professional Forecasters (first quarter, 1997). Although subjective uncertainty is not identical to expected volatility, the survey results are consistent with a short-term volatility of around 1% per annum in both inflation and GDP growth; that is, they are about equally volatile.

Economists' forecasts recognize that both inflation and real yields are volatile, and that they have comparable volatilities. It is tempting to conclude that nominal bond yields should indeed reflect an inflation risk premium, since returns on nominal bonds are affected by both inflation volatility and real yield volatility, while returns on inflation-linked bonds are only affected by real yield volatility. But this conclusion is not necessarily correct.

Based on an analysis of 30 years' worth of cross-country panel data, Judson and Orphanides have shown that — as one might expect — there is a strong negative correlation between inflation and growth.[9] Thus, as inflation rises, real yields should fall, and vice versa; in other words, the risks arising from fluctuations in inflation and fluctuations in real yields at least partly offset each other, at least over the medium to long term. It is therefore conceivable that, over the medium to long term, a portfolio of nominal bonds may be less risky, not more risky, than a portfolio of inflation-linked bonds. Certainly the situation is more complex than it seems at first.

We can actually use the earlier "economists' estimates" of volatility in real GDP growth and inflation, together with the implied volatility of short-term rates, to compute a rough estimate of the correlation between inflation and growth. Assuming that nominal rates are solely determined by growth and inflation, we have:

---

[8] For an explanation of the methods that can be used, see Chapter 4 in W. Phoa, *Advanced Fixed Income Analytics* (New Hope, PA: Frank J. Fabozzi Associates, 1998).

[9] R. Judson and A. Orphanides, "Inflation, Volatility and Growth," *Federal Reserve Board* (May 1996).

Exhibit 4: Economists' Uncertainty about Future Inflation and GDP Growth

Probability attached to possible changes in GDP price index

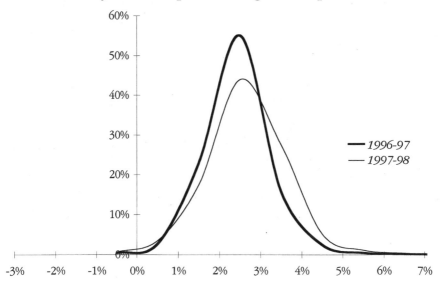

Probability attached to possible changes in real GDP

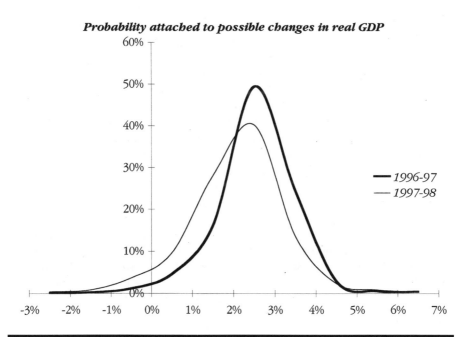

$$\sigma^2_{\text{nominal}} = \sigma^2_{\text{growth}} + \sigma^2_{\text{inflation}} + 2\rho\,\sigma_{\text{growth}}\,\sigma_{\text{inflation}}$$

If all three volatilities are around 1% per annum, then solving this formula for ρ gives the estimate $\rho \approx -0.5$. However, it would not be meaningful to try to compute a more precise estimate this way.

Incidentally, Judson and Orphanides also found a strong negative correlation between inflation volatility and growth.[10] In other words, if inflation is expected to become more volatile, real yields should fall, i.e., inflation-indexed bond prices should rally. However, in this scenario inflation-linked bonds should outperform nominal bonds, since the inflation risk premium should rise.

INFLATION-INDEXED BONDS IN A NOMINAL PORTFOLIO

Inflation-indexed bonds are often used for specialized purposes (e.g., asset/liability management for insurance companies offering inflation-linked life annuities), and may thus be segregated from other fixed-income holdings. However, if they are held in the same portfolio as nominal bonds, an interesting problem arises when attempting to define their "duration." We first examine the simplest possible definition of duration, and its consequences; then we look at some alternative definitions.

What is the Duration of an Inflation-Indexed Bond?

It is easy to compute the duration of an inflation-indexed bond using exactly the same method as one would use for a nominal bond. Because of its low real coupon and low real yield, an inflation-indexed bond tends to have a much longer duration than a nominal bond of comparable maturity.

But what does this duration mean? The duration of a nominal Treasury bond measures its sensitivity to changes in nominal yields, i.e., to changes in inflation and real interest rate expectations. By contrast, the duration of an inflation-linked bond measures its sensitivity to changes in real yields, i.e., to changes in real interest rate expectations alone. In other words, the two durations are not comparable: they are measuring different things. So, for example, it does not make sense to look for a "reference" nominal yield for the TIPS real yield: while the TIPS yield may appear to trade off the 10-year Treasury during some periods, or off the 5-year Treasury during other periods, there is no fundamental reason why any such relationship should persist.

This creates a problem on the portfolio level. If we try to compute a portfolio duration by adding up the durations of nominal and inflation-indexed bond holdings, what does the resulting figure mean? Two portfolios could have the same duration but, depending on the relative weighting of index-linked bonds, might have a very different response to a change in investor's economic expecta-

---

[10] Judson and Orphanides, "Inflation, Volatility and Growth."

tions. A simple duration target is no longer an effective way of controlling portfolio interest rate risk.

Thus, when a portfolio contains both nominal and inflation-linked bonds, it is critical to monitor and report the relative weights and durations of the "nominal" and "real" components of the portfolio separately. One approach is to report two durations for the portfolio, which distinguish two sources of risk:

1. A "portfolio real yield duration" equal to the sum of the durations of both nominal and inflation-indexed bond holdings. This shows how the portfolio value will respond to a change in market real yields (which also affect nominal yields).
2. A "portfolio inflation duration" equal to the duration of the nominal bond holdings alone. This shows how the portfolio value will respond to a change in market inflation expectations (which affect nominal yields but not real yields).

Similarly, care must be taken when carrying out portfolio simulations. For example, when carrying out parallel interest rate simulations, it is standard practice to apply an identical yield shift to all securities in the portfolio. For a portfolio containing both nominal and inflation-indexed bonds, this actually corresponds to a "real yield simulation." One should also carry out "expected inflation simulations," where the yield shift is applied to nominal but not inflation-indexed bond yields.

There is one practical situation in which it makes sense to compare the durations of a nominal and inflation-indexed bond directly: when designing trading strategies based on expected inflation. Suppose the central banking authority is targeting a long-term inflation rate of no more than 3%; and suppose that the 10-year nominal yield is 7.50% while the 10-year real yield is 4.00%. This means that the market is predicting an average inflation rate, over the next ten years, of 3.5%. If one had faith in the central bank's ability to meet its inflation target, nominal bonds would look undervalued relative to inflation-indexed bonds.

How should one exploit this perceived opportunity without changing exposure to other sources of risk? The correct way is to execute a duration-matched swap, selling 10-year inflation-indexed bonds and buying 10-year nominal bonds. If inflation expectations fall, the strategy would realize a profit. If real interest rate expectations change (i.e., if real yields change), there would be no effect — which is the intention. Later in this chapter, we develop more accurate ways to derive market inflation forecasts from the real and nominal yield curves, and discuss some further implications for portfolio strategy.

The above duration calculation is based on the (known) real cash flows, and discounts at the real yield. There are other potential ways to compute the "duration" of an inflation-linked bond, which involve forecasting the (unknown) nominal cash flows and discounting using nominal yields, on a zero coupon curve basis. The three most obvious alternatives are:

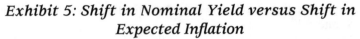

Exhibit 5: Shift in Nominal Yield versus Shift in Expected Inflation

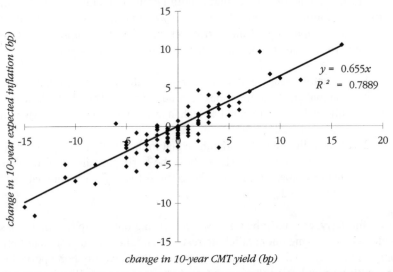

1. Using a fixed inflation forecast, generate projected bond cash flows (one should use a forecast which ensures that the net present value of the forecast cash flows, discounted using the current nominal zero coupon curve, is equal to the current bond price). Compute the duration of this fixed cash flow stream using ±100 bp shifts in the nominal zero coupon curve.
2. The same, except that when shifting the zero coupon curve by ±100 bp, one recalculates the bond's cash flows based on a new inflation forecast, adjusted by ±1%. That is, the cash flow stream is assumed to depend on the level of nominal yields.
3. The same, except that one adjusts the inflation forecast by an amount different from ±1%. For example, Exhibit 5 shows that in early 1997, a 10 bp rise in U.S. nominal yields corresponded, on average, to an 0.06%-0.07% rise in market long-term inflation expectations (we explain later in this chapter how the "expected inflation" figures were derived). Thus one might adjust the inflation forecast by (say) ±0.65%. The precise number depends on the reference Treasury yield, and historical period used to estimate the relationship.

In each case, some minor variations are possible; for example, either constant or time-varying inflation forecasts could be used. These calculations can be related to the above concepts of "real yield duration" and "inflation duration" in the following way:

1. Assuming a fixed cash flow stream (i.e., a fixed inflation scenario) amounts to assuming that the ±100 bp shift in nominal yields is due to a change in real yields, not a change in inflation expectations. Thus, this calculation determines the sensitivity to a change in real yields, i.e., it is essentially computing a *real yield duration*, and produces an answer very close to the duration calculation described above.

2. Assuming an inflation scenario that varies by ±1% amounts to assuming that the ±100 bp shift in nominal yields is due to a change in inflation expectations. Thus, this calculation measures an *inflation duration*, i.e., a sensitivity to a shift in market inflation expectations, which is conceptually different from the real yield duration. The inflation duration of a TIPS will be approximately zero, but may depend on the precise way the calculation is carried out.

3. Assuming an inflation scenario that varies by some amount based on the empirical relationship between nominal yields and market inflation expectations amounts to calculating a *nominal yield duration*, which attempts to measure the sensitivity of an inflation-linked bond to a shift in nominal yields.

Real yield duration is the most important of these risk measures — and, as we have seen, it can be calculated without using an inflation forecast. The inflation duration of a TIPS is not a useful risk measure; however, in the U.K. and Australian markets, where inflation-indexed Treasuries have some residual inflation sensitivity due to the lag in inflation indexation, inflation duration is perhaps worth monitoring. The definition of nominal yield duration makes essential use of an estimate about an empirical relationship which is probably unstable, severely limiting the usefulness of this risk measure.

Note that if inflation-indexed Treasury bonds did have stable nominal durations — i.e., if they did respond in an absolutely predictable way to a change in nominal yields — then there would be no point in issuing them, since they could be perfectly replicated by nominal bonds. In fact, experience shows that inflation-indexed bonds cannot be hedged perfectly with nominal bonds.

One can also attempt to compute a "tax-adjusted duration" for an inflation-linked bond, which takes its tax treatment into account; this may be of importance in the U.K., where inflation accruals are not taxed. In the U.S. market, inflation-linked and nominal bonds are taxed on a broadly consistent basis; in particular, by analogy with Treasury STRIPS, the inflation adjustment to the bond principal is taxable as it occurs, and not simply at bond maturity. Thus, just as one continues to use pre-tax durations for Treasury STRIPS despite their tax treatment, it seems reasonable to use pre-tax durations for TIPS as well. Additionally, the Australian experience suggests that pre-tax duration measures suffice for most day-to-day interest rate risk management. However, it is worth discussing taxes briefly.

The Impact of Taxation: An Outline

Inflation-indexed bonds attempt to eliminate inflation risk, but it reappears on an after-tax basis. We begin with the fact that tax affects returns on both nominal bonds and inflation-indexed bonds in an unfortunate way: high inflation results in lower after-tax real returns. For inflation-indexed bonds, an investor would reason as follows:[11]

> forecast after-tax real yield
> = forecast after-tax nominal yield − forecast inflation
> = tax rate × forecast pre-tax nominal yield − forecast inflation
> = tax rate × (pre-tax real yield + forecast inflation) − forecast inflation
> = tax rate × pre-tax real yield − (1 − tax rate) × forecast inflation

For nominal bonds, the reasoning is similar:

> forecast after-tax real yield
> = forecast after-tax nominal yield − forecast inflation
> = tax rate × forecast pre-tax nominal yield − forecast inflation
> = tax rate × (pre-tax real yield + market inflation) − forecast inflation
> = tax rate × pre-tax real yield − (forecast inflation − tax rate × market inflation)

where "forecast inflation" refers to the investor's inflation forecast and "market inflation" refers to the market's inflation forecast as reflected in the spread between market nominal yields and market real yields. Thus an investor who agrees with the market's inflation forecast and who is thus indifferent between inflation-linked bonds and nominal bonds on a pre-tax basis will also be indifferent on an after-tax basis.

The arguments show that projected after-tax real returns on both inflation-indexed and nominal bonds depend on forecast inflation. For example, assuming a tax rate of 40%, after-tax real yields will be negative unless expected inflation is less than 1.5 times the pre-tax real yield. In the second quarter of 1997, market real yields were around 3.60%. Thus an investor forecasting inflation of 5.4% or greater would expect negative real after-tax returns. Of course, the market inflation forecast, as reflected in the spread between nominal and real yields, is much lower than this.

An important consequence is that since U.S. inflation-indexed bonds and nominal bonds are affected equally, *inflation-linked bonds do not protect investors against the negative after-tax impact of high inflation*. Thus, TIPS real yields reflect only a premium for "pre-tax inflation risk." By contrast, since U.K. index-linked gilts receive preferential tax treatment, their yields also reflect a premium for "after-tax inflation risk." The price paid by U.K. investors, as observed by Roll[12] and by Brown and Schaefer,[13] is illiquidity: the market for index-linked

---

[11] For more details, see Roll, "U.S. Treasury Inflation-Indexed Bonds: The Design of a New Security."
[12] Roll, "U.S. Treasury Inflation-Indexed Bonds: The Design of a New Security."
[13] Brown and Schaefer, "Ten Years of the Real Term Structure: 1984-1994."

gilts is confined to investors with high marginal tax rates. (By the way, this provides a neat example of the tax clientele effects analyzed by Dybvig and Ross.[14])

Roll points out a further consequence: if the demand for inflation-indexed or nominal bonds is a function of expected after-tax returns, pre-tax real yields should rise as expected inflation rises, to maintain a constant after-tax real yield. It is not clear whether real yields on inflation-indexed bonds actually behave in this way, although the Australian experience in 1994 suggests that they do. In any case, this introduces a further source of uncertainty about the future behavior of real yields.

Inflation-Indexed Bonds and Portfolio Efficiency

Inflation-indexed bonds have a risk profile quite different to that of nominal bonds. In fact, it could be argued that for asset allocation purposes, they should not be grouped with nominal bonds but should be treated as an entirely separate asset class. We will use portfolio theory to explore the consequences of adopting this point of view. More specifically, we will try to determine what weight TIPS should have in efficient portfolios with varying degrees of risk, and what impact their inclusion has on expected returns.

For simplicity, we focus on maximizing nominal returns in the U.S. market, and we work in a total return framework. Other kinds of analysis are possible: for example, Eichholtz, Naber, and Petri discuss the problem of matching inflation-indexed liabilities in the U.K. and Israeli markets.[15] We summarize their results below.

The results of any Markowitz-style analysis are always highly dependent on the expected returns, volatilities, and correlations used. The assumptions we use are set out in Exhibit 6, and are broadly based on market data and presumed market expectations. They were derived as follows:

- Expected nominal returns for bills and nominal bonds are based on current market yields — this is more meaningful than using historical returns. We assume that nominal bonds and TIPS have the same expected return. (Since they are generally viewed as less risky, TIPS are unlikely to have a higher *expected* return than bonds.) The expected return for equities is obtained by adding a risk premium of 3.5% to that for bonds; this roughly corresponds to the average historical excess return in the period 1970–1995.
- Return volatilities for bills, nominal bonds, and equities are historical, calculated over the period 1970–1995. Since there is no meaningful return history for TIPS in the United States, two different volatility assumptions are made: a "realistic" 7.5% volatility (which is somewhat lower than the historical return volatility of inflation-indexed bonds in Australia) and a "low" 4.5% volatility (an optimistic scenario, which assumes that real rates will be quite stable).

---

[14] P. Dybvig, and S. Ross, "Tax Clienteles and Asset Pricing," *Journal of Finance* (July 1986).

[15] For the U.K. market, see Eichholtz, Naber, and Petri, "Index-Linked Bonds in a Liability Framework."

Exhibit 6: Assumptions Used in Efficient Portfolio Analysis

	Bills	Bonds	TIPS	Equities
Expected return	5.5%	6.5%	6.5%	10%
Return volatility	1%	8.5%	7.5%/4.5%	16%
Correlations				
Bills	1.0	0.1	0.0	−0.1
Bonds		1.0	0.5	0.1
TIPS			1.0	0.3
Equities				1.0

- Correlations between returns on bills, nominal bonds, and equities are historical. Correlations with TIPS returns are based on those observed in the
  Australian and U.K. markets.[16] In particular, we assume a small positive
  correlation of 0.3 with equities, which is consistent both with the historical
  data and with the observation, made earlier in this chapter, that inflation-
  indexed bonds and equities are somewhat related.

For simplicity, we focus on maximizing nominal returns, and we work in a
total return framework. Other kinds of analysis are possible: for example, Eichholtz,
Naber, and Petri discuss the problem of matching inflation-indexed liabilities.

At first glance, the results seem highly dependent on the volatility assumption used for TIPS. Exhibit 7 shows the composition of theoretically efficient portfolios with varying degrees of risk, using the realistic volatility assumption. Exhibit 8
shows the same, using the low volatility assumption. Using a 7.5% volatility, TIPS
play almost no role in any efficient portfolio; for example, at moderate risk levels,
nominal bonds are preferred because of their lower correlation with equities. However, using a 4.5% volatility, TIPS have a much more important role to play. They
partly displace bills at low risk levels, and largely displace nominal bonds at moderate to high risk levels. Only the equity weightings remain more or less unchanged.

But how much value do TIPS actually add? Exhibit 9 shows the efficient
frontier, i.e., expected returns from efficient portfolios, calculated using both the
realistic and low TIPS volatility assumptions. Above the 2% risk level, they are
very close: expected returns differ by no more than 14 bp. That is, even assuming
that TIPS will have a very low return volatility does not significantly increase
their expected value added to portfolio returns.

Exhibit 10 is even more telling. It shows expected returns from efficient
portfolios under the low TIPS volatility assumption, for both unconstrained portfolios and portfolios from which TIPS have been excluded. Even at moderate risk
levels, where TIPS are most important, the difference in expected returns is only
14 bp. Moreover, an investor who currently held a TIPS-free portfolio, and who
wanted to capture this additional 14 bp by purchasing TIPS, would have to turn
over 60% of the portfolio to achieve the optimal asset class weightings.

---

[16] Eichholtz, Naber, and Petri, "Index-Linked Bonds in a Liability Framework."

Exhibit 7: Composition of Efficient Portfolios, 7.5% Volatility Assumption

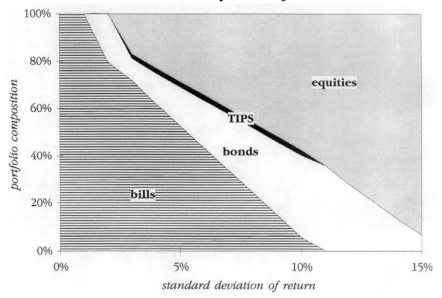

Exhibit 8: Composition of Efficient Portfolios, 4.5% Volatility Assumption

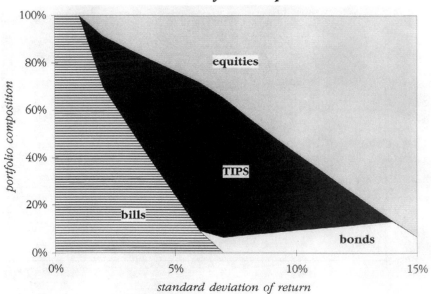

Exhibit 9: Efficient Frontier for the Two Different Volatility Assumptions

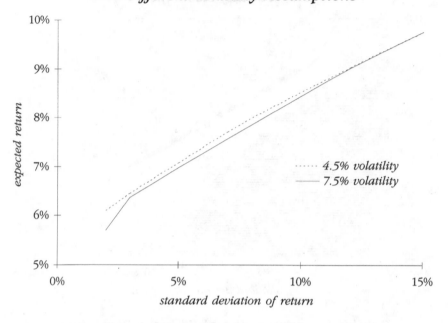

Exhibit 10: Efficient Portfolios Including and Excluding TIPS

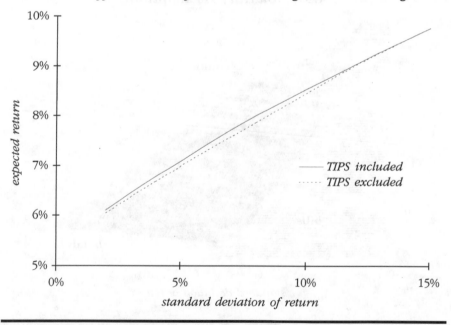

The overall conclusions are that (1) a realistic TIPS return volatility assumption, consistent with historical experience, implies that TIPS do not add value to asset allocation and (2) even under a very optimistic TIPS return volatility assumption, the value added by TIPS is very modest. The main reasons are that TIPS do not have a higher expected return than nominal bonds, but have a slightly higher assumed correlation with equities.

These results should be compared with the findings of Eichholtz, Naber, and Petri who used data from 1983–1991, and discovered a significant difference between relatively low inflation countries such as the U.K., and countries such as Israel where inflation has been extremely high and volatile.

- *Results for the U.K.:* If the goal is to maximize total return, inflation-linked bonds do not appear in any efficient portfolio. If inflation-linked liabilities are included in the problem, they appear in very low risk efficient portfolios, but with negligible weight (less than 1%).
- *Results for Israel:* If the goal is to maximize total return, inflation-linked bonds play a minor role in low risk portfolios but a major role in risky portfolios, sometimes having a weight of over 50%. If inflation-linked liabilities are included in the problem, inflation-linked bonds play a major role at all levels of risk, with weights between 44% and 88%.

U.S. investors will have to decide which set of results provides more useful guidance. Readers are encouraged to run the analysis themselves, based on their own portfolio objectives, and using volatility and correlation assumptions derived, not just from historical data, but from their own views on the nature of the U.S. economy. The computing resources required are very modest, and the exercise is likely to yield valuable insights.

ADVANCED ANALYTICAL APPROACHES TO INFLATION-INDEXED BONDS

Exhibit 3 showed the spread between the TIPS real yield and the 10-year CMT nominal yield, which provided an estimate of the market's implied inflation forecast. While this simple measure has been reasonably accurate, it has the following shortcomings:

- it ignores the maturity mismatch between the TIPS and the 10-year CMT, and it also ignores the cash flow mismatch between the TIPS and nominal coupon streams; and
- it assumes a constant nominal yield and a constant real yield over the whole 10-year period, and produces a single, constant inflation forecast for that whole period.

Deriving a Term Structure of Inflation Forecasts and Real Yields

Better results can be obtained by adopting a zero coupon approach, which analyzes securities on a cash flow by cash flow basis and which recognizes that real and nominal interest rates and inflation can vary as we move forward in time. This gives a more accurate estimate than taking a simple yield spread and, more importantly, gives additional information about the term structure of inflation forecasts and real yields, and (to some extent) the inflation risk premium.

In the Australian market, where inflation-linked Treasuries have been issued across a range of maturities, one can build a real zero coupon or forward rate curve using methods similar to those used to construct a nominal zero coupon or forward rate curve. (There are some complications, mostly arising from the indexation lag.) The spread between the real and nominal forward rate curve may be interpreted as the market's implied inflation forecast — possibly incorporating an inflation risk premium. This forecast need not be constant, but can vary through time.

The difficulty in the U.S. market is that, for much of the available history, there is only one TIPS outstanding: only the 10-year real yield is observable. How can we reconstruct an entire real forward rate curve or an entire implied inflation curve? This can be done in two steps:

1. Estimate short-term real interest rates by comparing short-dated nominal Treasury yields to short-term consensus inflation forecasts. This assumes that market short-term real rates should be consistent with these consensus forecasts, which seems reasonable since these forecasts are based on a great deal of data and analysis. Later on, we will discuss how sensitive the analysis is to a variation in the consensus forecasts used.

2. Interpolate between these short-term real interest rates and the observed long-term market real yield using a macroeconomic model.[17] More precisely, we assume that the forward real interest rate curve has the functional form implied by such a model, and fit this functional form to the given short- and long-term real yields. Note that this procedure only relies on the structure of the model. There is no need to estimate the model parameters separately since they are (implicitly) determined by market data.

One refinement is required. The short end of the yield curve can be idiosyncratic, and often has an unusual shape. This occurs partly because monetary policy is often perceived to be in disequilibrium compared to where the market thinks it currently "should be," and partly because short-dated yields can be based on detailed short-term economic forecasts: that is, short-term economic expectations can be more complex than long-term expectations. Thus, it is useful to allow for additional structure at the short end of the curve.

---

[17] For an example of such a model, see Chapter 1 in Phoa, *Advanced Fixed Income Analytics*.

Step 1 does this by using consensus inflation forecasts for both the next quarter and for the next year. Step 2 does this by assuming that the real yield curve can have a complex form. More precisely, if:

r^e = the market forecast long-term equilibrium real interest rate
r_0 = what the market thinks the short-term real interest rate should be
r_0' = what the short-term real interest rate actually is

then we assume that the real forward rate curve has the form:

$$r^e + (r_0 - r^e)\exp(-\delta t) + (r_0' - r_0)\exp(-\delta' t)$$

The first two terms of this expression are derived from a macroeconomic model;[18] the last term is chosen for its simplicity, and seems to give quite good results in empirical testing. To simplify the analysis, we also assume that the nominal forward rate curve (and hence the forward inflation curve) has the same functional form.

I explain how to estimate δ elsewhere.[19] δ' is estimated in an *ad hoc* fashion; in fact, the analysis is not too sensitive to the choice of δ and δ'. We choose to fit 3-month, 2-year, and 10-year nominal Treasury yields precisely, and observe that this generally gives a good fit to intermediate nominal yields. Mid-range nominal bond yields can be distorted by maturity-specific supply/demand factors. Mid-range real yields are unlikely to be affected by these factors, and so we adopt a method which does not transmit these distortions to the estimated real yield curve.

Recall that nominal yields may reflect an inflation risk premium. This must either be modeled separately, or absorbed into the market implied inflation curve, which then represents a "risk-adjusted inflation forecast." It is preferable to adopt the latter approach, in the absence of additional information enabling us to estimate the risk premium separately. This ensures that the estimation procedure is stable and does not rely on any assumptions about an unobservable (and possibly maturity-dependent) variable. However, one must remember that the resulting inflation forecast is risk-adjusted.

Exhibit 11 shows the results of this analysis, as of 1/31/97, 5/12/97, and 6/13/97. This exhibit has the following interpretation. On 1/31/97, the implied market forecast said that inflation would rise from a current level of around 3% to a long-term equilibrium rate of around 3.4%, while short-term real interest rates would rise from a current 2.5% to around 3.4%. (Note that this level is consistent with historical long-term real yields as shown in Exhibit 2.) These estimated market forecasts are consistent with a long-term scenario of moderately strong growth leading to some upward pressure on inflation. The market forecast for 10-year average inflation was around 3.25%, significantly higher than the consensus forecast produced by the Society of Professional Forecasters (SPF).

---

[18] See Chapter 1 in Phoa, *Advanced Fixed Income Analytics*.
[19] See Chapter 4 in Phoa, *Advanced Fixed Income Analytics*.

Exhibit 11: Estimated Forward Real Rates and Inflation on 1/31/97

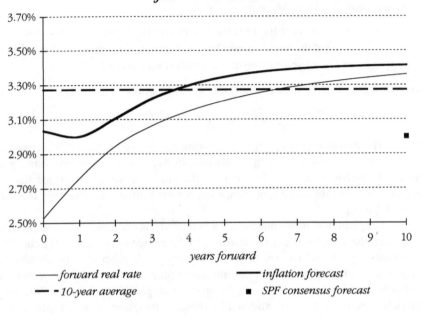

5/12/97

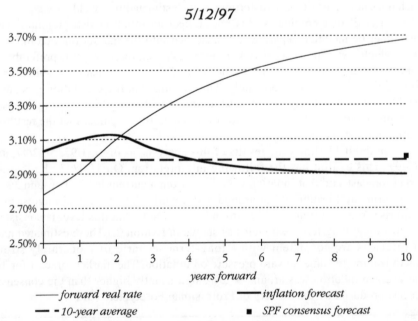

Exhibit 11 (Continued): 6/13/97

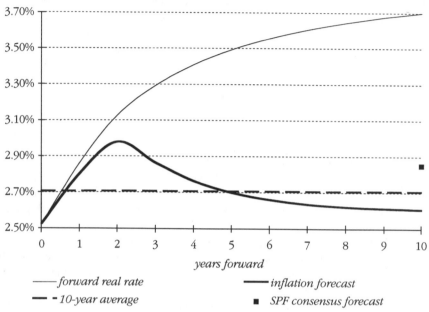

forward real rate ——   *inflation forecast* ——
10-year average — -   ▪ *SPF consensus forecast*

By 5/12/97, after a monetary tightening and the release of economic data which eased inflation concerns, the situation had changed. The implied market inflation forecast said that inflation would remain relatively stable: it would rise moderately over the remainder of the cycle and then drift down to an equilibrium level somewhat lower than 3%. Short-term real interest rates would rise from a current 2.8% to around 3.7% (reflecting expectations of slightly more aggressive monetary policy). These estimated forecasts are consistent with a long-term scenario of strong growth but muted inflation. Note that the market forecast for 10-year average inflation was now very close to the consensus forecast.

By 6/13/97, inflation expectations had eased even further; in fact, the implied 10-year average inflation forecast was by then somewhat lower than the SPF consensus forecast, which had itself been revised downwards since the previous quarter. In detail, inflation was expected to rise from 2.5% to 3%, and then ease back to around 2.6%. Since real interest rates had not changed appreciably, the fall in long-term inflationary expectations was not due to a belief that the Fed would act more aggressively to contain inflation, but was probably due to a positive reassessment of the economy and its ability to sustain non-inflationary growth.

This interpretation ignores the fact that the market inflation forecast is risk-adjusted, and incorporates an inflation risk premium. However, one can see that this risk premium cannot be large: for example, if it were 70 bp then this would imply that market participants were expecting a long-term inflation rate of around

2% on 6/13/97, which seems improbable. In fact, a possible interpretation is that on both 1/31/97 and 5/12/97, market participants expected long-term inflation to average 3%, but that nominal yields on 1/31/97 reflected a 25 bp inflation risk premium while nominal yields on 5/12/97 reflected no inflation risk premium. This would seem reasonable, since when inflation expectations are muted, inflation risk is dominated by real interest rate risk. Thus, nominal yields on 6/13/97 appeared to reflect a "negative inflation risk premium," arguably due to the fact that in investors' minds, real rate risk by then assumed significantly more importance than inflation risk.

We thus conclude that, if market long-term inflation expectations are assumed to agree with the economists' consensus forecast, *the inflation risk premium in nominal bond yields has fluctuated between 25 bp and −15 bp*. However, we will see in a moment that the discrepancy between the observed market long-term inflation forecast and the economists' consensus forecast can be explained in other ways. Therefore, this evidence about the inflation risk premium is inconclusive. Evans uses different methods to measure time-varying inflation risk premia in the U.K. market.[20]

Note that, while the long-term equilibrium real rate and inflation forecasts are somewhat sensitive to the short-term consensus inflation forecasts fed into the analysis, the 10-year average market inflation forecast is not; varying the short-term inflation forecasts has little effect on the 10-year forecast. Therefore, it is probably more valid to focus on this figure than on the long-term equilibrium forecast. Exhibit 12 compares the 10-year market inflation forecast, computed as above, with the simple yield spread between the 10-year TIPS and the 10-year CMT nominal yield. The yield spread actually provides quite a good measure of expected inflation. However, note that the discrepancy would be much wider if the yield curve were very steep, if the short end of the yield curve had an unusual shape, or if there were a larger maturity mismatch. The zero coupon approach gives more accurate results under all yield curve environments, and also provides additional information.

One useful application of the analysis is the estimation of real yields: this can be done by integrating the estimated forward real rate curve. Exhibit 13 shows estimated semiannual par real yields for various maturities, again on 1/31/97 and 5/12/97. While the nominal curve flattened between January and May 1997, the real yield curve actually steepened. This illustrates how the dynamics of the real yield curve may differ from that of the nominal curve.

Real yield curves are useful to investors in a number of ways. Here are some applications which arise in insurance investment management and corporate finance:

1. They can be used to value inflation-linked liabilities, such as inflation-indexed annuities.
2. They can be used to value inflation-linked revenue streams, such as toll-road revenues; this is helpful when assessing potential returns from infrastructure projects.

---

[20] D. Evans, "Real Rates, Expected Inflation and Inflation Risk Premia," forthcoming in *Journal of Finance*.

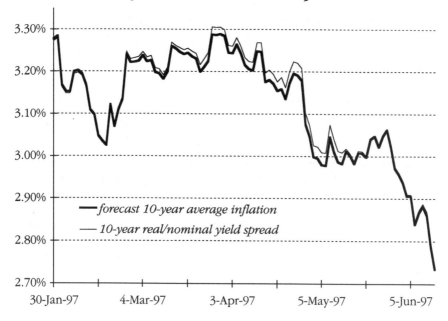

Exhibit 12: Implied Market Inflation Forecast versus Simple Real/Nominal Yield Spread

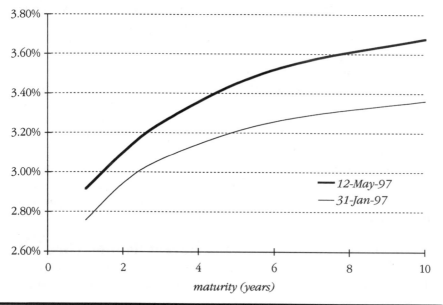

Exhibit 13: Estimated Real Yield Curves on 1/31/97 and 5/12/97

3. They can be used to estimate the present value of a company's future wage costs, which are broadly linked to inflation.

In each case, traditional valuation methods use nominal discount rates and an inflation forecast, which is usually taken to be constant. Using estimated market real yields is equivalent to using nominal discount rates together with the implied market inflation forecast, which need not be constant. This valuation method is consistent with the way nominal and inflation-linked bond holdings are valued.

For example, suppose a project will be completed in 1 year's time, and will generate quarterly real revenues of $25 million in today's dollars, for 5 years following. An investor wishes to value the project as of 5/12/97. Using a constant real rate of 3.66% (the TIPS market real yield) values the project at $439 million, whereas using the estimated real yield curve values the project at $444 million — that is, using more accurate real yields makes a $5 million difference. The discrepancy remains if we add a risk premium to the discount rates. The discrepancy would be larger if the yield curve were very steep, or oddly shaped.

Risk-adjusted market inflation forecasts are also useful in a number of ways, not all of them obvious. For example, if a prepayment model had to make certain assumptions about future house price levels (which affect loan-to-value (LTV) ratios and thus prepayment rates), these assumptions should not be specified arbitrarily, but should be derived from market inflation forecasts.

The analysis will be considerably sharpened once the Treasury has issued TIPS with a full range of maturities, including at least 2-, 5-, 10-, and 30-year maturities. This will make it possible to construct more accurate real yield curves and inflation curves. The availability of a 2-year TIPS real yield will also reduce the reliance of the analysis to the short-term consensus forecasts used, and thus improve the construction of a real yield curve. Note that if a 30-year TIPS is included, the estimation procedure must be modified to take the convexity bias into account.

Quality spreads in the inflation-indexed bond market are also worth analyzing. At the time of writing, inflation-indexed bonds have been issued by Federal agencies, financial institutions, and corporates. Since quality spreads depend on maturity, one would like to construct quality-specific real yield curves which permit accurate comparisons between different curves. This will suggest how new issues should be priced, and may also be used to identify arbitrages in quality spreads between the real and nominal markets.

Note that even with a range of TIPS maturities outstanding, it is likely that bond yield data for lower qualities will remain sparse. Thus, the interpolation method described above will still be useful for constructing real yield curves for lower qualities, even if it is no longer required to construct a Treasury real yield curve.

Economists' Forecasts versus Market Implied Forecasts

Why is there often a discrepancy between economists' inflation forecasts and market implied inflation forecasts? One obvious explanation is that traders and investors do not necessarily agree with economists. One must be careful here: this is only an explanation if one believes that the consensus among investors can differ from the consensus among economists, which is a much less obvious assertion. In fact, if this is true, it says something remarkable: in making economic forecasts, market participants do not always rely on the skills and resources of the "experts" which (in effect) they themselves have selected. On the face of it, this would seem to contradict market efficiency, i.e., the hypothesis that investors make use of all available information in what they believe to be an optimal way. One might argue that in an efficient market, either bond yields would reflect economists' predictions, or economists would be considered unreliable and would therefore not have jobs.

A second explanation is as follows. Investors do not make a single inflation forecast, but attach probabilities to future inflation scenarios; and this probability determines future bond yields (including the inflation risk premium, if it exists). Roughly speaking, if i is the unknown long-term inflation rate, which we regard as a random variable to which economists and market participants assign some probability distribution, then:

$$market\ implied\ inflation\ forecast \approx mean(i) + \lambda \times variance(i)^{1/2}$$

where the second term represents the inflation risk premium, i.e., λ is the market price of inflation risk. On the other hand, one could argue that:

$$economists'\ consensus\ forecast \approx median(i)$$

where the median is perhaps taken over a "trimmed" distribution, i.e., eliminating outliers. (The actual story is probably more complex than this, since different market participants and economists are using their individual probability distributions.)

Even if economists and market participants are using the same probability distribution, these two expressions need not be equal if this distribution is skewed. For example, if there is an upside skew, then the market implied forecast can be appreciably higher than the economists' consensus forecast for three reasons:

- the mean will be higher than the median, if there are wide outliers on the upside
- the inflation risk premium may be relatively more significant
- the "trimming" in the median will have eliminated more outliers on the upside

When inflation is low (below around 3%), there tends to be an upside skew and thus the market implied forecast is very often higher than the economists' consensus forecast. There are two main reasons for this skew. First, it is harder to cut real wages when inflation is very low, since workers tend to resist nominal wage cuts; this makes lower inflation scenarios seem less likely. Second, if low inflation is perceived to be the result of domestic policy rather than, for example, an external currency standard, political risk poses a threat to continued low inflation.

This seems to be the explanation advanced by Carmody and Mason.[21] It is important to note that wage stickiness and the absence of an external currency standard need not be unchangeable features of the economy. That is, the tendency for probability distributions to be skewed when inflation is low is not universal, but arises from particular institutional features of Western economies. These may be changing even now; for example, it is more plausible that real wages should fall in the United States over the next few years than it was in the early 1960s, when inflation was similarly low.

Note that the discrepancy between the market forecast and the consensus forecast may vary over time. For example, we saw earlier that it was around 0.25% on 1/31/97, but close to zero on 5/12/97; and on 6/13/97 it was −0.15%. An investor who believed that this discrepancy should theoretically be constant or nearly constant (e.g., because it reflects an inflation risk premium), might monitor the discrepancy from day to day, to detect potential trading opportunities.

For most practical applications, one should use market implied forecasts rather than economists' consensus forecasts. This ensures that one will obtain valuations of inflation-linked revenue streams or liability streams which are consistent with observed market prices of traded securities. In other words, using market implied forecasts ensures arbitrage-freeness, while using economists' forecasts admits the possibility of arbitrage.

---

[21] Carmody and Mason, *Analysis of Australian Index-Linked Securities.*

Chapter 9

Valuing and Trading TIPS

Gerald Lucas
Director, Govt/Derivative Strategist
Merrill Lynch & Company

Timothy Quek
Vice President, Govt/Derivative Strategist
Merrill Lynch & Company

INTRODUCTION

We divide this chapter into four segments in order to understand the factors driving real yields and the pricing of TIPS. The first part is a brief introduction to the theory of nominal yields, the risk premium, and the interaction between real rates and inflation expectations. In the second section, we examine the factors that determine the Fed funds rate, both nominal and real, and see how these factors influence long term real rates. The third section reviews the price performance of TIPS in 1997 and the factors that drive its price action. Finally, we examine how investors can view indexed-linked debt. We concentrate on their role from a fixed income portfolio context.

Throughout this chapter, we use either real yields or indexed-linked bonds (IL) to refer to inflation-linked bonds in a generic manner. The Treasury issued two 10-year and one 5-year TIPS in their first year of the program (with a new 30-year scheduled for April 15, 1998). However, this chapter concentrates on the first 10-year TIPS, the 3.375% 1/07 since it is the first issue and has the longest trading history. As such, when we use the term "TIPS" in this chapter, it refers just to the 3.375% 1/15/07, not the other maturities.

A BRIEF THEORY OF YIELDS

The Fisher rule states that the nominal yield on a conventional bond is equal to the sum of the real interest rate plus the expected level of inflation over the lifetime of the bond (to be precise, it is really the cross product). However, given that investors in conventional bonds are likely to be sensitive to the volatility of inflation as well as the average expected level, we should add a third component, the risk premium. In summary, we may decompose the curve into its three factors:

Spot Curve = Term Structure of
1) Expected Inflation +
2) Expected Real Yields +
3) Risk Premium

Expected inflation is self explanatory, although highly uncertain. We define expected real yields to equal the forward Fed funds rates minus expected inflation. Accordingly, the first two components will then equal the expected Fed funds curve. These two components form the basis for the expectations theory of interest rates, which implicitly assumes (1) that the return to owning any maturity bond is the same for a set holding period and (2) all rates will move to their forward rates.

However, the forward rates implied by the U.S. yield curve are generally higher than what is reasonably implied by pure expectations for future Fed funds. Historical analysis shows that forward rates are upwardly biased estimators of future spot rates and that the return for investments in long-term bonds generally outperforms that for short-term securities. Accordingly, the forward rates derived from the current spot curve do not give investors an accurate assessment of expected Fed policy. The primary reason for this upward bias in forward rates is the presence of a risk premium embedded in bonds. This premium results in the positive slope seen in most yield curves. Accordingly, we must combine the expectations theory with a risk premium to explain the shape of the curve (liquidity premium hypothesis).

Risk Premium

The risk premium is basically due to the fact that most investors are risk-averse. Due to the uncertainty in inflation forecasts and volatility of both inflation and the real rate, investors demand increased compensation for the additional market (price) risk they incur as they extend out the curve. One key reason for this risk premium is that most active managers are judged by their yearly performance, even if their benchmarks may be longer than a year. The risk premium may be described as the incremental yield or "cushion" that must be offered to induce them to extend their duration past their benchmark. Higher volatility translates into greater uncertainty and a higher risk premium. Without a risk premium, there would be a supply/demand imbalance since investors generally prefer to lend short while issuers prefer to borrow long.

We believe it is critical for investors to decompose the risk premium into its two sub-components: an inflationary and a real-rate risk premium. The inflationary risk premium may be defined as the premium required to offset the risk of a price decline that investors face due to an unexpected adverse change in inflationary expectations. Since inflation is of great concern to all bond investors, the inflationary risk premium is generally higher than the real rate risk premium. It is this cost that the Treasury anticipates saving since they (or the taxpayer), not the investor, are incurring this risk.

If we were to assume that the inflation risk premium is zero (i.e., investors are risk neutral with respect to inflation volatility), then inflationary expectations will simply equal the spread between the maturity matched yields of fixed coupon nominal and IL bonds (break-even inflation proxy). However, this approach is too simplistic; expected inflation would appear too high since this spread includes the inflationary risk premium embedded in nominal bonds.

The U.K. experience bears this out. If we assume that year-over-year RPI (Retail Price Index) may serve as a proxy for future expected inflation (on average), the spread of Gilt over IL yields has generally been higher than year-over-year RPI due to the inflation risk premium embedded in nominal bonds. The only exception was from 1988 to 1992 when RPI was so high (6%-11%) that it was not a valid proxy for long-term expected inflation. However, it is worthwhile to examine the change in this spread (nominal versus IL) since that will serve as a proxy for a change in inflationary expectations, assuming that the risk premia remains constant (a debatable assumption).

Expected Real Rate Risk Premium

Most investors have focused on the inflation risk premium and the give up in yield which IL investors should be willing to accept in return for the guarantee on inflation. However, there also exists a real rate risk premium. The real rate risk premium is the premium required to offset the risk of an increase in the real rate. Just as inflationary expectations may change over time, so does the expected real rate. The general upward term structure of real rates in the U.K. shows that a real rate risk premium exists. Further, history shows that the higher real rates are, the flatter the real rate curve; this implies that investors are willing to accept a lower overall risk premium to extend duration since they are already being amply compensated in real yields.

Long-term real rates are variable and are strongly correlated with short-term real rates. Since most active managers are sensitive to (at a minimum) yearly mark-to-market returns, they too will demand a real rate risk premium to compensate for an adverse change in that rate. Since the TIPS market is less liquid than the nominal market (this is certainly the case for all existing index-linked markets), then investors in real return bonds may also demand an illiquidity premium over the certain *ex ante* real return. However, the stability in both the Fed funds rate and TIPS real yield during 1997 has generally mitigated the real rate risk premium.

Although it is hard to precisely quantify the value of the overall risk premium, we may make some general observations. First, an increase in the yield volatility of the real rate and/or inflation expectations will increase these premia due to increased uncertainty. All else equal, high real yields should lower the risk premium since long-term real yields are mean reverting. Likewise, the risk premium will change over time, primarily due to the factors that affect long-term real rates (i.e., savings versus investment, public sector deficits versus return on capital, etc.).

Now that we have a basic understanding of the three components embedded in nominal yields, we would like to concentrate on how the first two, inflation expectations and real rates, interact with each other.

Exhibit 1: Inflationary Expectations versus Real Rate

Balanced Credible Fed	→	Positively Correlated
		IE ↑, RR ↑, Y ↑
Overly Aggressive Fed	→	Inversely Correlated
		RR ↑, IE ↓, Y?
Dovish Fed	→	Inversely Correlated
		RR ↓, IE ↑, Y?

Real Rates versus Inflation Expectations

Generally, real yields and nominal yields should be positively correlated. Exhibit 1 shows the likely effects of Fed policy on real rates and inflationary expectations. For example, with a balanced credible Fed (such as the current Greenspan Fed), any rise in inflationary expectations will generally be met with a rise in the real rate to slow the economy and keep inflation in check. In turn, both nominal and real yields will rise. Conversely, real yields may be negatively correlated with inflationary expectations if the Fed is overly hawkish or dovish. In such scenarios, IL bonds may have a marked increase in volatility relative to nominal bonds.

Real yields may also be negatively correlated with nominal yields if there is an unexpected change in inflation expectations. This is what happened during 1997 (Q2-Q4), when the curve flattened in a rally; TIPS were essentially uncorrelated with nominal yields, primarily because the primary force driving nominal yields was the major shift in inflation (year-over-year inflation declined from 3.30% to 1.70%). Conversely, Fed policy remained stable after the 25 bp tightening on March 25, 1997.

Real and nominal yields will be negatively correlated in deflationary (negative inflation) times. In order to maintain an effective gross income (i.e., both coupon and principal adjustment) of at least 0%, real rates must increase one for one against the negative inflation rate in order to offset the adverse effects of deflation on the adjusted principal. Few investors would purchase an IL bond if their expected gross income (real coupon plus adjustment to principal) were to be below zero. Conversely, nominal yields should decline with deflation, although there should be a floor of slightly greater than 0%.

However, inflation expectations are not the primary determinant of real rates; in reality, it is a secondary factor. We would now like to examine the other factor that drives real rates — the real GDP output gap — in order to better gauge how to price IL securities.

REAL RATES AND THE PRICE DETERMINANTS OF IL SECURITIES

With inflation remaining at relatively low and stable levels in the G7 economies, further potential declines in nominal interest rates may well depend on the trend for real interest rates. For fixed income investors, the potential increase in index-linked bond issuance over the next few years increases the importance of assessing real yield trends. At its simplest level, the long-term real interest rate may be seen as the price of capital and will be determined by the interaction of the demand and supply of capital. The primary determinant of supply of capital is the real level of national savings, which includes both private savings and public savings. (Note that budget deficits are defined as public sector dis-savings.) The main influence of the demand for capital is the real level of investment.[1]

However, long-term real rates are also based on expectations for forward monetary policy (i.e., the real Fed funds rate) and a real rate risk premia. The factors mentioned in the above paragraph primarily affect the risk premia embedded in long-term securities; these factors have minimal influence on the funds rate since the Fed (for the most part) conducts its monetary policy independent of these agents. Therefore, it is important to examine the two primary factors which drive the nominal Fed funds rate: the GDP gap and inflationary expectations. Exhibit 2 summarizes these interrelationships.[2] There exists both a positive reactive function between the funds rate and the GDP gap (i.e., as the GDP gap increases, the Fed reacts by raising real rates) and an expectative relationship between the GDP gap and expected inflation. Likewise, there is a reactive function between expected inflation and the real funds rate. In turn, the real funds rate has a positive expectative relationship with real long-term rates. As they rise, the output gap should then decrease, completing the cycle.

Exhibit 2: Factors Determining Funds Rate

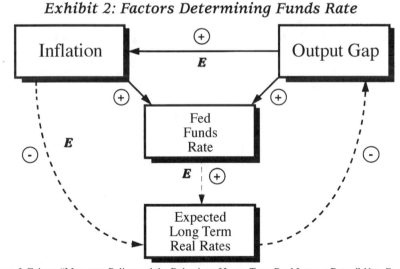

Source: J. Fuhrer, "Monetary Policy and the Behavior of Long-Term Real Interest Rates," *New England Economic Review* (September/October 1995).

[1] Ifty Islam, "Special Focus: Real Interest Rates," January 1996, Merrill Lynch publication.
[2] J. Fuhrer, "Monetary Policy and the Behavior of Long Term Real Interest Rates," *New England Economic Review* (September/October 1995).

Exhibit 3: Taylor Rule

$$FF = 0.5 \, (\text{Gap}) + 0.5 \, (I - 2.0)_I + I + 2.0_R$$

where

FF	=	Real Fed funds rate
Gap	=	$100 \times (G - G^*)/G^*$
G	=	Real GDP
G^*	=	Potential GDP
I	=	Year-over-year inflation
2.0_I	=	Target inflation rate
2.0_R	=	Equilibrium real rate

What Drives the Real Funds Rate?

In order to quantify the effect that these two factors have in determining the nominal funds rate, we have developed a model to predict the Fed funds rate, based on a modified Taylor rule. First, we examine the Taylor rule,[3] initially concentrating on the two factors that influence nominal funds: GDP output gap and inflation. We will then focus on the factor(s) determining the real rate since the real rate, not the nominal, determines how restrictive or accommodative monetary policy truly is. We find that the GDP gap is the primary force driving real rates.

Taylor Rule

Dr. John Taylor formally introduced the Taylor rule in 1993 to model the real Fed funds rate. The two primary factors that drive the model are the GDP gap and inflation (see Exhibit 3). Intuitively, these two factors have economic appeal. This policy rule states that if the economy is growing beyond potential or if the inflation rate is greater than the Fed's assumed target of 2%, the Fed will increase the funds rates to "lean against the wind." The long-term "equilibrium" real rate is estimated to equal 2%. From 1985 to 1992, this model appeared to provide a good correlation with target funds. However, the fit has been, at best, fair since then.

The original Taylor model was based on the fixed-weight GDP measurement, not the chain-weighted GDP as used in our model. In his original article, Dr. Taylor assumed a constant trend growth of 2.2% in potential real GDP. Conversely, our gap is relative to potential real GDP, as determined by the Congressional Budget Office (CBO). Exhibit 4 charts the level of real GDP versus CBO's non-inflationary GDP. We splined the quarterly GDP data into a monthly time series. Finally, we used core year-over-year inflation (released monthly) instead of the GDP deflator. While the results were quite similar with either of these inflation measurements, core inflation did provide a slightly better fit than the GDP deflator. Although the original Taylor model has not provided a very robust fit for the past four years, this does not detract from the theory behind his policy rule.

---

[3] J. Taylor, "Discretion Versus Policy Rules in Practice," *Carnegie-Rochester Conference Series on Public Policy 39* (1993), pp. 195-214.

Dr. Taylor correctly identified the two factors that drive the Funds rate; empirical analysis confirms this. The rule just needs a slight modification.

MODIFIED TAYLOR RULE

Using multiple regression analysis, we see in Exhibit 5 that nominal funds are correlated with the output gap and core year-over-year inflation, respectively. Combining these two factors increases the R^2 (0.86); this two factor modified Taylor model best explains nominal funds (Exhibit 6). The second equation transforms the original regression equation into a form compatible with Taylor's rule. Our estimated funds rate closely tracks the actual rate (Exhibit 7), confirming the importance of these two factors.

Exhibit 4: GDP: Actual versus Potential

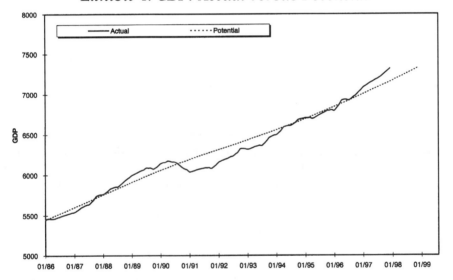

Exhibit 5: Nominal Funds

Indep Var =>	Gap+Infl	Gap	Infl
R-square	86.0%	46.0%	34.0%
F-test	428.4	118.2	72.7

Exhibit 6: Modified Taylor Model

$$FF_t = 1.0\,(\text{Gap}_{t\text{-}3}) + 1.3\,(I_t) + 1.35$$
$$= 1.0\,(\text{Gap}_{t\text{-}3}) + 0.3\,(I_t - 2.0) + I_t + 1.95$$

where
I = YOY Inflation

Exhibit 7: Regression Taylor Model: Fitted Nominal Funds versus Target Fed Funds

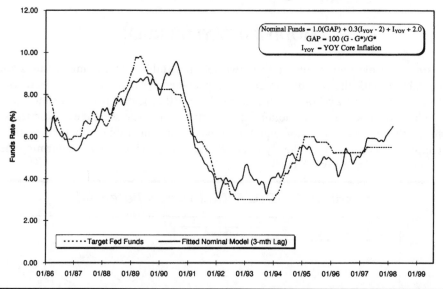

Nominal Funds = 1.0(GAP) + 0.3(I$_{YOY}$ - 2) + I$_{YOY}$ + 2.0

GAP = 100 (G - G*)/G*

I$_{YOY}$ = YOY Core Inflation

········ Target Fed Funds   ——— Fitted Nominal Model (3-mth Lag)

There are two differences between our model and the original Taylor rule. First, we found that the coefficients for the gap and inflation equaled 1.0 and 0.3 respectively, versus 0.5 for both coefficients in the original Taylor rule. These were the optimal coefficients, as determined by our regression analysis. Second, GDP gap appears to be a leading indicator; accordingly, we lagged this variable by three months with respect to Fed funds. (In actuality, the lead in the gap was time varying, with three months being the average. At times, the gap was coincident; other times, the gap led by more than six months.) Interestingly, the constant term (i.e., "equilibrium" real rate) equals 1.95%, very close to Taylor's estimate of 2.00%. We also found that there is zero correlation between gap (3-month lag) and inflation. Therefore, there is no multi-collinearity in our model. Since these two variables are independent, we feel confident that our model is a viable one. We should note that our model has the benefit of a certain degree of hindsight since both the GDP and gap have been subject to revisions over time.

While there is no guarantee that these relationships will hold in the future, the Merrill modified model definitely quantifies the two factors that drive the nominal funds rate: GDP gap and core inflation. The purpose of this model is not so much to predict the funds rate but rather to identify the factors driving the nominal rate. However, we should focus on the real funds rate, not the nominal, since it is the real rate that determines how restrictive or accommodative monetary policy really is. Here, the gap is the primary force driving real rates; it is much more important than inflation.

Exhibit 8: Real Fed Funds (Two Factor Model) $R^2 = 0.79$

$$
\begin{aligned}
\text{Real } FF_t &= (\text{Nominal } FF_t - I_t) \\
&= 1.0\,(\text{Gap}_{t-3}) + 0.3\,(I_t) + 1.35
\end{aligned}
$$

where
$I = \text{YOY Inflation}$

Exhibit 9: Real Funds

Indep Var =>	Gap+Infl	Gap	Infl
R-square	79.0%	76.0%	0.0%
F-test	262.4	439.1	2.0

Exhibit 10: Real Funds (YOY Inflation) versus Gap

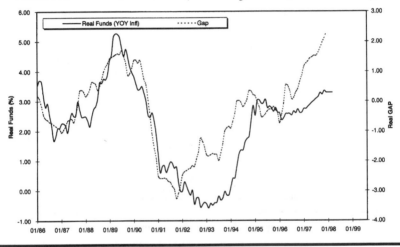

Real Gap Model

With a simple algebraic transformation of the modified Taylor rule, we then derive the equation for real funds (Exhibit 8, confirmed with regression analysis).

Although this two factor model has a reasonable R^2 (0.79), we believe it to be potentially misleading due to over-fitting. First, we found that there is zero correlation between the real rate and realized inflation on a coincident basis (Exhibit 9). Zero correlation implies that we should exclude inflation as a second factor. Although the goodness of fit decreased from 0.79 to 0.76 when using a one factor model, the F test (which adjusts for the degrees of freedom) was significantly higher. Second, Exhibit 10 clearly shows there is a strong inter-relationship between the real Fed funds rate and the GDP gap. We see that they closely track each other although the real funds rate seems to slightly follow the gap, reflecting the lag (three months) in the implementation of monetary policy. As such, we conclude that our one factor model is more appropriate than the two factor model when determining the real funds rate (Exhibit 11). In summary, the GDP gap, not realized inflation, is the critical factor in determining the real funds rate.

Exhibit 11: Real Fed Funds (1 Factor Model) R^2 = 0.76

$$\text{Real FF}_t = (\text{Nominal } FF_t - I_t)$$
$$= 1.0 \, (\text{Gap}_{t-3}) + 2.5$$

Exhibit 12: Regression GAP Model: Fitted Real Funds versus Actual Real Fed Funds

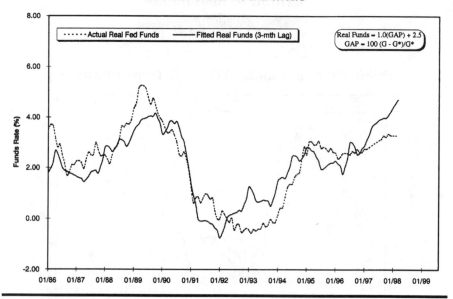

Although we did not find a relationship between the real funds rate and realized inflation on a coincident basis, it would be misleading to assume there is no relationship between real funds and inflation expectations. We think that inflation expectations are an important factor in determining the real rate. Perhaps it is more accurate to say that expectations are embedded in the GDP gap (the greater the gap, the higher the inflationary expectations). This explains why the gap alone is the primary determinant for real rates. However, we also saw that inflation, both realized and expected, declined in 1997 although the economy experienced high real growth and a concurrent increase in the gap. Perhaps, real growth and inflation really are independent, and inflation is not a determinant of real rates. If so, this may help explain the poor correlation between TIPS and nominal bonds during 1997.

Exhibit 12 illustrates the fitted real funds rate when using the one factor model (GDP gap is the single independent variable, lagged by three months). As is clearly evident, the fitted real funds rate closely tracks the actual real rate ($R^2 =$ 0.76). The equation is simple and has strong economic appeal: real funds rate equals the gap plus 2.5%. Interestingly, the constant term (2.5%) is very close to the long-term average for the non-inflationary growth in real GDP (2.34%, as determined by the CBO). Since gap is expressed as a percentage, the two terms are additive. In short, the real rate simply equals excess real growth (or shortfall) plus the long-term allowable real GDP growth (2.5%). This equation highlights the close relationship between real growth and real rates; in general, high real growth increases the demand for real borrowing, increasing real rates.

Further, a positive or negative gap can persist for extended periods; as shown in Exhibit 13, the 10-year rolling average for the GDP gap has been consistently negative from July 1969 to December 1987 (which covers the 10 years to December 1997). Only over the very long term (greater than 40 years) should the average gap be close to zero. Therefore, the estimated GDP gap is important for determining long-term real rates. The term will net out of our modified Taylor rule only if the gap maintains a zero average for the maturity of the IL security.

While there is not a one-for-one correlation between short- and long-term real rates, long-term real rates appear to be generally correlated with the real funds rate. It appears that expectations for the real long-term rate are based on the current real funds rate; intuitively, this is consistent. If short-term real rates are low, many investors may prefer to lock in higher long-term real rates by extending out the curve, thereby lowering long term real yields. Accordingly, we believe the real funds rate is an important determinant of the long-term real rate. Exhibit 14 compares the real funds rate relative to the real 10-year rate. Although the fit is not that precise, this is probably due to the fact that it is not always realistic to use year-over-year core inflation as a proxy for 10-year inflation expectations. We have found that a better fit exists when inflation expectations, based on either professional economic forecasts or a regression-based inflation model, is used.

Exhibit 13: GDP GAP: 10-Year Moving Average

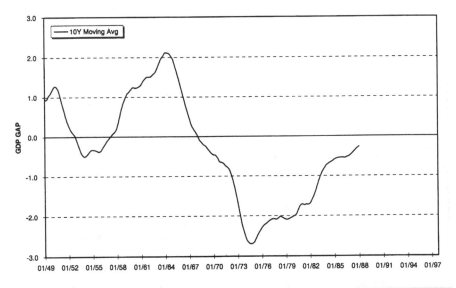

Exhibit 14: Real Funds (YOY Inflation) versus Real 10-Year (YOY Inflation)

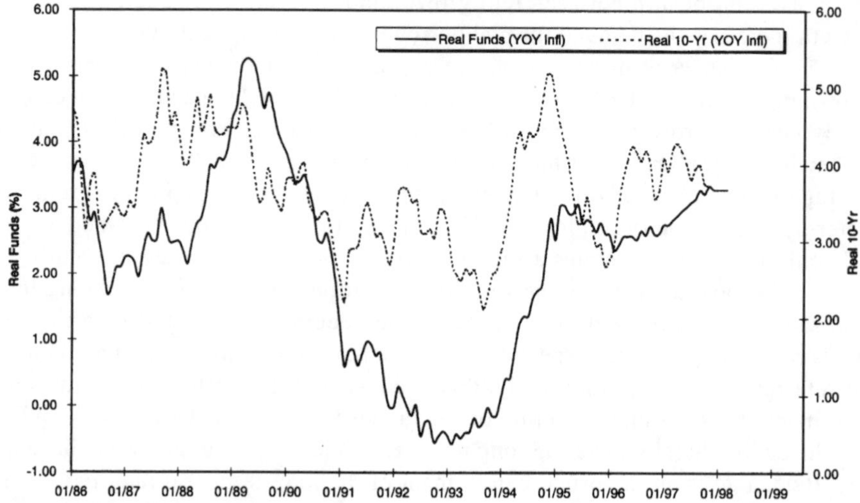

This basically completes the cycle shown in Exhibit 2. The key point of the modified Taylor model is not to predict the Fed funds rate but to ascertain the factors that drive the real Fed funds rate. We believe our historical analysis of the modified Taylor rule shows that the GDP gap is the primary factor determining both short- and long-term real rates. Further, the long-term real rate should be closely correlated with the short-term real rate. This relationship only breaks down when the short-term real rate is at an unsustainably high level. As will be discussed later on, the correlation between short- and long-term real rates has important implications regarding the use of IL bonds for fixed income portfolio management. Fixed income investors need to monitor these variables.

TIPS PRICE PERFORMANCE DURING 1997

While these theoretical factors have given us a better understanding as to how TIPS should trade relative to nominals, an examination of their price performance during the first year of trading should give us a better insight. However, their lack of liquidity and limited trading history still makes it difficult to make sweeping generalizations. First, supply/demand factors, especially around auction time, were a major price determinant. Although the clearing yields in three of the five auctions were lower than the 1.00PM WI yields, there were major price concessions going into each of the auctions. The attitude among many investors was "Why buy TIPS now when I can buy them cheaper at the auction." As a consequence of this view, secondary trading activity between auction periods was minimal.

Second, it is still uncertain as to how the market really prices TIPS. Is the real rate a plug, i.e., nominal rates minus estimated CPI-U plus an inflation risk premium? Or conversely, is the TIPS yield the markets expectation for the real Fed funds rate plus a real rate risk premium, making inflation the plug? While both factors are important to pricing TIPS, we do not believe the market prices TIPS based upon real rate expectations alone. Since nominal bonds are much more liquid than TIPS, the real yield is probably the plug, based upon the markets forecast for inflation. As will be seen later, the market's inflation forecast is heavily influenced by year-over-year CPI-U.

Until the advent of TIPS, it had been very hard to measure inflation expectations, let alone forecast it. However, given the biases in CPI and the inherent measurement problem, it is debatable that the breakeven inflation rate is an accurate representation for the future purchasing power of money. As Greenspan succinctly stated in a speech on September 5, 1997:

> The emergence of inflation indexed bonds does not solve the
> problem of pinning down an economically meaningful measure
> of the general price level...Returns on indexed bonds are tied to
> forecast of specified published price indexes, which may or may
> not reflect the market's judgment of the future purchasing power
> of money.

Finally, TIPS faced just one type of four potential growth/inflation environments in 1997 (albeit the worst one): high real growth (i.e., high real rates) and disinflation (i.e., low current income). TIPS have not traded in the following environments: (1) high growth and increasing inflation, (2) low growth and disinflation, and (3) low growth and increasing inflation. (We ignore deflationary environments.)

Accordingly, both the return and liquidity of TIPS were quite disappointing in their first year of trading. While their poor price performance can be attributed to the adverse environment they faced, their price action, in hindsight, does appear rational. Exhibit 15 compares the real yields for the 10-year TIPS (3.375% 1/07), the nominal yields for the 6.25% 2/07, and the breakeven inflation rate (nominal minus real yields), commencing February 15, 1997. In order to show the correlation (or lack thereof) between TIPS and nominals, Exhibit 16 plots the 2-month rolling real yield beta and the TIPS correlation with the 6.25% 2/07. During the selloff that occurred in the beginning of 1997 (2/15-4/15), the increase in TIPS yield almost matched that for nominals. Their real yield beta equaled 0.7 (i.e., TIPS yield increased 7 bp for each 10 bp increase in nominal yields). However, it was during this period that the Fed increased the funds rate from 5.25% to 5.50% (March 25, 1997), with the threat of more to follow, due to strong real growth and the potential for higher inflation. In summary, the TIPS yield closely followed that for the real funds rate, showing how sensitive TIPS are to Fed policy.

Exhibit 15: Treasury 6.25% 02/07 minus Treasury IL 3.375% 01/07 versus Treasury 6.25% 02/07 versus Treasury IL 3.375% 01/07

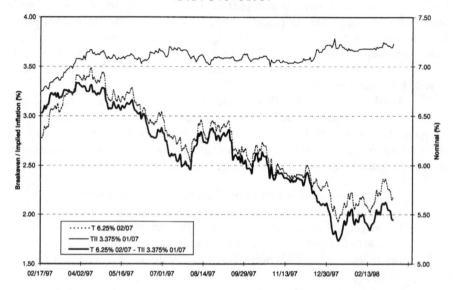

Exhibit 16: Treasury IL 3.375% 01/07 versus Treasury 6.25% 02/07: 2-Month Rolling Yield Beta and Correlation

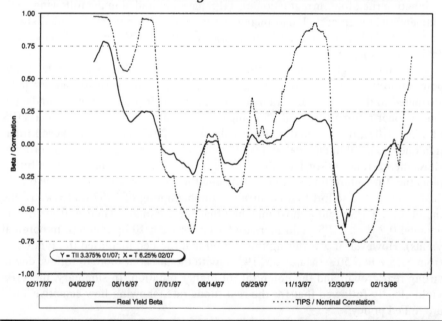

Conversely, TIPS had a low beta (–0.25< average beta <0.25) in a bull market that commenced in mid-April. On average, the TIPS beta has been zero (i.e., uncorrelated) since mid-April. Although the beta remained low, the correlation temporarily increased after Greenspan strongly hinted for a tightening with his October 8th speech. However, the Asian crisis quickly put the Fed back on hold and the curve flattened in a rally due to the possibility of deflation. During this period, the real yield beta then became negative (inverse correlation) since TIPS should perform poorly in a deflationary environment.

While real yields remained within a narrow range (3.50% to 3.75%), 10-year nominal yields declined by approximately 1.18% (6.98% to 5.80%) from April 15, 1997 to year end. Given the stability in real yields since mid-April, the breakeven inflation rate declined almost one for one with the decrease in nominal yields. Accordingly, the primary factor that caused the curve to flatten in the rally was the lowering of inflation expectations (YOY total inflation decreased from 3.30% to 1.70%). Conversely, real growth remained high and the Fed retained a tightening bias until the December 16, 1997 meeting. Given this decline in inflation, the real funds rate actually increased over this period. In such an environment, we should expect real yields to remain steady, and even to have an upward bias, similar to the real funds rate. In summary, it is not surprising that TIPS were basically uncorrelated with nominals since the Spring of 1997, given the stability in monetary policy but major change in inflation.

Three Price Factors for TIPS in 1997

While an uncorrelated asset class has value from a diversification viewpoint, the lack of correlation makes some investors hesitant to own TIPS since they do not seem to trade in a "rational" manner. While we too are occasionally perplexed by the price behavior of TIPS, there are three factors that basically explain how TIPS priced relative to nominals in 1997:

1. Year-over-year CPI
2. The inflation risk premium
3. The shape of the 2/10-year nominal curve

Breakeven Inflation Rate

The key factor for pricing TIPS (relative to the nominal rate) is predicting the breakeven inflation rate (i.e., 10-year nominals – TIPS; this spread equals expected inflation plus the inflation risk premium). As evidenced in Exhibit 17, the monthly average breakeven inflation rate[4] closely tracks YOY CPI-U (with food and energy), albeit with a lag of 1-2 months. In effect, the market's prediction for inflation over the next 10 years simply mirrors CPI-U over the past year.

---

[4] The monthly average breakeven inflation rate equals the average spread between the 6.25% 2/07 – 3.375% 1/07 from the CPI release date to the day prior to the following release date (i.e., the 2/19/97 value equals the average spread from 2/19 to 3/18).

However, using this simple trading rule can prove quite misleading; since 1950, the absolute prediction errors for CPI over the next 12 months (compared to the prior year CPI would have ranged between +7% to –6%.[5] Accordingly, TIPS investors should take an independent view and concentrate on predicting next year's inflation rate (but not necessarily the rate for the next 10 years). The breakeven inflation rate should then follow realized YOY CPI-U, assuming this rule continues to hold.

However, predicting inflation is a difficult job. The inflation prediction error, based on the Survey of Professional Forecasters, is quite similar to that for prior year CPI (since 1982, the error has ranged from +4% to –2%).[6] Romer and Romer have shown that the Fed is the only entity that can accurately predict inflation (perhaps because they have a measure of control).[7] They show that professional forecasters would have been better off using the Fed's prediction and discarding their own if it differed from the Fed's. Perhaps this is why the market uses YOY CPI as its inflation forecast; it is as good as any other method.

Exhibit 17: Monthly Average Breakeven Inflation Rate, YOY CPI versus Inflation Risk Premium

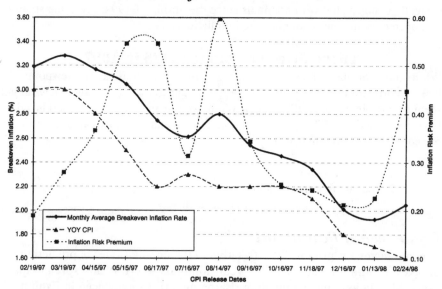

---

[5] B. Moore (SEI Investments), "Inflation Indexed Bonds," Presentation at Bloomberg/PIMCO/Barclays Conference (November 12, 1997).

[6] Moore, "Inflation Indexed Bonds."

[7] C. Romer and D. Romer, "Federal Reserve Private Information and the Behavior of Interest Rates," NBER Working Paper 5692 (July 1996).

Exhibit 18: Two-Month Rolling Beta: CMT Two Year versus CMT 10-Year and Real Yield Beta

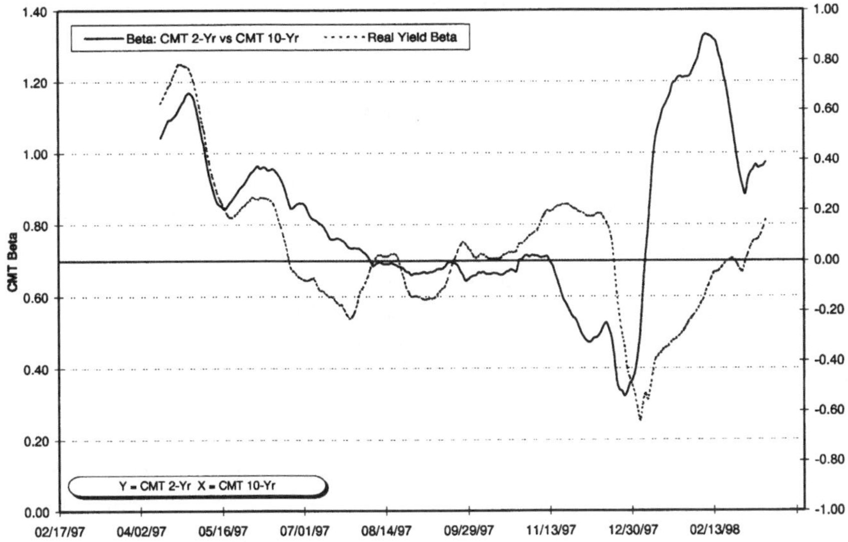

Inflation Risk Premium

Given that the market is currently using YOY CPI-U as a proxy for forecast inflation, the inflation risk premium should then "equal" the difference between the breakeven inflation rate and YOY CPI-U. All else equal, a low risk premium means that TIPS are cheap. Again, the inflation risk premium seems to follow a rational pattern. The relatively high inflation rate that prevailed at the beginning of 1997 (3.30%, the 6-year high) was associated with a low inflation risk premium; the market correctly perceived that there was little risk that future inflation would increase significantly over the long term. However, when CPI then declined, the risk premium increased since the market considered it highly uncertain that this low CPI rate could prevail going forward (excluding the July "dip"). As CPI then stabilized about the 2.20% level, the market started to feel increasingly comfortable that the Fed had achieved price stability; accordingly, the risk premium then declined to about 25 bp, starting in September.

TIPS Beta versus the Curve

More importantly, we notice that the TIPS beta increases when the 2/10-year curve steepens in a rally and flattens in a selloff or moves in a general parallel fashion. This curve behavior generally means that the front end (i.e., the Fed) is driving the curve. Conversely, there is a low correlation when the curve flattens in a rally and steepens in a selloff, (i.e., when inflation expectations drive the market). This has been the predominant curve behavior since mid-June 1997. These relationships are clearly shown in Exhibit 18, where we compare the rolling 2-month TIPS/nominal beta with the rolling curve beta (CMT 2-year relative to the CMT 10-year; a beta less than 1.0 means the curve flattens in a rally and steepens in a selloff). Note how the TIPS beta generally moves in tandem with the curve beta, showing the sensitivity of TIPS to the front end of the curve and the near term outlook for Fed policy. If anything, the curve beta seems to be a leading indicator for the TIPS beta.

USING TIPS IN A FIXED INCOME PORTFOLIO

Risk/Return versus Nominals

From April 15 to December 31, 1997, the risk for 10-year TIPS has been remarkably similar to the 6.25% 4/30/2001 (Exhibit 19). From a risk/reward perspective, perhaps we should compare TIPS to 4-year nominals, a similar risk security during 1997. However, this comparison could prove misleading; for example, the TIPS duration should increase when the Fed is changing monetary policy. Second, the correlation between real and nominal rates is highly variable, continually changing as the growth/inflation environment changes. This uncertain relationship (in terms of both risk and correlation) makes trading TIPS versus nominals a risky strategy, as many investors discovered in 1997. Accordingly, TIPS have fallen out of favor with many investors due to their underperformance in 1997. However, the problem is not with the security; the problem is that most investors view their TIPS buy/sell decision as an either/or decision versus nominals (i.e., investors compare the return performance of TIPS versus nominals, on either maturity matched or risk weighted basis).

TIPS/Nominal Portfolio

We believe the proper way for managers of both balanced and fixed income portfolios to view TIPS is from a portfolio approach. For example, TIPS should provide a good overall hedge in balanced equity/fixed income funds. While stocks may keep pace with inflation in the long run, an increase in inflation will generally hurt stocks in the short term. Obviously, TIPS will provide a much better hedge than nominal bonds in such a scenario. More importantly though is the relationship between real growth, real rates, and the equity market. As previously mentioned, real rates should rise (fall) during periods of high (low) real growth. All else equal, high real growth (or a forecast thereof) is normally associated with equity bull markets while low growth is associated with bear markets. TIPS should outperform in a low real growth environment due to the decline in real yields, again acting as an excellent hedge against an equity price decline. Obviously, deflation is as bad for equities as for TIPS; in this case, nominal bonds would be a much better hedge.

Exhibit 19: Risk/Return: 3.375% 1/07 versus 6.25% 4/30/01

(4/15/97 TO 12/31/97)

Security	Price Vol.	Absol. Return	Return/Risk
3.375% 1/07	2.53%	3.08%	1.22
6.25% 4/01	2.54%	7.70%	3.03

We believe fixed income investors should also view TIPS from a portfolio context. We think TIPS are a similar but separate asset class relative to nominals; their lack of correlation with nominals in 1997 reinforces this view. Accordingly, TIPS should provide an element of diversification, theoretically increasing the Sharpe ratio for the portfolio. More specifically, we think that investors should consider using a TIPS/nominal barbell to increase their risk/reward profile.

As stated earlier, TIPS have a higher real beta relative to 10-year nominals when the 2/10 curve beta is greater than 1 and a low/zero beta if the curve beta is less than 0.8. Given this conditional correlation with nominals, TIPS should act as a good hedge against nominals in certain curve environments. The basic tenets of modern portfolio theory is that a negatively correlated or an uncorrelated asset adds value due to diversification. We may also state that a bond with a conditional correlation (TIPS) should also add value. By incorporating the anticipated price action of TIPS with the dynamics of the nominal curve, we should be able to construct a lower risk portfolio with a TIPS/nominal barbell than that a cash/nominal barbell (or that built with nominals alone).

Accordingly, we would like to compare the price performance (both historical and theoretical) for a TIPS/long duration nominal barbell compared to (1) a nominal bullet, (2) a cash/long duration nominal, and (3) the master Treasury index (all coupons greater than one year). While we recognize that TIPS have a highly variable (both positive and negative) duration due to their conditional correlation with nominals, their average duration during 1997 was close to zero. Accordingly we assign a zero duration to TIPS in the following portfolio. In short, we are using TIPS instead of, but not as a proxy for, cash. Based upon an investor's view regarding real growth (i.e., GDP gap) and inflation, a TIPS/long duration nominal barbell (dollar and duration neutral, assigning a zero TIPS duration) may outperform a nominal bullet portfolio in most growth/inflation environments. Further, the TIPS/nominal barbell should have lower risk than a cash/nominal barbell. We think that the price/income performance of TIPS should help offset any potential underperformance in the long duration nominal (relative to the bullet) due to an erroneous growth/inflation forecast.

For example, a cash/nominal barbell strategy would underperform if the curve steepened in a selloff due to an increase in inflation expectations. However, TIPS should outperform in this environment due to higher coupon income received. Likewise, a nominal barbell would underperform a bullet if the curve steepened in a rally due to an easing of monetary policy. In such a scenario, real yields should also decline. Since the duration of TIPS/nominal barbell would then be greater than the benchmark, it should outperform both a bullet bond and the cash/nominal barbell. Of course, the risk to our TIPS/nominal barbell is an increase in the funds rate, causing a flattening in a selloff. Although the long duration nominal in the barbell would outperform the shorter duration bullet, real yields would also increase. In this scenario, the TIPS/nominal barbell would then be net long the Treasury Index in a selloff, hurting its overall performance. This was the scenario TIPS faced when they were first introduced in early 1997; from mid-February to mid-April, the curve flattened in a selloff due to Fed tightening. Although inflation was declining, the real yield beta was quite high (0.70). In short, this period was the worst of all possible worlds for TIPS. However, the negative performance for the TIPS/nominal barbell was just slightly worse than that for the bullet in this bear market (−2.433% versus −2.133% as shown in Exhibit 21).

Historical Returns

Exhibit 20 summarizes the initial (1/29/97) construction for the three portfolios. All three portfolios are dollar and duration neutral; we assign a zero duration for TIPS. Our benchmark is the Merrill Lynch Government Master Index (all coupons greater than one year). In order to eliminate the effects of coupon cash flows, we only use C-strips for the nominal portion of the portfolio. While this may be both a simplistic and extreme approach, our portfolio clearly shows the curve effects and seems to provide, from an empirical view, reasonable hedge ratios. However, investors may want to assign a 1-3 year duration for TIPS, lowering the risk of being net long their index in a selloff.

Exhibit 21 compares the price returns (annualized BEY) for the TIPS/nominal barbell, a 5-year bullet, a cash/nominal barbell, and the Master Treasury Index in 1997. We show the historical returns for three distinct periods: (1) from the first TIPS auction on 1/29/97 to year-end 12/31/97; (2) from 1/29 to 4/15, a period when the Fed tightened, the curve flattened in a selloff, and the TIPS yield increased by about 18 bp; and, (3) from 4/15 to 12/31, a period when the nominal curve flattened in a rally due to a lowering of inflation but the TIPS real yield increased by 9 bp. As mentioned earlier, the TIPS/nominal barbell slightly underperformed the bullet in the selloff from 1/29/97 to 4/15/97 (−2.43% versus −2.13%). However, the TIPS/nominal barbell outperformed the bullet from 1/29/97 to 12/31/97 (10.48% versus 9.70%). The outperformance was even greater from 4/15 to 12/31/97 (14.41% versus 13.28%). Since the 3.32% annualized return of TIPS was lower than that for cash (5.50%) during 1997, the TIPS/nominal barbell underperformed the cash/nominal barbell in all scenarios; however, we believe that the risk for the TIPS/nominal portfolio should be lower than that for the cash/nominal barbell. While the TIPS/nominal barbell slightly underperformed the Treasury index in 1997 (10.48% versus 10.98%), it basically matched the index from 4/15 to 12/31 (14.41% versus 14.43%). However, it should be noted that the performance of the Treasury index was enhanced due to its 0.5 year extension in weighted average life.

Even though TIPS were the worst performing U.S. fixed income asset class for 1997, this did not preclude a portfolio which contained them from outperforming the bullet or matching the Government index. In short, even a poor performing asset can add value to a portfolio if the security allows an increased exposure to curve risk.

Exhibit 20: Portfolio Construction

Instruments	Bullet	Tips & Nominal Barbell	Cash & Nominal Barbell
		Portfolios	
		Market Value (mm)	
Cash			54.43
Bullet Portfolio: 05/15/2002	71.61		
TIPS: 3.375% 01/15/2007		54.43	
Long Duration Strip: 5/15/2017		17.19	17.19
Total:	71.61	71.61	71.62
		Face (mm)	
Cash			54.43
Bullet Portfolio: 05/15/2002	100		
TIPS: 3.375% 01/15/2007		54.6	
Long Duration Strip: 5/15/2017		72.2	72.2
		$ Risk / Modified Duration	
Cash			0
Bullet Portfolio: 05/15/2002	$36,720		
TIPS: 3.375% 01/15/2007		"0"	
Long Duration Strip: 5/15/2017		$33,659	$33,659
Portfolio Modified Duration	5.12 Yr	4.7 Yr	4.7 Yr

We use the S 5/02 as the bullet security; its duration equaled 5.13 years, 0.5 years greater than that for the Treasury master index (4.62 years) on 1/29/97. The S 5/17 is the long duration bond in our TIPS/nominal barbell; the modified duration for both barbell portfolios equaled 4.7 years. In order to account for differential duration drift, the initial modified duration of the bullet is 0.5 years greater than that for the Treasury index while that for the two barbell portfolios is just 0.08 years greater. That is, the average modified duration for these three portfolios should be similar to that for the index during all of 1997; we estimate that the drift for the bullet portfolio should be 0.9 years while that for the barbell should only be 0.17 years. Implicitly, we assume that the duration for the Treasury index should remain the same. For the sake of simplicity, we do not dynamically adjust the durations for our bullet or barbell portfolio to match the Treasury index and we assume that the duration for the index should remain static. On 12/31/97, the duration for the bullet declined to 4.24 years while that for the two barbells increased to about 5.32 years, primarily due to the rally and high convexity of the S 5/17. The duration of the index increased to 5.1 years, primarily due to the extension in the average debt maturity (8.1 to 8.6 years).

Exhibit 21: Total Return Analysis (Annualized BEY)

	Yield			Annual Return		
	01/29	04/15	12/31	01/29–12/31	01/29–04/15	04/15–12/31
Cash				5.503	5.364	5.544
TIPS:						
3.375% 01/15/2007	3.449%	3.633%	3.719%	3.317	−1.360	4.705
Long Duration Strip:						
05/15/2017	7.200%	7.340%	6.095%	31.914	−5.810	44.266
Bullet Portfolio:						
05/15/2002	6.410%	6.770%	5.730%	9.695	−2.133	13.284
Portfolio:						
TIPS & Nominal Barbell				10.477	−2.433	14.407
Portfolio:						
Cash & Nominal Barbell				12.093	2.650	14.935
Treasury Master Index						
(GOQO)	6.35%	6.71%	5.79%	10.98	−0.04	14.43

Exhibit 22: TIPS/Nominal Barbell versus Bullet

1	2	3	4	5	6	7	8	9	10
					Price Performance		TIPS / S 5/17 Barbell vs S 5-02 Bullet		
Growth/ Inflation Environment	Fed Policy	Nominal Curve	TIPS Beta	TIPS Income	TIPS	S 5/17 vs S 5/02	Price Return	Income	Net
High Growth Dis-Inflation	Hold/Tightening Bias	Flatten in Rally	Low	Low	-	++	+	-	Even to +
Low Growth Dis-Inflation	Ease	Steepen in Rally	High	Low	++	-	+	-	Even to +
High Growth Increasing Inflation	Tighten	Flatten in Selloff	High	High	--	+	-	+	Even
Low Growth Increasing Inflation	Hold/Easing Bias	Steepen	Medium	High	++	-	+	+	++
High Growth Stable Inflation	Tightening Bias	Flattening	High	Even	-	+	Even	Even	Even
Low Growth Stable Inflation	Ease	Steepen/ Rally	High	Even	++	-	+	Even	+
Stable Growth Stable Inflation	Hold	Stable/ Parallel	Medium	Even	Even	Even	Even	Even	Even

Based upon this limited empirical performance, we theorize in Exhibit 22 how the TIPS/nominal barbell should perform in different economic environments. The first column — "Growth/Inflation Environment" — lists the seven major types of growth/inflation environments. By "Stable Inflation," we assume that inflation is either at or close to the Fed's target of 1% to 2%. For simplicity, we ignore deflationary environments. The second column — "Fed Policy" — summarizes the monetary policy that the Fed would conduct when faced with these economic environments. We base the Fed's anticipated policy actions on the aforementioned Taylor rule, favoring the GDP gap as the primary determinant for the funds rate. However, we recognize that some of these policy actions may be subject to debate since there is no clear correlation between real rates and inflation. For example, it may be unclear what the Fed would do in a low growth/ increasing inflation environment. However, the Fed started to ease in mid-1989 due to low growth even though inflation was actually increasing, peaking in November 1991.

The third column — "Nominal Curve" — predicts the dynamics of the nominal curve, given the Fed policy in the second column. The fourth column — "TIPS Beta" — predicts the real yield beta relative to 10-year nominal yields based on the conditional correlation between TIPS and nominal due to the curve. The fifth column — "TIPS Income" — compares the TIPS income due to the inflation over a 1-year holding period relative to that of a 1-year Treasury bill. Given these relationships, we then compare the anticipated "Price Performance" of the "zero duration" TIPS relative to cash in the sixth column. The seventh column compares the relative price performance of the S 5/17 (barbell) versus that for the S 5/02 (bullet); the net risk is the same for both of these Strips portfolios.

Finally, we then compare the "Net Return" (tenth column) of the TIPS/ nominal barbell against that of the bullet, taking into account both "Price Return" (eighth column) and "Income" (ninth column). Obviously, this can be a complex relationship due to three interrelated factors. First is the changing duration of the TIPS due to the curve. As mentioned earlier, if the 2/10 curve beta greater than 1, then both the TIPS correlation and beta increases, making the TIPS/nominal barbell long the benchmark. While advantageous in a bull market, this would penalize the performance in a bear market. Offsetting this is the relative performance of the long maturity barbell (S 5/17) versus the short maturity bullet (S 5/02 — equal risk) in a flattening or steepening curve. Note how the price performance for the TIPS is always opposite the relative price performance of the S 5/17 versus the S 5/02. This is what makes the TIPS a good hedge or a valuable addition to a barbell. However, it is not always clear which of these two factors should predominate: that is, does positive (negative) price action of TIPS offset the relative negative (positive) price performance of the long maturity barbell versus the short maturity bullet. The relative performance will depend upon the duration assigned to TIPS. Our empirical analysis for 1997 shows that zero duration appears reasonable. Finally, we must then factor inflation income in the TIPS return; again the holding period then becomes important in realizing the total inflation income that accrues to TIPS. For Exhibit 22, we assume a 1-year holding period.

The key point we wish to make is that TIPS can be a valuable addition to a portfolio, depending upon the investor's market view. Given our theoretical relative outperformance of the TIPS/nominal barbell relative to the nominal bullet in most scenarios, investors who favor a bullet portfolio should seriously consider using a TIPS/nominal barbell instead. Conversely, investors who prefer a cash/ long duration nominal barbell may wish to use a TIPS/long duration nominal barbell to lower their overall risk exposure to the curve. Obviously, there are no clear answers to constructing the portfolio with the best risk/reward profile; that depends upon an investor's view of the market, the shape of the curve, and the richness/cheapness of TIPS versus nominals. However, we do believe that TIPS can and should be an integral part of most investors fixed income portfolios due to their favorable risk/reward profile. TIPS may be especially valuable if the investor believes that real yields are close to their peak (3.75%), markedly reducing the risk of negative price performance.

Chapter 10

Understanding the CPI

William Kan
Senior Economist and Vice President
Merrill Lynch

INTRODUCTION

The Consumer Price Index (CPI) is the price index for retail consumer goods and services and is one of the most closely monitored economic indicators. Among the many different price indices available, the CPI is the most common benchmark measure used to gauge inflation and the cost-of-living. The CPI plays many important roles with direct implications on the formulation of monetary policy. The CPI is often used to calculate cost-of-living adjustments in labor contracts, and has a large influence on federal government tax receipts and outlays, such as Social Security benefits. Since the first auction of the Treasury Inflation Protection Securities (TIPS) in 1997, the CPI has been the price index used to determine the inflation accruals of TIPS and the price index that is most commonly used for the other inflation-linked securities in the United States.

Despite its many uses, the CPI is not perfect, and appreciation for its problems and nuances has become ever more important. At the core of its problems is the current consensus view that the CPI overstates inflation. The problems include inadequate accounting for shifts in consumer behavior and changes in product quality. The need for adjustments to improve the precision of the CPI is not new. The Bureau of Labor Statistics (BLS), the government entity that calculates the CPI, has been conducting an on-going program to improve its data and calculations for the last several decades. Nevertheless, estimates of the bias suggest that the CPI currently overstates inflation from several tenths of a percent to as high as 1.6% per year. Recent and upcoming adjustments to the CPI made with the BLS's on-going program are estimated to remove 0.7% of the upward bias. But some bias may still remain even after the adjustments.

The overstatement implies that adjustments for inflation or the cost-of-living using the CPI have been excessive. Without the overstatement, Social Security benefits would have grown more slowly, the federal budget surplus (deficit) should have been larger (smaller), and corporate profits may have been greater because of less wage growth. The overstatement also implies that TIPS investors

Copyright © 1998 Merrill Lynch, Pierce, Fenner & Smith Incorporated
The author thanks Stephen Antczak, Michele Chesnicka, and Martin Mauro for their valuable comments.

have been "over compensated" for inflation (to the degree it has not been factored into the market) since the inception of the program. Because of the CPI's far reaching effects, there is much momentum to improve[1] the data collection and calculations used to produce the CPI.

The focus of this chapter is on understanding the overall CPI index. We mention some technical aspects of the CPI, but do not go into great detail because it is beyond the scope of this chapter. Readers should refer to the papers that are footnoted for a discussion of the technical aspects. In this chapter, we highlight the current issues regarding the CPI, problems with the CPI as a measure of inflation, the BLS's on-going program to improve the CPI, and the linkage between CPI and TIPS.

BACKGROUND[2]

What is the CPI?

The CPI is a measure of prices paid by consumers for a fixed basket of goods and services. The BLS of the Department of Labor calculates the CPI based on monthly surveys of retail prices. The field representatives of the BLS visit or call retail stores, service establishments, etc. to collect prices for about 80,000 items each month. The CPI data are reported monthly, two to three weeks after the end of the month. The BLS estimates CPI figures for over 200 categories such as eggs, new cars, and cable TV services and arranges them into many different groups and aggregates. CPI indices are also available for different geographical areas across the country. The press and the financial markets typically focus on two figures in particular. They are CPI-U, the CPI for all urban consumers, and core CPI-U, the measure for CPI-U, excluding the food and energy components, which can be very volatile. We will generalize from this point and simply use CPI to refer to CPI-U over the balance of this chapter.

By surveying prices paid on expenditures by urban consumers, the CPI captures only 87% of the total U.S. population according to the BLS. Those covered include residents in urban and metropolitan areas. The portion of population not covered are those living in rural areas outside a metropolitan area, farms, prisons, mental institutions, and members of the Armed Forces.

For simplicity, we can say that the BLS staff asks two general questions to construct the CPI. First, it asks how prices have changed for a particular item. For example, it compares the prices paid for a red apple in January and February

---

[1] There were proposals in Congress to legislate a downward adjustment to the CPI to offset the upward bias during the debates on balancing the federal budget in 1996/1997. The proposals were not enacted.

[2] For more information see: (1) Dennis Fixler, "The Consumer Price Index: Underlying Concepts and Caveats," *Monthly Labor Review* (December 1993), pp. 3-12; (2) Bureau of Labor Statistics web site on the CPI (http://stats.bls.gov/cpihome.htm); and (3) Bureau of Labor Statistics, *BLS Handbook of Methods* (April 1988), pp. 154-215.

as inputs to estimate the CPI and to determine the inflation in red apples during February. Second, it looks at consumer expenditures for red apples versus overall expenditures to determine the relative importance of red apples. The relative importance helps the BLS to build a general index for all of the items in the basket of goods and services used to calculate the CPI.

The basket and the weights of the items in the basket are fixed over long periods of time. The basket is usually fixed for about 10 years, but the BLS plans to update it more frequently going forward. Because the CPI is based on a fixed basket of items purchased, it is formally known as a Laspeyrian[3] index. A Laspeyrian index generally asks "How much more must I spend in my current situation (period 2) to purchase the same quantities that I purchased initially (period 1)?"[4,5] As the question implies, the current CPI does not allow for consumers substituting between items in response to relative price changes in what they buy. However, consumers, indeed, are sensitive to price changes and do often adjust their buying patterns accordingly. This lack of flexibility is one reason why the CPI overstates inflation.

Brief History of the CPI

The CPI program was started during World War I. Prices were rising sharply and there was a need to construct an index to calculate cost of living adjustments in wages. The BLS started by reviewing what and how much consumers spent for different goods and services between 1917-1919 to construct the first basket. The CPI was published on a regular basis starting in 1921, with the history extending back to 1913. Since that time, there have been numerous updates to the basket of

---

[3] Brent Moulton, "Basic Components of the CPI: Estimation of Price Changes," *Monthly Labor Review* (December 1993) pgs. 13-24.

[4] Michael Boskin et al. "Toward a More Accurate Measure of the Cost of Living," final report submitted to the Senate Finance Committee, December 4, 1996.

[5] The Laspeyrian formula used to calculate the CPI is as follows:

Laspeyres-Type Estimate of a Price Change:

$$\text{Relative Price Change} = R^L_{i,\,t-1} = \frac{\sum_i W_{i,b} \times P_{i,t}/P_{i,b}}{\sum_i W_{i,b} \times P_{i,t-1}/P_{i,b}}$$

where

$W_{i,b}$ = the weight of the base period total expenditures share for item i
$P_{i,t}$ = price of item i at time t
$P_{i,b}$ = price of item i at the base period

Implicitly, the Laspeyrian index holds constant the quantity of an item.

Weighted Geometric Mean Estimate:

$$\text{Relative Price Change} = R^G_{t,\,t-1} = \prod_i (P_{i,t}/P_{i,t-1})^{S_{i,b}}$$

where, $S_{i,b} = W_{i,b} / \sum W_{i,b}$, the base-period expenditure share for item i. (Note that $P_i A_i = A_1 \times A_2 \times ... \times A_i$)
Implicitly, the geometric mean estimate holds constant the expenditure share (e.g., dollars spent) of an item constant.

goods and services to reflect changes in what consumers purchased and updates to the relative importance of the items. Although numerous, the updates are more akin to making adjustments based on snapshots taken at long intervals as opposed to using a movie camera recording changes as they occur.

Alternative Price Indices

There are many other measures of aggregate prices for the economy other than the CPI. Some measure prices in different parts of the economy, employ different measurement techniques or are released in weekly, monthly or quarterly intervals.

Some of the other price indices that are most closely watched by the financial markets and monetary policy makers are the producer price index (PPI), the GDP deflator, unit labor costs (ULC), and the employment cost index (ECI). The PPI is a monthly figure that measures producer prices at different stages of production. The GDP deflator is a quarterly index for prices across the entire economy, from commodities to wholesale to retail items, and purchases by the government, businesses, and consumers. The ULC is estimated quarterly to gauge the costs of production in businesses and are related to the national productivity figures. The ECI is a quarterly aggregate for wages and employee benefits and is the most comprehensive estimate for the cost of labor in the economy. Exhibit 1 shows the year-over-year change in the three indices. There are also aggregate commodity price indices such as the CRB and the JOC indexes that summarize agricultural, industrial metal, and precious metal prices and are updated daily.

Exhibit 1: Alternative Price Indices

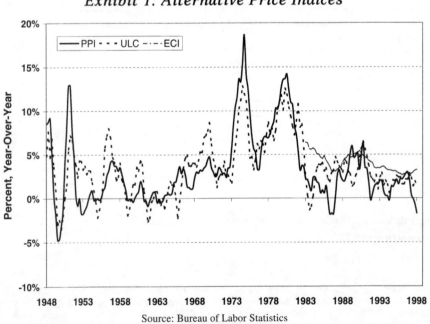

Source: Bureau of Labor Statistics

Exhibit 2: CPI Inflation

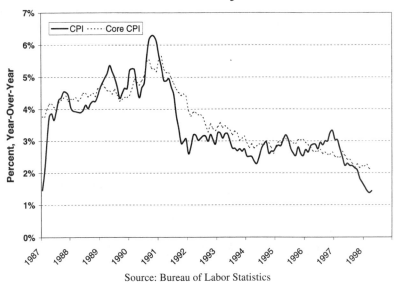

Source: Bureau of Labor Statistics

Aside from the ones described, there are many other price indices that we have not mentioned. They are meaningful in their particular application, but most do not reflect general prices to the consumer. Inflation in one stage of the economy, such as manufacturing as suggested by the NAPM price index, may not flow through to the end buyer because it was offset by declining prices in other stage of production. Another reason may be competition and the lack of pricing power, the inability of businesses to pass on higher prices. The BLS also recognizes that the quality of the new items purchased may vary over time and adjustments are needed to prevent "comparing apples with oranges," as products evolve.[6] These are key reasons why the CPI remains the most closely watched price index. It reflects prices to the consumer, the ultimate buyer.

The CPI Today[7]

CPI inflation as shown in Exhibit 2 has been trending down since its recent peak in the second half of 1990. A variety of factors have contributed to the decline. Fundamental forces such as greater productivity, deregulation, the trend towards free trade, increased global competition, slower money growth, and lower com-

---

[6] Mary Kokoski, "Quality Adjustment of Price Indexes," *Monthly Labor Review* (December 1993) pp. 34-46.

[7] For further discussion, see (1) Brent Moulton, "Bias in the Consumer Price Index: What is the Evidence," BLS working paper 294 (October 1996); (2) John Greenlees and Charles Mason, "Overview of the 1998 Revision of the Consumer Price Index," *Monthly Labor Review* (December 1996), pp. 3-9; and, (3) John Greenlees, Keynote address to the FRBSF and BLS seminar *Consumer Price Index (CPI) — The Ongoing Campaign of Improvement* (October 10, 1997).

modity prices largely account for the decline.[8] The recent mixture of disinflation and rapid economic growth has lead some to believe that the economy is operating within a new paradigm. Given the drop in inflation and questions about the inflation dynamics within the economy, there is much interest in the precision of the CPI as a measure of prices in the economy. However, the CPI is believed to have an upward bias that overstates inflation by several tenths to 1.6% a year. With year-over-year CPI inflation currently near 1.4% (for April 1998), a sizeable portion of measured CPI inflation may be attributed to measurement problems.

Interest in removing the upward bias in the CPI peaked in 1996 during the heat of the debates in Congress on ways to balance the federal budget. A reduction in CPI inflation would greatly reduce government outlays. Many items such as Social Security and civil service retirement benefits are indexed to the CPI. The Congressional Budget Office (CBO) estimated that a 1% downward adjustment to the CPI, if implemented, would reduce the budget deficit by $141 billion from 1998 to 2007 as shown in Exhibit 3. As a result, there were rumblings in Congress about legislating a reduction in the CPI to remove the upward bias. Although legislation to balance the budget was eventually passed without mandates for a change to the CPI, the debates added momentum to the BLS's on-going program to improve the CPI.

Problems with the CPI — The Boskin Commission Report[9]

Publicity regarding problems with the CPI heightened when the Congressionally appointed Advisory Commission to Study the Consumer Price Index, chaired by Michael Boskin, released its report on December 1996. The Boskin Commission found that the CPI overstates inflation by 1.1%. It also offered 13 recommendations to improve the quality of the data, remove the upward bias, and create new indices[10] that would represent better the cost-of-living.

Exhibit 3: Change in Budget Deficit if CPI Inflation was Reduced 1% ($ billion)

	1998	1999	2000	2001	2002	2003	2004	2005	2006	2007
Change in Revenues	−1.9	−6.0	−10.5	−13.9	−18.9	−24.1	−28.0	−33.0	−38.5	−44.2
Change in Outlays	−3.7	−9.2	−15.2	−21.1	−27.6	−34.3	−41.2	−48.9	−56.3	−63.9
Debt Service	−0.2	−0.8	−2.0	−3.8	−6.3	−9.7	−13.8	−18.9	−24.9	−32.0
Change in Deficit	−5.8	−16.0	−27.7	−38.8	−52.8	−68.1	−83.0	−100.8	−119.7	−140.1

Source: Congressional Budget Office

[8] The BLS has made improvements to the CPI over time, which we discuss later, that have also helped reduce CPI inflation over the last several years.

[9] Michael Boskin, "Toward a More Accurate Measure of the Cost of Living," final report submitted to the Senate Finance Committee (December 4, 1996). Readers interested in the BLS's response to the Boskin Commission's recommendations should refer to the testimony of BLS Commissioner Katherine Abraham before the Subcommittee on Human Resources House Committee on Government Reform and Oversight on April 30, 1997. The testimony can be found on the BLS's web site at http://stats.bls.gov.

[10] The Boskin Commission recommended that the BLS move away from a Laspeyrian index, such as the CPI, to a superlative index that would be more consistent with a cost-of-living index.

Exhibit 4: Estimates of Upward Bias in CPI* by the Boskin Commission

Sources of Biases	Estimate
Upper level substitution (e.g., substituting chicken for beef)	0.15%
Lower level substitution (e.g., substituting green apples for red apples)	0.25%
New products/quality change	0.60%
New products (e.g., updating/incorporating new products into the sample basket)	0.10%
Total	1.10%
Range	0.80 to 1.60%

* The size of the upward bias should be smaller now. Revisions to the CPI by the BLS subsequent to the release of the estimates by the Boskin Commission that are planned or already implemented are estimated to have reduced the upward bias by 0.7% as shown in Exhibit 5.

Source: Boskin Commission Report on the CPI, December 1996

The potential types of bias were categorized in five ways — substitution, outlet substitution, quality change, new product, and formula bias. Exhibit 4 lists the Boskin Commission's estimates of the upward bias. Quality change was determined to be the source of 0.6% of the total 1.1% upward bias. The Boskin Commission categorized the inability of the CPI to capture substitution into upper and lower level substitution. With the weights fixed across items in the basket, the current CPI implicitly assumes that consumers do not adjust their purchases when prices change. *Upper level substitution* refers to substituting across items, such as chicken for beef, when the price of beef increases relative to the price of chicken. *Lower level substitution* refers to substituting within items such as buying green apples instead of red apples when the price of red apples increase relative to the price of green apples.

The Boskin Commission found new products that entered the market and changes in quality as other sources of the upward bias. In other words, it found that the basket of goods and services in the CPI was not updated with sufficient frequency. As such, the prices of new items, which often decline after their introduction, may not be included in the basket. One example is cellular phones. For existing product categories, the Commission found that the BLS is not adequately adjusting for quality improvements, which may be another source of the bias. More adjustments are necessary to ensure that the CPI is comparing "apples with apples."

The most prominent recommendations were for the BLS to establish two new indexes and to adopt a new method of calculating the CPI. The Commission suggested that the BLS create a new monthly CPI to replace the current one. The reference market basket of the new index would be updated more frequently. The market basket for the current CPI is updated only about once every decade, with the most recent one released for the January 1998 CPI report. The second index suggested would be an annual cost-of-living index[11] (COLI) that would account

[11] The Boskin Commission highlighted the need for a price index that reflects a COLI more closely. A COLI would reflect the cost to maintain a standard of living and would encompass readily changes in consumer behavior. The BLS has stated that the CPI is not a COLI, but is estimated within a cost-of-living framework.

for changes in consumer spending patterns. The new method to calculate the CPI would allow for consumers responding to price changes by adjusting what they buy, i.e., substitution.

Several Congressional hearings on the CPI have been held since the release of the Boskin Commission report. There is broad consensus that improvements to the CPI are needed. Although a legislated change remains a possibility, improvements to the CPI will probably be left solely in the hands of the BLS.

The On-Going Program to Improve the CPI[12]

The BLS substantially updated the CPI with its benchmark revision that it released with the January 1998 report. The revision included a new geographic sample, a revised basket of goods and services purchased by consumers, a revised structure of items purchased, and updated weights for the items that comprise the CPI. The BLS estimated that the revision will lower CPI inflation 0.1% to 0.2%. Since World War II, such large revisions have been made in 1953, 1964, 1978, and 1987.

Explanation of Changes in the 1998 Benchmark Revision

The revision should remove some of the upward bias believed to be inherent in the current CPI. Exhibit 5 shows that recent and upcoming changes should remove 0.7% of the upward bias in CPI inflation. In particular, the revision addresses some of the bias stemming from new products and product substitution by updating the market basket. The new basket is based on consumer expenditures for goods and services between 1993-1995, which makes it more representative of current consumer expenditures. Previously, the basket was based on expenditures during 1982-1984. The revision incorporates new products, updates the weights of the items, assigns new product categories, and improves the quality adjustments. The update, however, is not a panacea. The new basket was already five years old when it first came into use for the January 1998 CPI report.

New Products and Weights[13]

The revision updated the sample basket to include new products and the relative importance of items purchased to reflect more current expenditure patterns. It also uses the 1990 census to update the geographical distribution of what and how items are purchased across the country. Some items that seem commonplace today were never included and just entered the CPI market basket with the revision. Cellular phone service, for example, was added to the basket with this revision. Many new products have been introduced or have become more important as a result of technological advances since the 1982-1984 basket was determined.

---

[12] For further reading, see (1) Greenlees and Mason, "Overview of the 1998 Revision of the Consumer Price Index;" (2) William Kan, "Upcoming Revision to the CPI," *Merrill Lynch Fixed Income Research Bulletin* (January 27, 1998); and, (3) Bureau of Labor Statistics, "Measurement Issues in the Consumer Price Index," letter to Jim Saxton, Chairman of the Joint Economic Committee (January 28, 1997).

[13] Greenlees and Mason, "Overview of the 1998 Revision of the Consumer Price Index."

Computers and software, for example, were assigned higher weights while items such as phonograph records were assigned lower weights.

New Definitions for Item Categories[14]

Some of the details of the CPI will not be directly comparable with its past values after the revision. Exhibit 6 shows that the revision increased the number of major categories from seven to eight and redefined four of the current categories. The three that were not changed are food and beverages, transportation, and medical care. Among the changes, entertainment was renamed as recreation, and it now includes items such as cable TV services, which were previously in housing. An education and communication category was created by shifting education, which was previously in other goods and services, and telephones and communications, which were also previously in housing.

Better Quality Adjustments for PCs

The BLS introduced new procedures to improve the adjustment for quality changes of some products. PC prices are now adjusted for quality using hedonic regression models.[15] In other words, the BLS estimates the implicit prices for key components and features to assess better how improvements in different components affect PC prices. This procedure has been used in the PPI calculation for PCs and is similar to what the BLS has been doing for the apparel category in the CPI for the last several years.

Exhibit 5: Effects of Recent & Forthcoming Changes to CPI Inflation

Change in Method	Year Introduced	Effect on CPI Percent Change
Pre-1998		-0.28
Generic prescription drugs	1995	-0.01
Food at home seasoning	1995	-0.04
Owner's equivalent rent formula	1995	-0.10
Rent composite estimator	1995	+0.03
General seasoning	1996	-0.10
Hospital services index	1997	-0.06
1998 and after		-0.41
Personal computer hedonics	1998	-0.06
Updated market basket	1998	-0.15
Geometric means	1999	-0.15
Rotation by item	1999	-0.05
Total		-0.69

Source: *1998 Economic Report of the President*

[14] Walter Lane, "Changing the Item Structure of the Consumer Price Index," *Monthly Labor Review* (December 1996), pp. 18-25.

[15] Bureau of Labor Statistics web site on the CPI. http://stats.bls.gov/cpihome.htm

Exhibit 6: Comparison Between Item Structure and Relative Importance

1998 Item Structure (NEW)	Weight (%)	1987-1997 Item Structure (OLD)	Weight (%)
1. Food & Beverages	16.3	1. Food & Beverages	17.5
2. Transportation	17.6	2. Transportation	16.2
— New Cars	5.1	— New Cars	3.8
3. Medical Care	5.6	3. Medical Care	7.4
4. Housing	39.6	4. Housing	41.5
— Shelter	29.8	— Shelter	28.6
— Fuels & Utilities	4.9	— Fuels & Utilities	7.0
		* Telephone Services	3.1
		* Information Processing	
		Equipment (include. PCs, etc)	0.1
5. Apparel	4.9	5. Apparel & Upkeep	5.3
6. Recreation	6.1	6. Entertainment	4.3
7. Education &	5.5	7. Other Goods & Services	7.4
Communication			
— Telephone Services	2.7		
— PCs & related items	0.4		
8. Other Goods & Services	4.3		

Source: Bureau of Labor Statistics

Previous Changes[16]

In addition to the benchmark revisions, the BLS also makes adjustments in periods between benchmark revisions. Many of the changes are to improve sampling, data collection, adjustments for quality, accounting for seasonality and other issues. Over time, the BLS has devised different approaches to construct the CPI for different items that it believes offers a better reflection of their prices. Exhibit 7 lists changes over the last 10 years. Examples of "special calculations" can be found in the measurement of items such as housing, generic drugs, and air fares. In housing, the BLS uses a concept of owner's equivalent rent to gauge how housing prices fluctuate as opposed to basing housing prices strictly on the price to buy a home, for example. In generic drugs, the BLS implemented in 1995 procedures for how generic drugs are priced after the brand name equivalent loses its patent. With air fares, the BLS adopted in 1991 substitution rules to account for the pricing of discount air fares.

The CPI of Tomorrow

There will be more improvements to the CPI in the years ahead as shown in Exhibit 8. The planned changes that the BLS have presented suggest that the development of the CPI will continue within the framework of a COLI. However, changing consumer buying patterns, product enhancements, and new patents make a "true" COLI a goal that the BLS will always be chasing.

---

[16] Greenlees and Mason, "Overview of the 1998 Revision of the Consumer Price Index."

Exhibit 7: Improvements to the CPI since the 1987 Benchmark Revision

Change	Year Implemented	Description
Aging bias correction	1988	Rental values adjusted for aging of the housing stock.
Imputation procedures for new cars and trucks	1989	Price changes for non-comparable new models are imputed using only the constant-quality price changes for comparable model changeovers.
Quality adjustment of apparel prices	1991	Regression models used to adjust prices for changes in quality when new clothing lines are introduced, and eliminate bias due to linking product substitutions into the CPI.
Discount air fares	1991	Substitution rules modified to expand pricing of discount air fares.
Sample augmentation	1992	Increase in the number of outlets from which prices are collected to replace sample lost through sample attrition.
Hotels and motels	1992	Samples for hotels and motels quadrupled to reduce variances related to seasonal pricing.
Seasonal adjustment	1994	Procedures for seasonal adjustment revised to eliminate residual seasonality effects.
Quality adjustment for gasoline	1994	Treat "reformulated" gasoline as a quality change and adjust the price to reflect quality difference. Impact of the change estimated.
Generic drugs	1995	Introduced new procedures that allow generic drugs to be priced when a brand drug loses its patent.
Food-at-home period prices	1995	Introduced seasoning procedures to eliminate upward bias in setting of base period prices of newly initiated items.
Rental equivalence	1995	Modified imputation of homeowner's implicit rent to eliminate the upward drift property of the current estimator.
Composite estimator used in housing	1995	Replaced current composite estimator with a 6-month chain estimator. Under-reporting of 1-month rent changes had resulted in missing price change in residential rent and homeowners' equivalent rent. Old estimator also produced higher variances.
Commodities and services base period prices	1996	Extended food-at-home seasoning procedures to remainder of commodities and services series. Base period prices left unchanged in most non-comparable substitutions.

Source: Extracted from John Greenlees and Charles Mason, "Overview of the 1998 Revision of the Consumer Price Index," *Monthly Labor Review* (December 1996), p. 5.

Exhibit 8: Summary of CPI Improvement Plans

Improvement	Year	Consumer Substitution	Quality/ New Goods	Efficiency/ Accuracy
Geometric Means (Experimental CPI)	1999		X	
New Housing Sample/Estimator	1999			X
Targeted New Goods Samples	1999	X	X	
Data Collection for Hedonic Regressions	1999		X	
Rotation by Item	1999		X	X
Consumer Expenditure Survey Expansion	2000			X
Accelerated Update System	2001	X	X	X
Superlative Index	2002	X		

Source: John Greenlees, BLS. Keynote Address to FRBSF & BLS Seminar on Consumer Price Index (CPI) — The Ongoing Campaign of Improvement

The BLS will make more strides toward a COLI in 1999 when it adopts elements of its experimental CPI index. Between that and enhancing its procedure to rotate the items in the CPI basket, CPI inflation should be lower by 0.2% to 0.3% as some of the upward bias from consumer substitution and new goods entering the market are removed. The BLS will also make other improvements, but many of the improvements that the BLS often makes do not have material effects on the CPI. Looking ahead, the marginal effects of the changes to remove the upward bias will decline as the improvements are made on a more frequent basis.

Experimental CPI/Geometric Means[17]

Adopting elements currently used in the experimental CPI is expected to have a large impact on reducing the upward bias. The difference between the experimental and the official CPI is that the experimental figures use a "geometric mean" procedure[18] to summarize price changes. The procedure assumes that consumers do indeed make substitutions in response to price changes and that they substitute one-for-one. However, it only allows for "lower level substitution," e.g., substituting green apples for red apples when the price of red apples increases relative to the price of green apples. The calculation does not allow for "upper level substitution," e.g., substituting chicken for beef when the price of beef increases relative to the price of chicken. According to the estimates by the Boskin Commission listed in Exhibit 4, lower level substitution accounts for 0.25% of the upward bias.

The BLS has been reviewing the validity of applying the geometric procedure across the different items in the CPI basket. We believe that it will be used in areas where the BLS deems appropriate such as our example of red and green apples. The BLS noted[19] that geometric means will be used in item categories that account for 61% of consumer spending represented in the CPI. It will not be applied to some items within the shelter service category, utilities, government charges, and medical care. The reasons why geometric means will not be applied vary across the items. Consumers cannot respond quickly to relative price changes in housing, hence, the adoption of geometric means will not affect the measurement of residential rent, owner's equivalent rent, and housing at school. In utilities, for example, it is often difficult for consumers to switch providers without moving, which would make geometric means inappropriate. For medical care, the BLS found it hard to assume that consumers are responsive to relative price changes when directly purchasing health care. The use of geometric means will be officially adopted for the January 1999 CPI report that will be released in February 1999.

---

[17] For a further discussion, see BLS Briefing on the CPI, "Research Issues Related to the Geometric Mean Formula for Elementary Indexes," Attachment E (December 4, 1996), William Kan, "The Experimental CPI," *Merrill Lynch Fixed Income Research Comment* (April 7, 1997), or BLS press release on "Planned Change in the Consumer Price Index" (April 16, 1998).

[18] Refer to footnote 5 for the formula.

[19] BLS press conference on the experimental CPI, April 16, 1998.

CPI AND TIPS[20]

With the introduction of Treasury Inflation Protection Securities (TIPS), financial market participants have followed developments regarding the CPI with greater attention. The returns on TIPS are directly linked to the CPI. As such, investors have closely watched efforts to "reduce the upward bias" in the CPI and have been exploring nuances how the CPI is produced. In this section, we focus our attention on how changes to the CPI may affect TIPS investors and the seasonality in the CPI figures.

How Changes to the CPI Should Affect TIPS[21]

The cash flows of TIPS are directly tied to the official CPI values. Unlike the Treasury's nominal coupon securities, which have fixed cash flows, the cash flows from TIPS vary depending on how the CPI fluctuates over time. Hence, revisions made to reduce the upward bias in the CPI may affect returns.

Not all the effects of the revisions to the CPI are necessarily passed onto investors. In setting the terms of the TIPS program, the Treasury recognized the uncertainties about the CPI index that lie ahead. Even before the TIPS program was announced in May 1996, the upward bias in the CPI was already well publicized (and apparently priced into the market for them). The TIPS program increased attention to the Boskin Commission report, the benchmark revision to the CPI, and the Congressional debates to legislate a change to the CPI. We highlight below several of the index contingencies that the Treasury established to handle changes to the CPI index:[22]

1. If a previously reported CPI is revised, Treasury will continue to use the previously reported CPI in calculating the principal value and interest payments.
2. If the CPI is rebased to a different year, Treasury will continue to use the CPI based on the base reference period in effect when the security was first issued, as long as that CPI continues to be published.
3. If, while an inflation-indexed security is outstanding, the applicable CPI is: (1) discontinued, (2) in the judgment of the Secretary, fundamentally altered in a manner materially adverse to the interests of an investor in the security, or (3) in the judgment of the [Treasury] Secretary, altered by legislation or Executive Order in a manner materially adverse to the interests of an investor in the security, Treasury after consulting with the Bureau of Labor Statistics, or any successor agency, will substitute an appropriate alternative index. Treasury will then notify the public of the

---

[20] For further reading see William Kan, "Deflation, CPI Index Risk, and TIPS," *Merrill Lynch Fixed Income Weekly* (June 20, 1997).

[21] See also Thomas Sowanick, et al, "Understanding Treasury Inflation-Index Securities," *Merrill Lynch Global Fixed Income Research Report* (January 29, 1997).

[22] Department of Treasury, Uniform Offering Circular (31 CFR Part 356), December 31, 1996.

substitute index and how it will be applied. Determinations of the Secretary in this regard will be final.

The first two points are clear but the third is subject to interpretation. In general, the Treasury does not spell out what "fundamentally altered in a manner that is materially adverse to the interests of an investor" means. Its meaning has not been tested and is beyond the scope of this chapter. However, our working assumption is that the effects of the adjustments, such as those made in the general context of BLS's on-going program to improve the CPI, would be passed onto investors. In other words, the effects of the benchmark revision that were implemented starting with the January 1998 CPI figures and the implementation of elements of the experimental CPI scheduled for 1999 will directly affect investors. What we have assumed will not be passed onto investors are adjustments such as those that are the result of a legislated change by Congress. In the case of a legislated change, we expect the Treasury to absorb the difference between measured inflation and adjusted inflation, so that investors are not adversely impacted.

Seasonality[23]

One of the nuances that relates CPI and TIPS is that TIPS are indexed to the non-seasonally adjusted (NSA) values of the CPI, not to the seasonally adjusted (SA) values that are more commonly discussed. (Note that the SA figures may be subject to revision as a result of new seasonal factors, whereas the NSA figures are not revised.) Market participants that buy and sell TIPS at different times of the year may be greatly affected by the seasonality of CPI inflation. The seasonal effects over a 12-month period cancel out. However, over shorter periods the inflation accrual[24] to TIPS investors can vary substantially.

The values of the NSA CPI follow a very distinct pattern over a 12-month period as shown in Exhibit 9. Items such as food, energy, heavy-and light-weight clothing follow seasonal patterns that affect the CPI. SA CPI inflation, for example, is about 0.21% greater than the NSA CPI inflation during December on a month-to-month basis. In other words, the inflation accrual in December is 0.21% less than what the "headline" SA CPI figure would suggest. The January figures suggest that the pattern reverses in January, when the SA CPI inflation is about 0.20% less than the NSA CPI inflation. Assuming that the monthly SA CPI inflation figures are flat for each of the 12 months in a year, an investor with a 2-month holding period would receive more inflation accrual during January and February (positive accrual), when NSA inflation would be positive, than in November and December (negative accrual), when NSA inflation would be negative.

---

[23] Bureau of Labor Statistics, *BLS Handbook of Methods* (April 1988), pp. 209-210. The BLS uses the Census Bureau's X-12-ARIMA seasonal adjustment software to estimate the seasonal adjustment factors.
[24] Gerald Lucas and Timothy Quek, "TIIS: Seasonally vs. Non-Seasonally Adjusted Inflation," *Merrill Lynch Fixed Income Weekly* (February 21, 1997).

Exhibit 9: Effects of Seasonal Adjustment, Average During 1993-1997

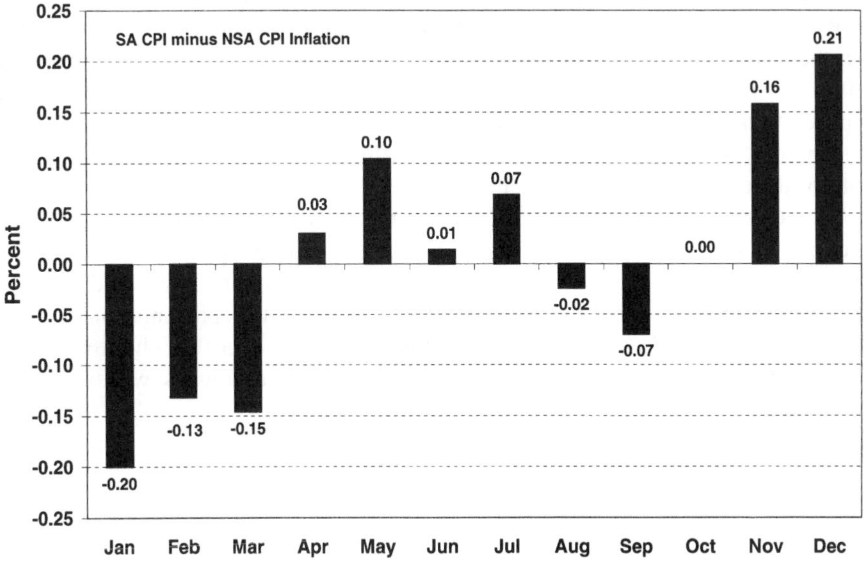

SA CPI minus NSA CPI Inflation

Source: Bureau of Labor Statistics and Merrill Lynch

CONCLUSION

Understanding the CPI requires an appreciation of the price trends within the items that comprise the CPI and the way that the CPI is calculated. This chapter has focused on the current problems in the CPI and the efforts of the BLS to remedy the problems and to improve the precision of the index. At present, the CPI is believed to overstate inflation because it does not adequately account for changes in consumer buying patterns, improvements in product quality, and new products entering the market. Although there is an on-going program to remove the upward bias and efforts to make the CPI more closely akin to a pure cost-of-living index, adjustments take time to implement and more changes are forthcoming. Some bias may still remain even after the adjustments.

Although this chapter has concentrated on the efforts to remove the upward bias in the CPI, some components within the CPI may also contain a downward bias, i.e., understate inflation. In some instances, one may believe that the deterioration of quality in some products have been ignored. Phone calls into customer service centers of companies, for example, are handled increasingly by a maze of computer options instead of the personalized attention of a human, which may be viewed as a drop in quality. Unfortunately, such a change in quality is difficult to incorporate into the CPI.

Another consideration is that CPI inflation is not universal for all consumers. Inflation to someone living in an urban area may be much different than to someone living in a rural area. What they consume and how they buy could vary substantially, as well as the relative importance of the different items that they buy. The age of the consumer will also play a large role in determining the inflation that they observe. Senior citizens, for example, are generally more exposed to medical care inflation than teenagers. As we noted at the beginning of this chapter, the BLS also publishes many different CPI indices to measure inflation for different products, geographical areas, and consumers.

Over time, the CPI as with any aggregate index will run the risk of mistracking what it is trying to measure. The sample of items purchased and procedures used to calculate the CPI need to be under constant review and updated periodically to ensure that the index provides an accurate representation of retail prices in the United States. The adjustments discussed in this chapter should improve the precision of the CPI, but more adjustments, as always, will be needed in the future as products and consumer behavior evolve.

Chapter 11

Understanding the Inflation Risk Premium

P. Brett Hammond
Manager, Corporate Projects
TIAA-CREF

Andrew C. Fairbanks
Senior Analyst
Prudential Securities

J. Benson Durham
Research Analyst
TIAA-CREF

INTRODUCTION

The inflation risk premium, a critical but mostly unexamined component of the value of ordinary bonds, is an issue raised in a very practical way, first by the introduction of and then by the need to value inflation-indexed bonds. For example, during the 1996-1997 introductory period, U.S. Treasury officials remarked repeatedly that among several advantages of an inflation-protected debt market, the most compelling is the opportunity for the U.S. government to enjoy long-term savings based on the existence of a positive *inflation risk premium* associated with ordinary bonds.[1] The idea is that investors are willing to pay for inflation protection, i.e., they will accept a lower real interest rate as compared to conventional debt.

[1] See, for example, the speech and accompanying handout by Lawrence Summers, Deputy Secretary of the Treasury, Investor Meeting, New York Federal Reserve Bank (New York, May 30, 1996) and the speech by Roger Anderson, Assistant Secretary for Financial Markets, Morgan Stanley Seminar on Inflation-Indexed Bonds, (New York, January 15, 1997).

The views expressed in this chapter are the authors' alone and do not necessarily reflect the position of TIAA-CREF. The authors wish to thank Mark Warshawsky, John Biggs, John Shoven, Olivia Mitchell, Andrew Lo, John Ameriks, Martin Leibowitz, and Eric Fisher for their helpful comments on earlier drafts of this paper.

The Treasury's stated motive for creating inflation-indexed government securities raises a fundamental question: Just how much will the government save by issuing inflation-protected bonds? Or, put another way: What are investors willing to pay to avoid inflation volatility?

However the question is posed, the answer will influence or even determine the future behavior of inflation bonds, because how investors evaluate inflation risk in practice will influence prices, yields, and returns. Without such knowledge, we can't be sure how the market will, over the long run, price inflation-protected securities, nor will the government be able to estimate the size of the hoped-for savings it expects from these new instruments. As an added benefit, through an analysis of the inflation risk premium, we can also gain a better understanding of how investors price ordinary or nominal bonds.

This chapter analyzes the concept and theory of the inflation risk premium and estimates its size. We estimate it to have averaged 41 basis points over the last several decades. This is generally consistent with other efforts to estimate the inflation risk premium.

But our presentation makes several key distinctions based on (1) a different, but realistic view of how market participants — investment professionals as well as nonprofessionals — actually evaluate and behave in response to inflation risk and (2) temporal versus inflation uncertainty effects. Both of these distinctions are key to understanding the role the inflation risk premium plays in pricing inflation-indexed and ordinary bonds. For example, governments and private firms might consider using shorter-maturity inflation-indexed debt to save term as well as inflation risk premiums, while pension funds and endowments might be interested in longer-maturity inflation-indexed debt to take advantage of term and inflation risk premiums.

THE INFLATION-RISK PREMIUM

The inflation-risk premium is one of many risk premiums that compensate market participants for uncertainty, in this case the possibility that bad things (i.e., low or negative returns) could happen. A far-from-exhaustive list of other sources of investment uncertainty would include market, reinvestment, and default risk. Of course, not every risk premium is germane to all assets. For example, compared to corporate coupon bonds, government zero-coupon bonds enable investors to eliminate default and reinvestment risk. But until the introduction of inflation bonds, no single security — public or corporate, coupon or zero — could eliminate the risk of inflation uncertainty.

To put it another way, in pricing a nominal or ordinary bond, we must separate inflation expectations from inflation uncertainty. An ordinary bond purchaser can make an estimate of future inflation (inflation expectations), which she then factors into the price she is willing to pay. If the purchaser's prediction is always correct (i.e., actual inflation never fails to match the prior estimate), then the bond is fully and accurately priced, with no need for an inflation-risk premium.

But if, as can happen, future inflation turns out to be higher than the prior esti-mate, then the purchaser, and the bond, will lose out. Because of the uncertainty surrounding future inflation, the purchaser will demand a compensating premium.

To account for this inflation uncertainty, we can modify the venerable Fisher return formula for the *ex-ante* nominal bond return:

$$(1+n_{xa}) = (1+r_{xa})(1+ \pi_e)(1+P_{xa,\pi}) \tag{1}$$

where n_{xa} is the bond's *ex-ante* nominal return, r_{xa} is its *ex-ante* real interest rate, π_e represents inflation expectations, and $P_{xa,\pi}$, is the inflation risk premium, or the extra portion investors require to compensate them for bearing the risk that actual and expected inflation will differ.

In theory, if government, corporate and other borrowers can issue infla-tion-indexed bonds for which all payments are tied to a true inflation index that is applied instantaneously, they can promise to eliminate inflation uncertainty risk. In exchange, they thereby save $P_{xa,\pi}$. Conversely, because real post-inflation cash flows are certain, inflation-indexed bond purchasers willingly forgo the extra return associated with the inflation-risk premium. In either case, by understanding the nature and behavior of the inflation-risk premium we can better analyze the true price, yield, and return on all bonds.[2]

Assuming Risk Neutrality in Modeling the Inflation-Risk Premium

Although the inflation-risk premium is (1) an important element of any nominal bond and (2) key to understanding the differences in pricing between nominal and inflation-indexed bonds, there have been few efforts to price this risk. Three approaches that have been tried are to (1) compare historical returns on nominal and indexed debt,[3] (2) examine the covariance of bond returns with relevant state variables,[4] and (3) apply a pure expectations hypothesis.[5] A fourth approach would employ forward pricing models. These approaches share an analytical commitment to risk neutrality.

---

[2] Some researchers are skeptical about the interests of governments and corporations in saving the inflation risk premium (e.g., John Y. Campbell and Robert Shiller, "A Scorecard for Indexed Government Debt," *NBER Macroeconomics Annual, 1996*). But, there is considerable evidence, drawn from work on collective interests and principal/agent theory, that supports the notion that governments and firms can and should wish to can save the inflation risk premium if it exists.

[3] See Shmuel Kandel, Aharon F. Ofer, and Oded Sarig, "Real Interest Rates and Inflation: An Ex-ante Empirical Analysis," *The Journal of Finance* (March 1996), pp. 209-10.

[4] Campbell and Shiller, "A Scorecard for Indexed Government Debt;" Zvi Bodie, "Inflation Risk and Capi-tal Market Equilibrium," *NBER Working Paper No. 373* (July 1979); Zvi Bodie, "Inflation, Indexed-Linked Bonds and Asset Allocation," *The Journal of Portfolio Management* (Winter 1990), pp. 48-53; and Zvi Bodie, "An Innovation for Stable Real Retirement Income," *The Journal of Portfolio Management* (Fall 1980), pp. 5-13; and Christopher Good, "The Inflation Risk Premium in Government Bond Returns," work-ing paper, Harvard University (December 1996), pp. 2-3.

[5] Campbell and Shiller, "A Scorecard for Indexed Government Debt."

Premium-estimation methods that employ data from existing sovereign index bond markets are perhaps most intuitively appealing. For actual government bonds, *ceteris paribus*, the discrepancy between either *ex-ante* or *ex-post* returns on nominal and indexed zero-coupon debt should approximate P_π. That is, given an ideal empirical comparison,

$$P_\pi = R_{nz} - R_{iz} \qquad (2)$$

where R_{nz} is a nominal zero, and R_{iz} is a zero indexed to inflation. Unfortunately, there are few actual cases of simultaneously traded nominal and inflation-indexed zeros of equal maturity, coupon rate, and duration. (Note that ordinary bonds are true fixed income assets in nominal but not real terms. Inflation bonds are true fixed income assets in real but not nominal terms. This contrast results in very different cash flow structures and durations, thus making true comparability difficult to achieve.) A deep and liquid market for Treasury indexed-bond STRIPs would facilitate U.S. comparisons.

Despite these challenges, some researchers[6] estimate the general inflation risk premium from the *ex-post* real rate, *ex-ante* nominal rate, and *ex-post* inflation identities by assuming that market participants don't systematically over or underestimate inflation. They account for lagged CPI values and tax treatment in the Israeli sovereign debt market from September 1984 to March 1992 and produce monthly estimates for the *ex-ante* real interest rate for each period in which the necessary quintuple set of bonds. (See the appendix for a more complete explanation.)

This approach assumes zero mean inflation expectation error, which is classic risk neutrality where market participants equally weight positive and negative returns as well as the probability of unexpected inflation versus no unexpected inflation. Thus, inflation expectations (π_e) are presumably based either on historical means or forecast values that assume risk neutrality.[7]

Estimation techniques that rely on CAPM are germane to markets, such as the United States, where inflation-indexed assets are only recently arrived (i.e., little or no opportunity for *ex-ante* and *ex-post* comparisons). Using bond covariances and relevant state variables, a second approach uses asset pricing theory to ascertain the implied inflation risk premium associated with the covariance of bond returns with relevant state variables. Bodie modifies the traditional CAPM to predict equilibrium prices in *real* returns,[8]

$$R_i = R_f + \beta(R_m - R_f) \qquad (3)$$

[6] Kandel *et al* use bonds of different coupons, indexation rates, and maturities in their estimate of the general *ex-ante* real rate. Israeli indexed bonds are partially or fully indexed ranging from 80% to 100%, coupon rates are paid annually and range from 2% to 7%, and maturities range from six to 20 years. Nominal bonds deliver a single par payment at maturity, which range from one month to one year. See Kandel, Ofer, and Sarig, "Real Interest Rates and Inflation: An Ex-ante Empirical Analysis."

[7] See Bodie, "Inflation Risk and Capital Market Equilibrium;" Bodie, "Inflation, Indexed-Linked Bonds and Asset Allocation;" and, Bodie, "An Innovation for Stable Real Retirement Income."

[8] Bodie, "Inflation, Indexed-Linked Bonds and Asset Allocation."

where

$$\beta = \frac{\sigma_{im}}{\sigma_m}$$

is measured in real terms, R_i is the expected real return on an individual asset, R_f is the real risk free rate, R_m is the real return on the market portfolio, σ_{im} is the covariance of the individual asset and the market portfolio, and σ_m is the variance of the market portfolio. Under this version, therefore, ordinary government bonds are risky assets, and the difference between the rate of return on ordinary bonds and the implied riskless real rate of return approximates the inflation risk premium.

Similarly, Campbell and Shiller employ state variables such as the return on the proxy for the "market portfolio," the traditional CAPM, and the growth rate of aggregate consumption, the consumption CAPM. They regress excess bond returns on excess market return, consumption growth and a convex combination of both market return and consumption growth. And Good assumes that asset returns are log-normally distributed under a version of the conditional CAPM and derives the risk premium as "a function of the conditional price of market risk and the conditional variances and covariances of the news components of the bond's return and the excess market return."

The CAPM has attracted an extensive critical literature, which undermines our confidence in its ability to determine inflation risk premiums.[9] For our purposes, the CAPM assumes a number of conditions that may affect the size and stability of an inflation-risk premium: perfect competition and price taking, a normal or log-normal distribution of returns, identical holding periods, limited investments in publicly traded financial assets, a fixed risk-free interest rate for borrowing and lending, no taxes, no transaction costs, universal mean-variance optimization and homogenous expectations. Further, as Roll's seminal critique suggests, to approximate the market portfolio with measures like the S&P 500 is problematic.[10] Even setting aside concerns about simplifying assumptions and measurement a well-known set of empirical findings suggests that beta does not accurately explain divergent returns. Fama and French find, for example, market value (size) and book-to-market equity explain the cross-section of stock returns in the United States, while beta is insignificant.[11] Other empirical anomalies from various studies include, but are not limited to, various other accounting valuation measures such as earnings-to-price ratios, the momentum of past returns, January seasonals, or weekend effects. Perhaps most important, the CAPM requires normally or log normally distributed returns and the market portfolio in order to produce helpful results. In the case of inflation, Exhibit 1 shows that inflation "returns" are far from normally distributed.

---

[9] See George M. Frankfurter, "The Rise and Fall of the CAPM Empire: A Review on Emerging Capital Markets," *Financial Markets, Institutions and Instruments* (1995), pp. 104-27.

[10] Richard Roll, "A Critique of the Asset Pricing Theory's Tests: Part 1: On Past and Potential Testability of the Theory," *Journal of Financial Economics* (March 1977), pp. 129-76.

[11] See Eugene Fama and Kenneth French, "The Cross-Section of Expected Stock Returns," *Journal of Finance* (1992), pp. 427-66.

Exhibit 1: Normality and Inflation Rates
Annualized Rolling 10-Year Inflation Rates (January 1957 to February 1991)

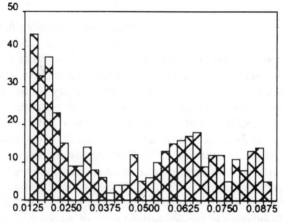

Series: INFLAT
Sample 1957:01 1991:02
Observations 410

Mean	0.044047
Median	0.042856
Maximum	0.088385
Minimum	0.012537
Std. Dev.	0.024855
Skewness	0.234064
Kurtosis	1.561789
Jarque-Bera	39.07975
Probability	0.000000

Source: CPI Index, Bureau of Labor Statistics

A third approach to modeling the inflation risk premium applies a pure expectations hypothesis of the interest rate term structure. Using this approach to supplement their CAPM analysis, Campbell and Shiller assume that the excess return for an "inflation sensitive asset" compared to a "comparatively riskless asset" is "entirely accounted for by its inflation risk premium." That is, the yield on an inflation sensitive asset — a 5-year Treasury zero — less the yield on an inflation insensitive security — a rolled-over 3-month Treasury bill — produces the inflation risk premium. This third procedure rests on two basic assumptions. The first is that the risk premium accounts for the entire excess return because the yield curve was flat during the period measured. Put somewhat differently, the approach assumes that the yield discrepancy between short- and long-term bonds is zero.[12] For this to be true, the term premium must be zero, which is unlikely except during short transition periods.[13]

The second assumption is that the key benchmark in the calculation — 90-day T- bills — contains no inflation risk. This is a common and therefore understandable assumption, but it is hard to reconcile with empirical research that suggests such short-term instruments are not a suitable inflation hedge.[14] Overall,

---

[12] They do not advance the weaker form of the expectations hypothesis, which posits a constant non-zero difference in yields across maturities.

[13] From a borrower's perspective, the yield curve has certainly not been flat, as the U.S. and Italian governments have recently issued more short-term debt obligations as a proportion of total debt explicitly to save the term premium associated with longer maturities. For a useful discussion of sovereign debt management and strategy, see John Y. Campbell, "Some Lessons from the Yield Curve," *Journal of Economic Perspectives* (Summer 1995), pp. 129-52, for a useful discussion of sovereign debt management and strategy.

[14] See Alicia H. Munnell and Joseph P. Grolnic, "Should the U.S. Government Issue Indexed Bonds?" *New England Economic Review*, Federal Reserve Bank of Boston (September/November 1986), pp. 3-21.

this approach might be strengthened (1) by comparing an inflation-sensitive asset with one that is relatively inflation proof and (2) taking steps to separate term-risk and inflation-risk effects.[15] We will return to the term premium/inflation risk premium question below.

A fourth approach to modeling the inflation risk premium would use forward pricing methodology to approximate the inflation risk premium. A nominal bond price includes an inflation expectation, and given uncertainty, the bond resembles a forward contract on the realized inflation rate. The inflation expectations component of the price of the bond reflects a strike price. If actual inflation is greater (less than) expected inflation, the real value of the bond will be lower (higher) than expected and the bondholder will suffer a loss (gain).

To set the return demanded on a nominal bond, expected inflation represents the mean of the distribution of all potential inflation outcomes over the life of the bond weighted by their probabilities. This fourth approach assumes, like the first (as suggested by Kandel *et al.*), a zero mean inflation expectation error. To price the inflation forward component of a nominal bond under the conventional forward pricing approach, one would simply price a value equal to an inflation expectation. Then there would be no additional inflation-risk premium to distort the expected future rate. In other words, if the real rate on the indexed asset is equal to the expected real rate on the nominal asset, risk-neutral, rational investors would be indifferent to owning either.[16] But if the realized spot rate consistently exceeds the forward price, then this is evidence either of a positive nonzero prediction error or an inflation-risk premium. Therefore, one might (1) examine historical data on bond prices, (2) calculate or assume a real yield, (3) evaluate any deviations from long term expectations, and (4) take an average of those deviations to derive the inflation risk premium.

But one cannot separate the prediction error from the inflation risk premium given one equation and two unknowns. Moreover, the real rate of return fluctuates from year to year. Empirical studies of forward (noninflation) risk premiums in foreign exchange and interest rate contracts have produced results confirming a risk premium in some contracts of long maturity and finding no consistent premium (unbiased expectations hypothesis) in other instruments such as short-term interest rate futures.

In summary, critical but probably unrealistic assumptions make recent analyses of the inflation-risk premium problematic. These include pure expectations of the term structure, benchmarks for supposedly riskless assets, reliance on the CAPM, and identification problems. These largely follow from the dearth of empirically observable instruments to approximate the riskless asset. *But the most*

---

[15] While both assets have risk premiums, differing maturities might affect its precise size. Therefore, the yield discrepancy might consist of term premiums and the effect of maturity on the inflation risk premiums between the two debt instruments.

[16] For example, investors would see no difference between a guaranteed fixed real return of 3% or a single draw from a distribution of real returns with a 3% mean.

critical assumption common to each approach is that investors are risk neutral, while abundant empirical evidence suggests that market participants are far from risk neutral, especially when it comes to inflation-related behavior.[17]

Perhaps the most widely noted empirical violation of risk neutrality is the discrepancy between returns on equities and bonds. As Mehra and Prescott show,[18] previous efforts to accommodate risk-averse investors do not sufficiently explain equilibrium pricing problems similar to the inflation risk premium (e.g., the equity premium puzzle). They find a coefficient of relative risk aversion of 30 is required to explain the magnitude of the historical gap between equity and risk-less-in-nominal-terms government bonds, while economists estimate that the coefficient is approximately four in the U.S. economy. Thus, given the general prevalence of risk aversion in asset pricing, modeling approaches that assume risk neutrality do not accurately capture inflation index bond pricing in actual and hypothetical government bond markets. Rather, given *empirically observed* risk aversion, investors more likely overstate the outcomes *and* probabilities of unexpected inflation. Thus, individual utilities in a rational expectations model must be weighted appropriately to accommodate the way in which investors actually treat the inflation risk premium component of a bond's price.

Prospective Decision Making and Asset Pricing

Given the challenges of preserving risk neutrality when it comes to inflation, we sought a more appropriate way to price inflation-indexed bonds. We turned to *behavioral* evidence concerning the way people actually assess real-life risks, including how they differentially weight potential outcomes *and* probabilities. This evidence led us to a model that more accurately assesses preferences and, we think, plausibly estimates the inflation risk premium. We employ three findings from the field of behavioral finance, all of which rest on the notion that investors' choices have a psychological basis that can sometimes differ from the choices they might make from a purely rational expectations point of view:

1. *Certainty Effect.* People are relatively phobic about uncertainty — they are likely to differentially overweight the probability of unexpected bouts of increased inflation. In a by-now–famous experiment, Kahneman and Tversky present the following choice-set in a hypothetical gamble presented to survey respondents:[19]

---

[17] For example, see Paul A. Samuelson, "Risk and Uncertainty: A Fallacy of Large Numbers," *Scientia* (1963), pp. 108-13; and Sanford Grossman and Robert Shiller, "The Determinants of the Variability of Stock Market Prices," *American Economic Review* (May 1981), pp. 222-27.

[18] Rajnish Mehra and Edward C. Prescott, "The Equity Premium: A Puzzle," *Journal of Monetary Economics* (March 1985), pp. 145-61.

[19] Daniel Kahneman and Amos Tversky, "Prospect Theory: An Analysis of Decision Under Risk," *Econometrica* (March 1979), p. 266.

A: ($4000, 0.80) or B: ($3000, 1.00).

Choice A has an 80% chance of returning $4,000 (but with a 20% chance of returning nothing), while choice B will return $3,000 with complete certainty. Even though the expected value of A is greater than ($3,200>$3,000), about 80% of respondents (including graduate students in statistics and business) consistently prefer B to A in clear violation of the rational choice. For example, rather than the expected value, respondents prefer the *certain* result among positive outcomes. By analogy and *ceteris paribus*, given the choice between a nominal or index bond, which yields a *certain* real return, investors might exhibit similarly preferences for the latter in the realm of positive returns.

2. *Loss Aversion Effect.* People are more than twice as averse to the prospect of real losses (i.e., increases in inflation) than they are attracted to the prospect of real gains (i.e., decreases in inflation) of the same magnitude. Returning to the equity premium puzzle — the view that the gap between equity and bond returns is larger than expected utility models would predict — Thaler and Benartzi provide a compelling explanation based on behavioral alterations to expected utility valuations.[20] They show that loss aversion helps explain the willingness to invest in bonds, despite the consistently greater historical return on equities *in relation to the relative risk of equities and bonds.* More generally, survey-research suggests that investors, even those trained in business and statistics, are not risk neutral. For example, most people will accept a bet involving a potential loss only at a discount to its statistically expected value.[21]

3. *Small Probability Effect.* People evaluate small-probability events differently than events that are relatively more likely. For example, in experiments, people willingly pay more than the expected value of a gamble when bets involve small probabilities of very large gains. This effect is especially noticeable in the area of environmental protection, airline safety, and lottery tickets.[22]

   In sum, investors and others often give subjective responses to objective choices about future events. In other words, their choices may make sense psychologically, but not from a rational expectations point of view.
   To reflect how people really behave with respect to the prospect of losses and gains, we employ what has been labeled "prospect theory" to modify expected-value calculations of inflation-related outcomes and probabilities.[23]

---

[20] Richard H. Thaler and Shlomo Benartzi, "Myopic Loss Aversion and the Equity Premium Puzzle," *NBER Working Paper No. 4369* (May 1993).

[21] See Amos Tversky and Daniel Kahneman, "Rational Choice and the Framing of Decisions," *Journal of Business* (October 1986), pp.251-278; Amos Tversky and Daniel Kahneman, "Advances in Prospect Theory: Cumulative Representation of Uncertainty," *Journal of Risk and Uncertainty* (1992), pp. 297-323.

[22] Kahneman and Tversky, "Prospect Theory: An Analysis of Decision Under Risk."

[23] Kahneman and Tversky, "Prospect Theory: An Analysis of Decision Under Risk," p. 309.

Using historical data, we generate a *prospective* utility for holding nominal bonds, set this equal to the utility of holding indexed bonds, solve for the riskless real return and the inflation risk premium, and finally extrapolate an estimate of real indexed bond yields. In this way, the gamble of buying a nominal bond can be compared to the option of buying and holding a riskless indexed bond. A positive premium implies that a risk-neutral borrower, perhaps like the U.S. Treasury or a firm, can lower borrowing costs by issuing inflation-indexed debt to risk-averse investors who prefer *certain* (loss-protected) real returns to *potentially* higher returns on nominal bonds.

Modeling the Prospective Inflation-Risk Premium

We modify the (1) outcome values and (2) probability weights in the conventional expected value formula to more accurately reflect risk-averse behavior. The prospect theory value function modifies the potential outcome states depending on sign and magnitude, and the transformed *values* correspond to the following:

$$V(x) = x^\alpha \tag{4}$$

for every $x \geq 0$ and

$$V(x) = -\lambda(-x)^\beta$$

for every $x < 0$ — where x is the outcome, $V(x)$ is the weighted prospective value of the outcome, α is a nonlinear scalar adjustment factor equal to 0.88, β is the nonlinear scalar adjustment factor also equal to 0.88, and λ is a loss aversion adjustment factor equal to 2.25. Values for the scalars and adjustments are drawn from experimental data and modeling results from Kahneman and Tversky.[24] The resulting outcome and probability weights are shown in Exhibit 2 and Exhibit 3, respectively. Given the scalars in equation (4), the prospective transformations reflect the assumption that market participants are more averse to losses than attracted to gains, with losses weighted more than twice gains of the same magnitude. The transformed *probabilities* follow

$$W(p) = \frac{p^\gamma}{[p^\gamma + (1-p)^\gamma]^{1/\gamma}} \tag{5}$$

for every $x \geq 0$ and

$$W(p) = \frac{p^\delta}{[p^\delta + (1-p)^\delta]^{1/\delta}}$$

---

[24] Kahneman and Tversky, "Advances in Prospect Theory."

Exhibit 2: Prospective Inflation Decision Weights Versus Actual Outcome Probabilities

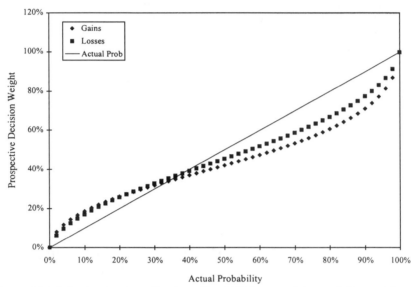

Source: Calculation based on Amos Tversky and Daniel Kahneman, "Advances in Prospect Theory: Cumulative Representation of Uncertainty," *Journal of Risk and Uncertainty* (1992), pp. 297-323.

Exhibit 3: Prospective Values Versus Expected Values

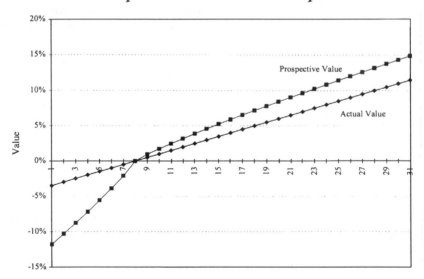

Source: Calculation based on Amos Tversky and Daniel Kahneman, "Advances in Prospect Theory: Cumulative Representation of Uncertainty," *Journal of Risk and Uncertainty* (1992), pp. 297-323.

for every $x < 0$ — where γ is an adjustment factor equal to 0.61 and δ is an adjustment factor equal to 0.69. Furthermore, in the realm of gains, π is the cumulative probability of obtaining an outcome at least as good as x, minus the cumulative probability of obtaining an outcome strictly better than x. But in the realm of losses, π is the cumulative probability of obtaining an outcome at least as bad as x, minus the cumulative probability of obtaining an outcome strictly worse than x. In short, these scalars imply that market participants overweight the probabilities of negative real returns. Finally, we multiply and add these transformed outcomes in the same manner as conventional expected utilities. Given the weighted outcomes and probabilities, the prospective utility or modified expected value is

$$V(f) = \left[\sum_{i=-m}^{n} W(p)V(x) \right]^{1/\alpha} \tag{6}$$

where $V(f)$ is the prospective utility, n is the greatest outcome, m is the smallest outcome, and $W(p)$ and $V(x)$ are the weighted probabilities and outcomes, respectively, of the ith observation.

Calculating the Prospective Inflation-Risk Premium

To calculate variability in nominal bond real returns induced *strictly* by inflation volatility, we eliminated all other sources of price fluctuations, including coupon reinvestment risk, changing inflation expectations, changing real yield requirements, liquidity risk, and default risk. Given a nominal financial asset that fits this description, we compared that bond to an identical one in all respects *except* sensitivity to inflation. Since there is no long pricing history of such riskless assets in the United States, especially for buy-and-hold assets, we used hypothetical Treasury zeros. We compared this hypothetical, riskless, non-callable, nominal zero-coupon bond series to a hypothetical, riskless, indexed zero-coupon bond series trading simultaneously, which approximates *ex-post* estimation of simultaneously traded nominal and index zero coupon government debt in equation (2).

We employed several assumptions to reduce the differences between the two (hypothetical) series to inflation sensitivity. First, we assumed that the hypothetical nominal bonds are bought at 10 years to maturity and held to the redemption date. Given this buy-and-hold strategy, we avoided the complexity of incorporating interest rate changes, capital gains and losses and option pricing. Second, by using government bonds, we eliminated default risk from the analysis. Third, by using zero-coupon bonds, we eliminated the complexity surrounding coupon reinvestment rates. Finally, the duration of zero coupon instruments is simply the number of periods for both the hypothetical indexed and nominal Treasuries, a 10-year holding period.

Based on these simplifying assumptions, we took the following steps to generate a hypothetical nominal zero coupon bond time series and an inflation-risk premium:

- Using McCulloch and Kwon's data set of historical bootstrapped zero coupon interest rates from January 1947 to February 1991,[25] calculated the price of hypothetical, 10-year zero-coupon bonds, P, given nominal market yield, r, according to the formula:

$$P = \frac{1,000}{(1 - r)^{10}} \tag{7}$$

- Included monthly changes in inflation that actually transpired over each 10-year holding period using the Consumer Price Index for All Urban Consumers (CPI-U) as an indicator of the price level.
- Calculated the real, or inflation-adjusted, value of the 1,000 nominal principal payments, F_i,

$$F_i = \frac{1,000}{CPI_f / CPI_i} \tag{8}$$

where, CPI_i and CPI_f represent the CPI at initial purchase, i, and final maturity, f, respectively.

- Calculated the real rate of return, R, experienced by investors who hold the bond to maturity.

$$R = \left(\frac{P}{F_i}\right)^{1/10} - 1 \tag{9}$$

- Created a time-series of 410 real returns on the 10-year hypothetical zeros from January 1957 through February 1991.
- Loaded the hypothetical zero coupon distributions into the prospect theory model to determine the prospective value of a nominal zero-coupon bond held to maturity, $P(v)_{nominal}$. Equate this to the prospective value of indexed bonds, $P(v)_{indexed}$, as in

$$P(v)_{nominal} = P(v)_{indexed} \tag{10}$$

The real-return distribution of these indexed bonds consists of a single class with 100% probability of occurring.

- Solved for the real yield, R_y (equal to real return since this is a zero-coupon bond), and subtract this amount from the expected value, $E(v)$, of the distribution to derive the inflation risk premium, P_π, as in

$$R_y = [P(v)_{indexed}]^{1/\alpha} \tag{11}$$

where, α is the parametric factor $= 0.88$, and

$$P_\pi = E(v)_{nominal} - R_y \tag{12}$$

This result quantifies how much less investors are willing to accept for the privilege of avoiding the volatility in real returns induced by uncertain inflation.

---

[25] See Huston J. McCulloch and Heon-Chul Kwon, "US Term Structure Data, 1947-1991," *Ohio State University Working Paper No. 93-6* (1993).

RESULTS AND COMPARISON WITH ALTERNATIVE CALCULATIONS

In our formulation, prospect theory produced an inflation risk premium of 40.6 basis points. This represents the *average* risk premium on hypothetical 10-year nominal zero-coupon Treasuries held to maturity and maturing from January 1957 to February 1991. Exhibit 4 illustrates the models results using a smaller data set.

Comparing Results: Different Methods and Data Sets

This estimate is consistent with other approaches but it is more intuitively, methodologically, and theoretically appealing. Other approaches include alternative methods using approximately the same data set, as well as our prospect theory model using different data.

Pure Expectation Models

Using the CAPM approach outlined above, Campbell and Shiller produced an inflation risk premium of about 50 basis points, while Good's result using 5-year Treasuries from August 1953 to November 1995 was 61 basis points, both of which are somewhat above our prospect model's estimate. Based on the discrepancy between Treasury bond and bill yields under the pure expectations hypothesis of the term structure, Campbell and Shiller estimated an average inflation risk premium of 70 to 100 basis points, significantly above our prospective estimate.

To address these differences, we reestimated our own model, using, as the others do, 5-year instead of 10-year bonds in our prospect model (again, for January 1957 to February 1991). We found that the prospective inflation-risk premium rose to 58 basis points. Further, we also estimated a prospective risk premium average of 62 basis points by constructing our own series of hypothetical 10-year Treasury zeros over a longer time frame (1953-1994). In short, while the applications of these other models aren't perfectly consistent, the results range between 50 to 100 basis points. They support the conceptually and methodologically more appealing prospect theory calculation. We believe any remaining difference between the results of the two approaches may be explained by the term premium. We focus on this question below in the next major section.

Prospect Model Using Sovereign Bond Data

Perhaps the most persuasive comparison would be one based on actual inflation-indexed bonds, despite the difficulty of controlling for noninflation risks. We used Israeli inflation-indexed bond data from Kandel et al. by loading the ex-post real returns from their data set into our prospect model.[26] The prospective value of the real returns represents the certainty associated with an inflation-proof security, while the conventional expected value resembles the inflation sensitive asset that yields the general *ex-post* real interest rate that Kandel et al. derive.

---

[26] The returns from Kandel et al., represent the *general* real interest rate not associated with any particular asset. Again, they use both index and nominal bonds of varying maturities and coupons in the *ex-ante* estimation. The replication, then, also considers the real interest rate on some arbitrarily defined hypothetical asset.

Exhibit 4: Prospect Theory Calculation of the Inflation Risk Premium

Parameters:

alpha	0.88
beta	0.88
lambda	2.25

	if x is gain	if x is loss
gamma	0.61	0.69

N	Date 10 Year Zero	Monthly Returns Class x	v(x)	Prob	Actual Cumulative Probabilities (as good/better)* p	Trans-formed Probabilities (strictly better)* p'	P(outcome) w(Px)	P(outcome) w(Px)	Decision Weight π	Comp-onents π*v(x)	Prospective Utility V(G)	Real	Nominal Expected	PREMIUM
8	02-Dec-84	8.45%	11.36%	9.09%	9.09%	0.00%	17.78%	0.00%	17.78%	0.020	-5.79%	-1.745%	-1.03%	0.72%
3	01-May-85	4.83%	6.95%	9.09%	18.18%	9.09%	24.90%	17.78%	7.12%	0.005				
7	02-Jan-85	2.66%	4.12%	9.09%	27.27%	18.18%	30.35%	24.90%	5.45%	0.002				
11	02-Sep-84	-0.75%	-3.03%	9.09%	72.73%	63.64%	60.84%	54.25%	6.59%	-0.002				
2	02-Jun-85	-0.90%	-3.55%	9.09%	63.64%	54.55%	54.25%	48.27%	5.98%	-0.002				
5	03-Mar-85	-1.61%	-5.95%	9.09%	54.55%	45.45%	48.27%	42.56%	5.71%	-0.003				
9	01-Nov-84	-1.77%	-6.45%	9.09%	45.45%	36.36%	42.56%	36.88%	5.69%	-0.004				
10	01-Oct-84	-2.07%	-7.41%	9.09%	36.36%	27.27%	36.88%	30.92%	5.95%	-0.004				
6	03-Feb-85	-5.36%	-17.14%	9.09%	27.27%	18.18%	30.92%	24.29%	6.63%	-0.011				
4	01-Apr-85	-5.93%	-18.74%	9.09%	18.18%	9.09%	24.29%	16.07%	8.23%	-0.015				
1	03-Jul-85	-8.88%	-26.71%	9.09%	9.09%	0.00%	16.07%	0.00%	16.07%	-0.043				

Note: Prospect calcualtion using data from Shmuel Kandel, Aharon F. Ofer, and Oded Sarig, "Real Interest Rates and Inflation: An Ex-Ante Empirical Analysis," *The Journal of Finance* (March 1996), pp. 209-210.

Using our prospect model, the average general inflation risk premium in the Israeli sovereign bond market from September 1984 to March 1992 is about 42 basis points, which compares with Kandel et al.'s own average estimate of approximately 34 basis points.

Estimating the Riskless Rate to Determine the Inflation Risk Premium

A third approach follows basic theory and empirical research on the relationship between risk and reward in asset pricing. Briefly, the method considers varying volatility and returns to estimate an implied "riskless" interest rate. The "riskless" rate *is the real return on an asset with no default, reinvestment, inflation or interest rate risk.* This implies that the asset exhibits zero volatility for the holding period. If so, the riskless rate, α, is

$$r_{xa} = \alpha + \beta X + \mu \tag{13}$$

where r_{xa} is the *ex-post* real rate, α is the constant, X is some functional form of the standard deviation of the real return for each maturity year, and μ is the "normal" residual. While the CAPM and the security market line suggest a linear relationship between risk and reward, different functional forms that might capture the relationship between linear-log and quadratic expressions of X. As the specification suggests, the estimation of α is an out-of-sample prediction of r_{xa} when X, again the standard deviation, is zero. McCulloch's yield curve for hypothetical zeros, which again have no default or reinvestment risk, informs the estimate of α.[27]

Given α, the value of the risk premium follows from the following decomposition of the *ex-post* real rate of return:

$$(1 + r_{xa}) = (1 + \alpha)(1 + P_{\pi}) \tag{14}$$

where r_{xa} is the *ex-post* real return for a given maturity, α is the riskless real rate, and P_{π} is the inflation risk premium. Solving for P_{π} yields

$$P_{\pi} = \frac{1 + r_{xa}}{1 + \alpha} - 1 \tag{15}$$

Turning to results, as Exhibit 5 indicates, the equation implies a riskless real rate of approximately 0.98%, and both parameter estimates are statistically significant at the 1% level. Given our decomposition of r_{xa} and the observed real return on 10-year zeros of 2.22%, this produces an inflation risk premium of approximately 123 basis points. Similarly, the approximate 2.09% return on 5-year zeros produces a result of 111 basis points.

---

[27] Equities and corporate bonds, of course, exhibit default risk, and government coupon bonds are subject to reinvestment risk. Besides these substantive concerns, the econometric rationale for omission of riskier assets from the sample is that the greater volatility (standard deviations) associated with higher returns is considerably removed from the out-of-sample value of the riskless rate (which, again, exhibits zero standard deviation for the holding period).

Exhibit 5: Zero-Coupon Yield Curve Regression

January 1957 to February 1991
Yearly Returns and Annualized Standard Deviations
Dependent Variable
Real Return

Independent Variable(s)	β	p value
Constant	0.00977	0.010
Standard Deviation of Real Return	1.48505	0.000
chi2	20.68	
Prob. > chi2	0	
Number of Observations	455	
N	13	
T	35	

Note: The data for estimation consists of 13 zero maturities (1-year through 13-year zeros) from January 1957 to January 1991 and yearly real returns based on 1-year holding periods and annualized standard deviations based on the monthly returns. There are 35 yearly returns for each maturity, which yields a total pooled sample size of (13 * 35) 455 maturity-years. Since the panel design is temporally dominant (N < T, 13 < 35), we use feasible generalized least squares with panel corrected standard errors. Given Cook-Weisberg and Durbin-Watson test statistics for heteroskedasticity and serial correlation, respectively, we also correct for heteroskedasticity across maturities and a first-order AR(1) process specific to each maturity. (The alternative assumption of a common error disturbance does not alter the parameter estimates.) For details on this procedure, see Nathaniel Beck and Jonathan Katz, "What to Do (and Not to Do) with Time-Series Cross-Sectional Data, *American Political Science Review* (1995), pp. 634-47.
Source: Huston J. McCulloch and Heon-Chul Kwon, "US Term Structure Data, 1947-1991," *Ohio State University Working Paper No. 93-6* (1993).

The problem with α is that it is sensitive to specification bias. Following Kandel et al. and others, we might believe that, contrary to the Fisher hypothesis, real returns are negatively correlated with inflation. A regression of the real returns on standard deviations *and* the yearly CPI growth rate implies a riskless rate of about 4%, which in turn produces a premium of about −1.8% with respect to 10-year zeros. This sharply contrasts with the 123 basis point premium based on the model without the inflation regressor. In short, one might have more confidence in extrapolating a riskless rate from a model that more thoroughly specifies the determinants of real returns.

Besides specification issues, this model overestimates the inflation risk premium because the previous decomposition of the real rate of return for a given maturity does not include interest rate risk. A more comprehensive decomposition might be

$$(1+ r_{xa}) = (1+ \alpha)(1+ P_{\alpha})(1+ \varepsilon) \tag{16}$$

where ε is the interest rate risk associated with the realized standard deviation during the holding period. By definition, α exhibits zero volatility and is therefore not a proxy for the return on (hypothetical) indexed bonds, which vary over any reasonable holding period. According to equation (16), equations (14) and (15) overstate P_{π} by a factor of $(1+ \varepsilon)$. Put differently, given the two unknowns associated with the more comprehensive specification of r_{xa}, one cannot determine the precise proportions of the approximate 123 basis points in the calculation that correspond with the inflation risk premium or the interest rate risk premium. Since the prospect calculation of about 41 basis points is less than the term-structure regression result from equation (14), perhaps the difference, approximately 82 basis points, might approximate the prevailing *interest rate* risk premium.

HOW DOES THE INFLATION RISK PREMIUM VARY?

Our prospect theory risk premium of 41 basis points represents the *average* risk premium on hypothetical 10-year nominal zero-coupon Treasuries held to maturity and maturing from January 1957 through February 1991. As we noted above, by using a different time frame and different data, the prospect model produced a premium of about 62 basis points. These estimates are all averages that don't capture dynamic changes in the premium over time or provide a point estimate.

A key question for anyone interested in the price of bonds is how the inflation risk premium changes. The inflation risk premium should vary systematically with changing inflation uncertainty over time, the quantity of inflation-indexed bonds relative to nominal issues or, as Campbell and Shiller suggest, increased experience with indexed bonds in a given market as "the public becomes more familiar with indexed bonds."[28]

For example, Kandel et al. calculate a highly volatile monthly inflation risk premium for Israel during the 1980s and 1990s with a standard deviation of about 235.9 basis points for the entire sample period (see Exhibit 6).[29] Their risk premium for January 1992 was approximately 2.33% but fell dramatically to −1.11% in March 1992. To address the effect of inflation levels and changes in the risk premiums, they also divide the sample into two regimes, a higher-inflation period from September 1984 to July 1985 and a lower-inflation period from August 1985 to March 1992. They derive two average premiums of about 235.8 basis points and 4.8 basis points, respectively. Kandel *et al.*'s assumption of a zero mean inflation expectation error suggests to us that the existence of a *non*-zero inflation expectation error likely contributes to the high standard deviations and disparate regime estimates.

Using our prospect model, we similarly divided the sample and calculated premiums of about 71.6 basis points and 23.9 basis points, respectively. Our results reflect the general direction of the change away from the hyperinflationary period in Israel, but the disparity of our estimates is less pronounced, perhaps because we avoided the assumption of zero inflation expectation error.

We also devised a way to make instantaneous estimates of the inflation risk premium. We did this by incorporating a temporal scheme that relaxes a basic assumption built into the original prospect model, namely that every monthly return — early or late — has an equal probability of informing the total average premium. For example, the November, 1981, return of −2.56% (with a prospective weight of

---

[28] Campbell and Shiller, "A Scorecard for Indexed Government Debt," p. 7.
[29] Again, see Exhibit 6, which indicates several negative premiums during the period according to Kandel *et al.*

−8.95) is the lowest value in the 410 monthly return data set. It receives the second greatest prospective weight — 7.3 times the average. (Note that in the standard expected value formula, each monthly return, whether from January 1957, February 1991 or sometime in between, has a probability weight of 1/410.)[30] In order to arrive at an *instantaneous* measure, one would have to heroically assume that investors equally vividly remember all 410 monthly returns over the previous 30-year period. Just as investors overweight negative outcomes and the probabilities of unlikely outcomes, they also remember recent events more vividly.

Ideally, we should simultaneously incorporate the prospect outcome weights, prospect probability weights, and a set of prospect temporal weights to accommodate the effects of memory. We tried several alternative methods for doing this and report the most promising below.

Indexed Correlations that Retain Prospect Probability Weights

Since we have little or no experimental evidence on the weights people implicitly assign to recent versus distant events, we modeled market participant memory with a basic time-series econometric concept — indexed autocorrelation coefficients (*ACs*) from the hypothetical distributions of indexed and nominal bond returns. The general objective is to augment $W(p)$ in equation (5) that proxies the return on indexed bonds and the standard expected value calculation that proxies the return on a comparable nominal bond, to incorporate a temporal measure. Again, absent experimental evidence, the additional temporal component assumes that market participants weight recent events more heavily, and the temporal component is equal to the prospect probability component of the comprehensive weight. That is, the general augmented probabilities are

Exhibit 6: Kandel Inflation Risk Premium (Mean = 0.34%)

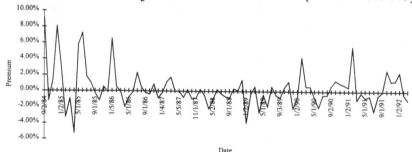

Date

Source: Calculation based on data from Huston J. McCulloch and Heon-Chul Kwon, "US Term Structure Data, 1947-1991," *Ohio State University Working Paper No. 93-6* (1993).

---

[30] Incidentally, and by the remote chance of one in 410, the greatest weighted observation in the data set is also the most recent. The calculation weights the 8.2% (11.1% prospective weight) February 1991 real return about 11.6 times the average prospective weight. This coincidence suggests that the temporal bias in this calculation is lower than might occur in data sets in which magnitude and temporal characteristics do not so coincide. Hypothetically, if the real return was, say, 8.5% in January 1957, the earliest return would receive the greatest weight.

$$W(P_{P,T}) = \frac{W(P_P) + P_T}{2} \tag{17}$$

and

$$P_{i,t} = \frac{(p_i + p_t)}{2} \tag{18}$$

where P_T is *some* temporal weight for the *prospective indexed bond* distribution of real returns, and p_t is *some* temporal weight for the *nominal bond* distribution of real returns. The temporally transformed prospect theory calculation equation (6) becomes

$$V(f_T) = \left\{ \sum_{i=-m}^{n} W(P_{P,T})V(X_p) \right\}^{1/\alpha} \tag{19}$$

and the transformation of the standard expected value calculation is

$$E(x_t) = \sum_{i=1}^{410} P_{i,t}x_i \tag{20}$$

Finally, the temporally adjusted premium calculation based on equation (12) is therefore the difference between equation (20) and equation (19) or

$$P_{P,T} = E(x_t) - V(f_T) \tag{21}$$

Methods to determine P_T and p_t in equations (17) and (18), *respectively,* are critical. We compute P_T and p_t by indexing the *ACs* from the respective *level* time-series of indexed and nominal real returns, $V(X_p)$ and x_i, respectively. The standardized temporal weight for each is the positive statistically significant *AC* for each lag k divided by the average statistically significant *AC* for the entire distribution, multiplied by p_i. *ACs* from any time-series seem to decline geometrically until the final statistically significant kth lag. Interestingly, this pattern broadly resembles a Koyck model such as

$$\beta_k = \beta_0 \lambda^k$$

where

$$k = 0,1,2...$$

and some λ, such that $0<\lambda<1$, is the rate of decline in market participant memory. While we do not impose a precise λ, the weight, $W_{k,AC}$, for the kth lag is

$$W_{k,AC} = (AC_k / \overline{AC})p_i$$

P_T and p_t are the respective $W_{k,AC}$s, from the prospect weighted and nominal real return distributions.

Exhibit 7: Temporally Adjusted Prospect Theory Inflation Risk Premiums: March 1981-February 1991

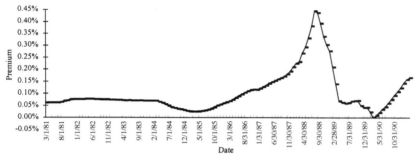

Source: Calculation based on data from Huston J. McCulloch and Heon-Chul Kwon, "US Term Structure Data, 1947-1991," *Ohio State University Working Paper No. 93-6* (1993).

This preferred method using indexed *AC*s was an iterative process that produces instantaneous risk premium estimates. We first limited the probability distribution that enters steps (17) through (21) — how many returns do investors remember, or consider relevant in their assessment of risk aversion? We turned to the simple level correlogram from the time-series of real returns and assumed that market participants do not consider statistically insignificant *AC*s. That is, they remember the respective returns through all positive statistically significant *AC*s but do not recall figures after last significant return. Therefore, only returns with statistically significant *AC*s were used in computing each monthly estimate.

Using the hypothetical McCulloch and Kwon zeros from January 1957 through February 1991, Exhibit 7 presents the results given the 10-year period from March 1981 through February 1991 for this iterative process. The average monthly risk premium for the period is approximately 10 basis points, which peaked at about 44 basis points in July 1988 and reached its lowest point at −0.03 basis points, the only negative premium in the distribution, in February 1990.

We also pursued three additional strategies, all of which produced positive inflation risk premiums. These methods include two strategies alternatively based on *AC*s and partial autocorrelation coefficients (*PAC*s) that, unlike our preferred method, do not limit the data set to those returns that have statistically significant *AC*s and *PAC*s. Rather, those returns with statistically insignificant lagged coefficients simply receive no temporal weighting in addition to the prospect weights. With the same data as before, these procedures rendered risk premiums of approximately 51 and 74 basis points, respectively. The third technique employs simple Box-Jenkins methodology and eschews the prospect *probability*, but not the *outcome* weights (like Kandel *et al.*, it assumes a zero inflation-expectation error). This procedure produced a risk premium of about 8 basis points circa March 1, 1991.

The results produced by these four alternative methods aren't definitive, but they strongly suggest some ways to track inflation risk premium changes over time.

Exhibit 8: Varying Holding Periods — Inflation Risk Premium and McCulloch Zero Maturity

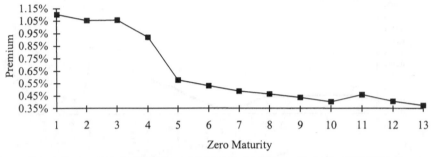

Zero Maturity

Source: Calculation based on data from Huston J. McCulloch and Heon-Chul Kwon, "US Term Structure Data, 1947-1991," *Ohio State University Working Paper No. 93-6* (1993).

Next Steps: The Yield Curve, Prospect Theory Inflation Risk Premiums and Real Interest Rates

In addition to changing premiums, three important issues remain for academics and practitioners alike regarding the yield curve and real interest rates. First, we explore a persuasive hypotheses about the yield curve and inflation risk premiums, which suggests that as maturity lengthens, *ceteris paribus*, investors pay more for inflation protection. Second, we ponder the same question but under the assumption of a constant holding period. Third, this exercise recommends reflection on whether the inflation risk premium is independent of the real interest rate level, notably holding volatility constant.

Inflation Risk Premiums and Varying Holding Periods

Given a hold to maturity strategy, an unexpected inflationary spike seems more probable the longer the investment horizon. That is, an investor holding a 5-year bond to maturity is less likely to see their principal erode substantially due to unexpected inflation than an investor holding a 10-year bond. Thus, the latter investor pays a greater premium for inflation insurance. With respect to borrowers such as the U.S. Treasury, this suggests that sovereigns will save more with respect to the *inflation risk* premium, which might offset losses regarding the *term* premium.

Unfortunately, one cannot observe the *ex-ante* inflation risk premium across multiple maturities. To explore this notion, we took zeros ranging from one to 13 years and assumed each bond is held to maturity. We then loaded the resulting *ex-post* monthly rolling real returns into the (static) prospect theory model to calculate the respective premiums. Risk premiums for longer maturities should be greater than those for shorter periods. *But the data contradict this view.* As Exhibit 8 indicates, premiums seem to actually decrease as the maturity increases. As some simple regressions indicate, the functional form of this relationship is not linear, but linear-log, as the effect tapers off around the 5-year zero. Of course, all things are not equal in this *ex-post* design. The standard deviations across maturities are not the same. Holding the mean constant across probability distributions, prospect theory should produce a higher premium for distributions with higher variance.

Inflation Risk Premiums and Constant Holding Periods

We also examined the effect of maturity given constant holding periods. Is the risk premium equal, *ceteris paribus*, for a 5-year bond held to maturity and a 10-year bond sold after five years? To produce more comparative leverage, we tested 1-year holding period and the same 13 zero maturities. Turning to Exhibit 9, the data generally suggest a positive linear-log relationship between zero maturity and the prospect theory inflation risk premium, which tapers off around the 5-year bond. Does prospect theory actually capture *term premiums*, given the "normal" upward sloping yield curve and ambiguous theory regarding the inflation risk premium and maturity given constant holding periods?

The Level of Real Interest Rates and the Inflation Risk Premium

A question that perhaps we have yet to ask is whether the inflation risk premium correlates with the *level* of real interest rates. Previously, we suggested that, holding the mean of two probability distributions constant, prospect theory would produce a greater premium for the more volatile sample. Conversely, *holding volatility constant*, would a probability distribution with a greater mean have a higher premium?

The data seem to support this view. Both simple scatter plots from the varying and constant holding period samples, Exhibit 10 and Exhibit 11, respectively, suggest a positive general relationship between the level of real interest rates and the inflation risk premium. Also, *despite the high collinearity between real return and volatility and the small sample size*, regressions on the inflation risk premium that control for the standard deviation produce positive and significant coefficients for the real interest rate in both holding period samples.

Exhibit 9: One-Year Holding Period Inflation Risk Premium and McCulloch Zero Maturity

Source: Calculation based on data from Huston J. McCulloch and Heon-Chul Kwon, "US Term Structure Data, 1947-1991," *Ohio State University Working Paper No. 93-6* (1993).

Exhibit 10: Varying Holding Periods Inflation Risk Premia and Real Returns

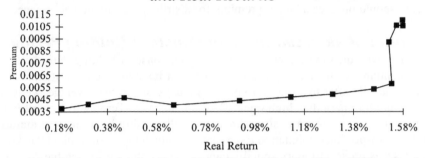

Source: Calculation based on data from Huston J. McCulloch and Heon-Chul Kwon, "US Term Structure Data, 1947-1991," *Ohio State University Working Paper No. 93-6* (1993).

Exhibit 11: One-Year Holding Period Inflation Risk Premium and Real Return Levels

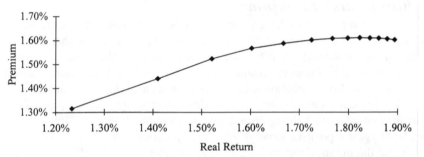

Source: Calculation based on data from Huston J. McCulloch and Heon-Chul Kwon, "US Term Structure Data, 1947-1991," *Ohio State University Working Paper No. 93-6* (1993).

However robust this evidence, does the theory suggest any relationship between the real interest rate level and the risk premium? Perhaps the premium is a proportional component of nominal return — that investors in nominal bonds demand higher premiums proportional to prevailing interest rate levels. Perhaps the inflation premium is germane to *relative* rather than *absolute* risk.

CONCLUSIONS AND IMPLICATIONS

By using prospect theory as a rationale for generating risk outcome weights, and with supporting evidence from conventional pricing techniques, our research demonstrates a substantial, positive inflation risk premium in the range of 40 to 60 basis points for 5- and 10-year U.S. Treasuries (based on historical data from the 1950s to the early 1990s). The risk premium can also vary significantly over time, but is independent of other temporal effects, such as the term premium. Most important, we are confident that these results reflect the way in which people — professionals as well as ordinary investors — actually perceive inflation and then behave in light of those perceptions.

Policy Implications for Borrowers: Sovereigns and Corporations

We have shown that the U.S. Treasury and other organizations — public and private — that issue inflation-indexed bonds will, on average, save an amount equal to the inflation risk premium in comparison with ordinary debt. Depending on the size of the portfolio and the proportion of inflation-indexed instruments in it, this could be a substantial amount (e.g., about $2.5 billion per year on $500 billion in inflation-indexed bonds outstanding). This sounds like a reasonable reward for any institution willing to bear the risk of inflation for the life of the bond.

Policy Implications for Investors

On the other side of the inflation-indexed coin, investors who are averse to inflation risk will be willing to forgo some return in order to remove that uncertainty from their real returns. Prior to development of an inflation-indexed bond market, some especially risk-averse investors may drive up returns on ordinary bonds in order to compensate themselves for being forced to bear a risk they fear. Examples may include people, such as retirees or people nearing retirement, who are no longer able to take advantage of the relatively high correlation between their own salary growth and inflation, and institutions, such as insurance companies or employer pension plans, whose future liabilities are affected by inflation, but whose asset base is not inflation-protected. Once inflation-indexed bonds became an option, and once these types of investors choose to buy them, their influence on the pricing process of nominal bonds could be reduced.

As an interesting speculation, it is possible that when a substantial amount of indexed debt becomes available, investors will become, on balance, more inflation risk tolerant with respect to the rest of their portfolios. Some mean-variance analyses suggest that, depending on the correlations between inflation-indexed bonds and other assets, this could be so. Individuals and portfolio managers, for example, might be able to buy more risky assets than before because they can use indexed bonds to hedge their overall portfolios.

The Holy Grail: The Search for the Riskless Asset

With a buy-and-hold strategy, investors can use inflation-indexed bonds to eliminate inflation uncertainty, one of the biggest threats to successful investing. But, since real interest rates vary, government-issued inflation indexed bonds *are not truly riskless securities*. Their prices decline if real rates increase just as nominal bonds do if nominal rates go up. This is clearly the experience of the United Kingdom where indexed gilts (i.e., bonds) have traded in a range of 2.0% to 4.8% during the last 14 years. The final step in creating a truly riskless-in-all-dimensions bond would be to have the Treasury offer an inflation-indexed, floating real yield, zero coupon security traded in a continuously deep and liquid debt market. No country has gone this far yet.

APPENDIX

Kandel et al. account for lagged CPI values and tax treatment in the sovereign debt market from September 1984 to March 1992 and produce monthly estimates for the *ex-ante* real interest rate for each period in which the necessary quintuple set of bonds exist. Given a time-series of *ex-ante* real rate values, Kandel et al. define the *ex-post* real rate, r_{xp}, in (continuously compounded) log differences, as

$$r_{xp} = n - \pi$$

where n is the nominal return, and π is the realized inflation rate. They further decompose the nominal rate into

$$n = r_{xa} + \pi_e + P_\pi$$

where r_{xa} is the *ex-ante* real interest rate, π_e represents inflation expectations, and P_π is an inflation premium. The realized inflation rate is

$$\pi = \pi_e + \delta$$

where δ is a zero-mean expectation error, as market participants purportedly neither systematically overestimate nor underestimate inflation. Substituting equations (4) and (5) into equation (3) yields

$$r_{xp} = (r_{xa} + \pi_e + P_\pi) - (\pi_e + \delta)$$

and solving for P_π simplifies to

$$P_\pi = r_{xp} - r_{xa} + \delta$$

Therefore, *assuming a zero* δ, the risk premium is the difference between the *ex-ante* and *ex-post* real interest rates. Kandel et al. find an average *general* 34 basis point premium, notably not associated with any particular security, based on monthly figures from September 1984 to March 1992.

Section III:

Global Environment:
Past and Present

Chapter 12

The U.K. Experience

Mark Deacon, AFIMA
Quantitative Analyst
U.K. Debt Management Office

INTRODUCTION

The U.K. index-linked gilt (IG) market was launched in March 1981 with the auction of a 15-year bond. Since then the market has expanded significantly and by the end of December 1997 stood at almost £58 billion (approximately $95 billion) in uplifted terms — 19% of total marketable debt in the U.K. — making it the largest indexed bond market in the world. This chapter provides a detailed account of how the IG market has evolved since 1981 and also briefly touches on some of the ideas for changes to the market that have been discussed in early 1998 as part of a Treasury consultation exercise with market players.

HISTORICAL PERSPECTIVE

In the U.K., one of the earliest advocates of indexation was Sir George Shuckburgh Evelyn who, in his 1798 article "An Account of Some Endeavours to Ascertain a Standard of Weight and Measure," attempted to construct an index to represent the general change in prices. Inspired by Evelyn, Joseph Lowe advocated the widespread use of indexation in his 1822 book *The Present State of England in Regard to Agriculture and Finance*. Support for indexation also came from John Maynard Keynes. In 1924, he proposed to the Royal Commission on National Debt and Taxation that the British government should issue index-linked bonds. Besides offering investors an opportunity to protect their purchasing power, Keynes argued — to no avail — that the government might also be able to save on its interest costs since risk-averse investors might be prepared to pay a premium for such bonds.

      The U.K. government demonstrated a similar lack of enthusiasm for indexation in the 1959 Radcliffe Report on the Working of the Monetary System, which declared that indexation would constitute "a confession of failure" in the face of inflation. However, by the early 1970s rising (unexpected) inflation (see

The author thanks Andy Brookes and Gurminder Bhachu for their assistance.

Exhibit 1) meant that holders of nominal debt were experiencing significant erosion of the real value of their assets. As a result, when the Page Report on National Savings was published in 1973, it recommended the use of indexation for national savings certificates aimed at small investors. In 1975, the government acted on this advice and began issuing non-marketable national savings contracts with returns linked to the Retail Prices Index (RPI). Although investment in these certificates was initially limited to pensioners (earning them the nickname of "granny" bonds), this restriction was later removed.

Further anxieties over the effects of inflation on the U.K. financial system were expressed in the Wilson Report of 1980. A chief concern was that the substantial number of high coupon bonds issued during the 1970s left the government vulnerable to the risk that the real burden of its debt interest would rise should inflation and hence nominal interest rates fall. The Wilson Report also emphasised the adverse effects of inflation on the real value of investors' savings. Given the important role played by pension funds in the gilt market and their need to provide pensions based on earnings, the Wilson Report recommended that the government should issue earnings indexed gilts, which only pension funds would be eligible to purchase.

In March 1981, doubtless influenced by the Wilson Report, the Government began issuing marketable inflation-protection bonds. These securities are officially referred to as index-linked gilts (IGs) though many in the market refer to them simply as "linkers". Rather than indexing to the average earnings index the authorities opted instead to use the Retail Prices Index. The main reasons behind this decision were that the RPI is published frequently, is seldom revised, and is widely understood — unlike earnings based measures of inflation. Although ownership of IGs was initially restricted to pension funds (as had been suggested by Wilson), these restrictions were lifted in March 1982.

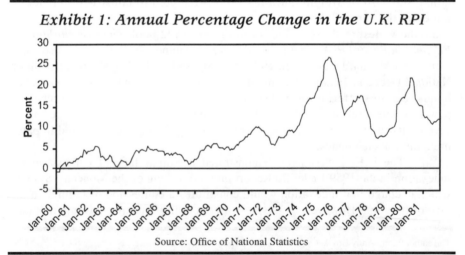

Exhibit 1: Annual Percentage Change in the U.K. RPI

Source: Office of National Statistics

Exhibit 2: Growth in the U.K. Index-Linked Gilt Market

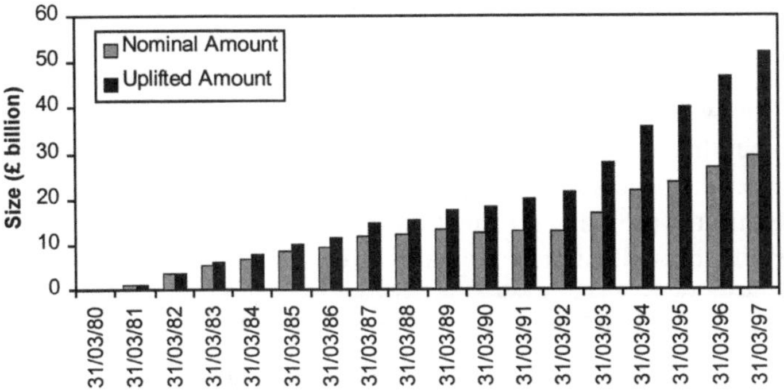

Source: Bank of England

There were three official reasons given for the introduction of indexed bonds: (1) to reinforce belief in the government's anti-inflation policy by reducing the ability of the government to reduce the real value of its liabilities (and hence investors assets) via an unexpected rise in inflation; (2) to reduce the cost of funding by reducing inflation risk for investors; and, (3) to improve monetary control by increasing the flexibility of funding — indexed gilts would be saleable in times of uncertainty about inflation without the need to raise nominal interest rates, thereby reducing the government's vulnerability to surges of growth in the monetary aggregates.[1]

The first index-linked gilt, a 15-year bond, was issued on March 27, 1981 by single price auction. As Robert Price reports, the market found pricing the first index-linked gilt difficult, with bids at the auction ranging from £80 to £130 per £100 nominal.[2] However, since a single price format was used for the auction, the entire issue was allocated at one price (par), saving some investors from an exceptionally large "winners' curse." Over the subsequent 18 months six additional index-linked gilts were issued, with maturities of between six and 29 years. Because significant amounts of the bonds remained unsold on several occasions, single price auctions were abandoned in 1988. Since then index-linked gilts have been issued entirely by tap, the authorities arguing that this format enables them to time issuance in response to market demand. As with the earlier auctions, taps are used both for the issue of new bonds and for building up existing issues, although no new index-linked gilts have been introduced since September 1992.

Exhibit 2 shows the growth in the index-linked gilt market since 1981. By the end of December 1997 the market size was £57.8 billion ($95.2 billion) in uplifted terms, amounting to 19% of total government marketable debt in the U.K. Target index-linked issuance for the 1998/99 financial year is 25% of gilt sales. Despite the size of the market, it is noticeably less liquid than the conventional gilt market. Two of the most commonly used indicators of liquidity are turnover and

[1] HM Treasury, "Indexed Gilts," *Economic Progress Report No.133* (May 1981), pp. 1-2.
[2] Robert Price, "The Rationale and Design of Inflation-Indexed Bonds," *International Monetary Fund Working Paper* 97/12 (January 1997).

the size of bid-ask spreads. For large trades, spreads are reportedly £½ (16 "ticks" or 32nds) per £100 for a £50 million trade of index-linked gilts compared with £¹⁄₁₆ (2 "ticks") for conventional gilts.[3] Analysis of U.K. data for 1994 shows that turnover in the conventional gilt market was 25 times greater than in the index-linked gilt market by value, though only five times greater by volume (i.e., number of bargains). To put this into perspective: in terms of market value, the conventional market is between five and six times greater in size than the index-linked market.

Exhibit 3 provides information on the 13 index-linked gilts currently in existence; Exhibit 4 illustrates the maturity distribution of these bonds.

Exhibit 3: U.K. Index-Linked Gilts

Coupon (%)	Maturity Date	Date of First Issue	Nominal Amount Outstanding (£ mn)
4.625	27/04/1998	18/09/1992	800
2.500	22/11/1999	05/05/1983	2
2.500	24/09/2001	26/08/1982	2150
2.500	20/05/2003	27/10/1982	2500
4.375	21/10/2004	22/09/1992	1150
2.000	19/07/2006	08/07/1981	2500
2.500	20/05/2009	19/10/1982	2625
2.500	23/08/2011	28/01/1982	3100
2.500	16/08/2013	21/02/1985	3750
2.500	26/07/2016	19/01/1983	3975
2.500	16/04/2020	12/10/1983	3800
2.500	17/07/2024	30/12/1986	3850
4.125	22/07/2030	12/06/1992	1300

Source: Bank of England. Figures as at December 31, 1997.

Exhibit 4: Distribution of Index-Linked Gilts by Residual Maturity (Position as of December 31, 1997)

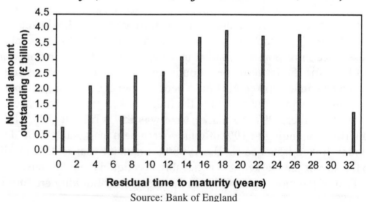

Source: Bank of England

[3] Bank of England, *Index-Linked Debt — Papers Presented at the Bank of England Conference September 1995* (August 1996).

Exhibit 5: U.K. Private-Sector Issues of Index-Linked Bonds

Issuer	Bond	Issue Size (£ mn)	Issue Date
Halifax Building Society	3 7/8% IL 2020	15.00	Oct 1985
Nationwide Building Society	3 7/8% IL 2021	30.00	Jul 1986
		30.00	Apr 1987
Nationwide Building Society	4 1/4% IL 2024	50.00	Feb 1989
Dartmoor Investment Trust	6 1/4% IL 2005	16.00	Apr 1990
		3.00	Jun 1992
Anglian Water	5 1/8% IL 2008	100.00	Jun 1990
Severn River Crossing	6% IL 2012	131.00	Oct 1990
The Housing Finance Corporation	5.65% IL 2020	60.00	Nov 1990
(Indexed) [THFC]		40.00	Mar 1993
New City & Commercial Investment Trust	5.06% IL 2006	12.64	Feb 1993
The Housing Finance Corporation	5 1/2% IL 2024	31.25	Dec 1994
(Indexed 2) [THFC]		24.75	Dec 1995
Abtrust New Preferred Income Investment Trust	5 3/8% IL 2007	7.50	Mar 1997

Source: Mark Deacon and Andrew Derry, *Inflation-Indexed Securities* (Hemel Hempstead: Prentice-Hall Europe, 1998).

Despite the fact that the index-linked gilt market is currently the largest inflation-indexed government bond market in the world, as yet there has been little interest in indexed issuance by the private sector in the U.K. Exhibit 5 provides a detailed list of private sector indexed bonds, the first of which was issued more than four years after the first index-linked gilt was introduced. This contrasts starkly with the rapid development of the non-Treasury inflation-indexed bond market in the United States. Roger Bootle attributes the small number of index-linked private sector issues in the U.K. to past tax regimes, which "seemed vague or penal or both," as well as to the innate conservatism on the part of issuers.[4] However, tax reforms have not led to a rush of issuance, with just one new issue being successfully brought to the market since December 1994. Another possible explanation for the lack of issuance is a lack of demand — investors preferring a product that is free from both credit and inflation risk.

INSTRUMENT DESIGN

Index-linked gilts are capital-indexed bonds which pay semiannual coupon payments indexed to the RPI. Should there be a change in the coverage or the basic calculation of the RPI that would be materially detrimental to index-linked gilt holders, prospectus terms require the government to offer investors the opportunity to have their bonds redeemed. The tax treatment of index-linked gilts is at odds with how indexed bonds are taxed in most markets since the inflation uplift

---

[4] Roger Bootle, *Index-Linked Gilts — A Practical Investment Guide* (2nd Edition) (Hemel Hempstead: Woodhead-Faulkner, 1991).

on the principal is tax-free. Also, since April 1996, the total return on index-linked gilts has been taxed on a real basis.

An eight month indexation lag is used in the U.K. — two months to allow for the compilation and publication of the RPI and six months to ensure that the nominal size of the next coupon payment is known at the start of each coupon period, for accrued interest calculations. In order to calculate each cash flow on an IG, two RPI figures are required: that applicable when the bond was originally issued (the "base" RPI figure) and that relating to the cash flow concerned. In each case, the RPI figures used are those for the month eight months before the relevant dates.

So, standard coupon payments are calculated using the formula:[5]

$$\frac{c}{2} \times \frac{RPI_{M-8}}{RPI_{I-8}}$$

and the redemption payment from:

$$100 \times \frac{RPI_{R-8}}{RPI_{I-8}}$$

where:

c	=	annual coupon rate (%)
RPI_X	=	published RPI for month X
I	=	month in which the bond is issued
M	=	month in which the interest payment falls
R	=	month in which the bond redeems

Interest and redemption payments are rounded *down* to 2 decimal places for 2% Index-Linked Treasury 2006 and 2.5% Index-Linked Treasury 2011. For all other index-linked gilts payments are rounded *down* to 4 decimal places.

For example, the base RPI figure for 4 1/8% Index-Linked Treasury 2030 (originally issued in June 1992) is 135.1 — the RPI figure for October 1991 (published in November 1991). This bond pays coupons in January and July for which the relevant RPI figures are those relating to the previous May and November, respectively. So, the coupon payment in January 1998 was calculated as:

$$\frac{c}{2} \times \frac{RPI \text{ for May } 1997}{RPI \text{ for October } 1991} = \frac{4.125}{2} \times \frac{156.9}{135.1} = 2.3953$$

Similarly, the redemption proceeds on maturity in July 2030 of a £100 nominal holding of this bond will be:

$$100 \times \frac{RPI \text{ for November } 2029}{RPI \text{ for October } 1991}$$

---

[5] Index-linked gilts are often issued part-way through a dividend period, in which case the size of the first dividend payment is adjusted accordingly. Also, index-linked gilts have in the past been issued in partly-paid form, adding further complications to the calculation of the first dividend.

All index-linked gilts issued to date, bar one, have had the same cash flow structure — the exception being the May 1983 issue of £1 billion of a convertible index-linked gilt (2.5% Index-Linked Treasury Convertible 1999). This bond gave investors the option to convert (all or part of) their holdings into a conventional gilt (10.25% Conversion 1999) on any one of three dates.[6] The value of the option would have tended to increase (decrease) as inflation fell (rose) since the nominal return on the indexed gilt would be falling (rising) whilst the nominal return on the conventional gilt would, *ceteris paribus*, be fixed — increasing (decreasing) the incentive to switch into the conventional gilt. In the event, 97% of the bond was converted at the first available opportunity and a further 2.8% on the subsequent conversion dates, leaving only a tiny rump unconverted (£1.7 million) which is rarely traded.

Possible changes to the structure of index-linked gilts were considered at a conference hosted by the Bank of England in September 1995 to discuss ways in which the U.K. market could be improved.[7] One proposal put forward by Robert Barro was an alternative method for index-linking gilts which potentially improves the quality of the inflation protection offered. Although Barro's formulation is actually for an index-linked gilt with a six month lag (for ease of exposition), the methodology can easily be extended to indexed bonds with any length indexation lag. Barro suggests that inflation in the six months prior to a coupon or principal payment should be proxied by giving double weight to the previous six months (the most recent for which data are available when the coupon must be fixed) rather than by including in the calculation the six months before the bond's issue date. The intuition behind this is that inflation for the most recent usable six month period is likely to be a better indication of current inflation than that from the six months before the bond was issued.[8]

Another possibility discussed at the conference was whether the government should introduce *Limited Price Indexation* (LPI) gilts. The motivation behind this was that in the U.K., the 1995 Pensions Act[9] requires pension funds to guarantee that — as a statutory *minimum* — the future benefits to which their members are entitled increase at a rate matching the *lower* of the increase in the RPI or 5% (i.e., a 5% inflation cap). LPI bonds would have coupons and principal indexed to the lower of the increase in the RPI or some fixed percentage (e.g., 5%), and should thus provide an ideal hedge for such pension fund liabilities. In the event there was little enthusiasm at the conference for either of these innovations — or the suggestion that earnings-linked gilts (EGs) should be issued — and so rather than risk segmenting the market (by having more than one type of indexed gilt) and thereby reducing liquidity, the authorities did not take the proposals any further.

---

[6] November 22, 1983, May 22, 1984 or November 22, 1984.

[7] *Index-Linked Debt — Papers Presented at the Bank of England Conference September 1995.*

[8] A more technical description of Barro's proposal appears in Mark Deacon and Andrew Derry, *Inflation-Indexed Securities* (Hemel Hempstead: Prentice-Hall Europe, 1998).

[9] This Act took effect on April 6, 1997.

Exhibit 6: Total Return of Index-Linked Gilts (IGs) versus Conventional Gilts and the FTSE All Share Index (1988-1996)

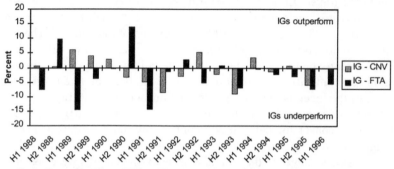

Source: Karim Basta, Ifty Islam, William Kan, Gerald Lucas, Timothy Quek, and Thomas Sowanick, "Understanding Treasury Inflation Protected Securities (TIPS): A Fundamental and Analytical Framework," *Merrill Lynch Global Fixed Income Research* (December 20, 1996).

PERFORMANCE OF INDEX-LINKED GILTS

Research published by Merrill Lynch examined the performance of index-linked gilts relative to both conventional gilts and the FTSE All Share Index over the period 1981 to 1996 by comparing six month returns.[10] Exhibit 6 shows the differential between index-linked total returns and the total returns on conventional gilts and the FTSE All Share Index for the period from 1988 to 1996. Although index-linked gilts underperformed both conventional gilts and equities for most of this period there are some periods when they clearly outperformed the other asset classes. For instance, index-linked gilts outperformed conventional gilts from the beginning of 1988 to mid 1990 as a result of the sharp increase in inflation following the "Lawson boom" of 1987/88. Similarly, following sterling's exit from the European Exchange Rate Mechanism in September 1992 and the subsequent increase in long-term inflation expectations, index-linked gilts again outperformed conventional gilts. This appears to support the assertion that investors are attracted to indexed bonds in periods of emerging inflation risk.

Although index-linked gilts have generally provided a lower return than conventional bonds and equities, their returns have — as expected — proved much less variable, demonstrating their appeal to investors looking for real value certainty. This is illustrated in Exhibit 7, which compares the standard deviation of quarterly real holding period returns on index-linked and conventional gilts of different maturities between 1982 and 1996.[11] Clearly, over the period examined, the returns on index-linked gilts are noticeably less volatile than those on conventional gilts.

---

[10] Karim Basta, Ifty Islam, William Kan, Gerald Lucas, Timothy Quek, and Thomas Sowanick, "Understanding Treasury Inflation Protected Securities (TIPS): A Fundamental and Analytical Framework," *Merrill Lynch Global Fixed Income Research* (December 20, 1996).

[11] In the U.K. market, *short* is used to denote bonds with residual maturities of up to 7 years; *medium*, bonds with maturities of between 7 and 15 years; and *long*, bonds with maturities of over 15 years.

Exhibit 7: Volatility of Real Holding Period Returns in the U.K.

Maturity	Annualised standard deviation of real holding period returns (Q3 1982 - Q2 1996)	
	Conventional Gilts	Index-Linked Gilts
Short	4.6%	3.9%
Medium	9.7%	6.6%
Long	11.8%	8.4%

Source: Mark Deacon and Peter Andrews, "The Use and Value of Index-Linked Bonds," *The Financier: Analyses of Capital and Money Market Transactions* (November/December 1996), pp.13-25.

FUTURE DEVELOPMENT

In March 1997, the U.K. Treasury announced that it saw "positive merit" in the re-introduction of index-linked gilt auctions once it had consulted market participants on the precise form that the auction programme should take. As a result, in January 1998 it published a wide-ranging consultation paper[12] which considered not only the issue of auctions but also questions on whether a separate IG market maker list should be established and on whether index-linked gilts should be re-designed along the lines of US inflation-indexed securities.

The Treasury published the outcome of the consultation exercise in its Debt Management Report (DMR) of March 1998.[13] Given the generally favorable reaction from the market towards the idea of index-linked auctions, the Treasury confirmed its intention to introduce auctions in 1998-99. However, in order to allow sufficient time for the U.K. Debt Management Office (DMO)[14] to establish a separate list of index-linked market makers, index-linked auctions are not scheduled to start until October 1998. The DMO plans to hold two index-linked auctions in 1998-99, one in October 1998 and one in January 1999. Each auction will be for between £0.5 billion and £1.0 billion cash of one bond on a uniform price basis. The authorities intend to reduce gradually the supply available for tap issuance between auctions, with the aim that in the longer term, auctions will constitute the primary means of index-linked issuance.

The Treasury has also pre-committed to a minimum annual level of £2.5 billion cash of index-linked gilts gross issuance for the foreseeable future. For 1998-99, on current forecasts the DMO is aiming to raise £3.6 billion cash through index-linked gilt sales. On the issue of index-linked redesign, while many of those consulted saw advantages to such a move, the consensus was that these advantages did not justify the transitional costs of fragmented market liquidity or holding large scale conversion offers. Given this, the Treasury announced in the DMR that it does not intend to undertake a redesign at present.

---

[12] HM Treasury, "Consultation on Index-linked Gilts Auctions," January 5, 1998.

[13] HM Treasury, "Debt Management Report 1998-9," March 19, 1998.

[14] The responsibility for debt management was transferred from the Bank of England to the DMO on April 1, 1998.

As in other index-linked bond markets, one of the biggest challenges facing the U.K. authorities is how to improve market liquidity. Over recent years the approach adopted to tackle this problem has been to build up progressively the size of existing issues rather than issue new bonds. Liquidity could be improved if an index-linked gilt futures contract was established since it would provide a hedge for those with positions in IGs. However, the London International Financial Futures and Options Exchange (LIFFE) has indicated that its members perceive insufficient demand for such a contract until the underlying cash market is more liquid. It is possible that over the long term the switch to auctions may improve liquidity by increasing and better focusing demand.

Chapter 13

The Australian Experience

Michael Chadwick
CPI Product Manager
ABN AMRO Australia Ltd.

INTRODUCTION

The inflation-linked securities market in Australia has been in existence since 1983. Since then, the total volume of inflation-linked securities on issue has grown steadily to reach approximately AUD$10 billion by the end of 1997. Issuance has been dominated by the Australian Commonwealth government, although there have been a number of state government authorities and corporate entities who have also issued inflation-linked securities. The primary investors in the Australian market have been superannuation (pension) funds, life insurance companies, and professional fund managers. A unique characteristic of the Australian inflation-linked market is the multitude of issues and the array of borrowers who have utilized this market.

Before describing the development of the market from its infancy stages in 1983 to the present day, I will review the various types of inflation-linked securities that are available in Australia.

TYPES OF INFLATION-LINKED SECURITIES IN AUSTRALIA

The two major types of inflation-linked securities in Australia are Capital Indexed Bonds and Indexed Annuity Bonds.[1] As of the end of 1997, they represented 60% and 40% of the outstanding inflation-indexed securities, respectively. We examine each type in more detail with illustrations of the relative cash flows.

Capital Indexed Bonds

Capital Indexed Bonds (CIBs) are the oldest form of inflation-linked security in the Australian market (the first issue occurring in 1983) and at present account for about 55% of the total inflation-linked securities on issue. As the name suggests, the indexing of this security occurs quarterly on the capital, or principal amount

---

[1] Another type of inflation-linked security issued in Australia is Interest Indexed Bonds. These bonds are structured so that the interest payments have a fixed rate component (coupon payment) and a floating component which is added to the fixed coupon payment. The latter varies with the indexation adjustment which is usually the inflation rate. The principal is repayable at maturity at the original face value. IIBs were briefly issued in the late 1980s but have never become a significant part of the inflation-linked market.

of the bond which is repaid at maturity. The indexation factor is usually based on the rate of consumer price inflation represented by the Australian Bureau of Statistics' CPI, although other price and wage indices can be used. Interest is generally payable quarterly on the then-current indexed capital amount at a fixed coupon rate (usually 4.00% per annum). As the inflation indexation increases the principal value of the security over time, the amount due at maturity becomes greater. This increases the credit risk to the holder over time.

Exhibit 1 illustrates a typical cash flow profile of a 10-year CIB. Note that cashflows increase over time as the indexed principal amount increases with inflation. This indexed principal is repayable at maturity. Note that the structure of the above securities is essentially similar to that of all other major sovereign issues, including the U.S. and the U.K.

Indexed Annuity Bonds

Indexed Annuity Bonds (IABs) are simply regarded as a stream of revenue which has attached no principal and hence there is no distinction between principal and interest payments. The original payment amount (before indexation) is called the *base payment*. This payment is grossed up by the inflation indexation each quarter. If the inflation rate was zero, the only payments from an IAB would be the quarterly base payment. However, more typically, as the CPI increases each quarter the base payment is grossed up by the factor: the previous highest CPI index over the original value.

Exhibit 1: Capital Indexed Bond

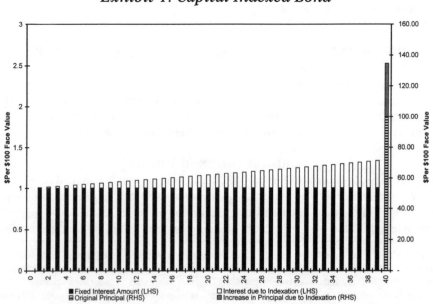

Fixed Interest Amount (LHS)
Original Principal (RHS)
Interest due to Indexation (LHS)
Increase in Principal due to Indexation (RHS)

Exhibit 2: Indexed Annuity Bond

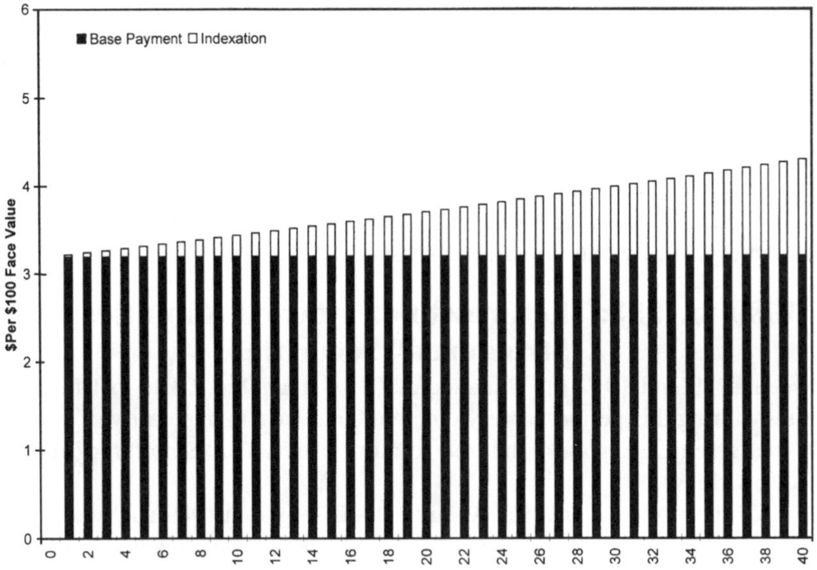

Base Payment ☐ Indexation

Exhibit 2 shows a typical 10-year Indexed Annuity Bond given positive inflation.

HISTORY OF THE INFLATION-LINKED SECURITIES MARKET

The inflation-linked bond market began with the issuance of a CIB in 1983 by the former electricity authority, the State Electricity Commission of Victoria. The total volume on issue has risen reasonably consistently since that date to reach approximately AUD$10 billion by the end of 1997. Over this period the issuance of different structures has ebbed and flowed as investors and issuers have discovered the specific features or benefits of each structure. (See Exhibit 3.)

The development of the Australian inflation-linked securities market can be divided into three distinct stages. These are:

1985 to 1989: the birth of the market
1989 to 1993: the growth in IABs and "structured" securities
1993 to present: acceptance and "liquidity"

1985 to 1989: The Birth of the Market

Although the first issue of inflation-linked securities was in 1983, it was not until 1985 that the first issue of Commonwealth Government Capital Indexed Bonds was held. This time could arguably be described as the "birth" of the market in

Australia. In the period 1985 to 1988, the Commonwealth continued regular issuance of CIBs by public tender, but then withdrew from the market as investors focused on the newer indexed annuity style-security being issued by various other vehicles. State Governments followed a similar pattern, issuing only Capital Indexed Bonds regularly from 1986 through to 1989.

During the market's formative years, the primary type of issuance was the Capital Indexed Bond. Investors in the market were relatively few, dominated by some large life insurance companies, and liquidity was poor. Commonwealth tenders regularly had wide yield ranges, and the securities had seemed to have fallen out of favor by both investors and issuers alike by the late 1980s.

1989 to 1993: The Growth of Indexed Annuities and "Structured" Securities

Between 1989 and 1992 the issuance of CIBs stagnated. CIBs lost favor with investors during this period, largely due to the increase in popularity of new types and issuing vehicles, namely Indexed Annuity Bonds and "Structured" inflation-linked securities.

The issuance of Indexed Annuity Bonds began in 1989 and were initially marketed as a tax-effective inflation-linked bond. These were readily embraced by semi-government authorities over the ensuing four years as an alternative to the Capital Indexed Bond style. Investors appreciated this structure not only for the tax benefits obtained but also for its liability matching capabilities. The tax benefits associated with this structure were removed in 1994 but the appetite for this style of security remains to this day.

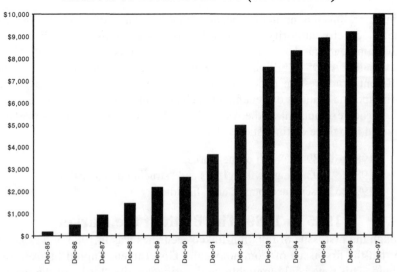

Exhibit 3: Total Issuance (in Millions)

A logical extension of the inflation-linked securities market has been the packaging of projects and/or assets whose cash flows are implicitly or explicitly related to inflation. Such issues have not been limited to public or quasi-private infrastructure projects with some form of claim against the relevant State or Commonwealth Government. Many existing and proposed assets held in the private sector have inflation-linked cash flows which can be supplemented by commercial obligations and/or capped reserve (sinking) funds, isolated on commercial terms, to provide the necessary credit quality.

Since the late 1980s, the Australian inflation-linked market has been supplemented by the introduction of these "structured" or project-related issues. These have been issued primarily in the form of Indexed Annuity Bonds. "Structured" issues have been used to finance such diverse projects as the construction of the Sydney Harbour Tunnel, the construction of the Great Southern Stand at the Melbourne Cricket Ground, and construction of a hospital at Port Augusta, South Australia. In each instance, the proposed cash flows of the project are in some way inflation-related and hence match with a fair degree of accuracy the liabilities of an inflation-linked security.

1993 to the Present: Acceptance and "Liquidity"

Until 1992, inflation-linked securities were predominately the preserve of a few large investors who had inflation-linked liabilities. The market still suffered from poor liquidity, and although the variety of issuers had increased, appetite for credit risk amongst investors had not extended much beyond the state-government backed or credit-enhanced variety.

The years 1992 and 1993 were characterized by an increasing acceptance amongst investors and asset consultants alike that inflation-linked securities constituted a separate asset class. In this period, the investor base multiplied considerably and new issues were in hot demand.

In 1993, the Commonwealth Government re-entered the inflation-linked market, starting a new program of CIB issuance with the objective of creating an active liquid market in inflation-linked securities. This commitment has continued to the present day. The Commonwealth is now the predominant issuer of such securities in Australia.

State government authorities have reduced issuance considerably in recent years, given an increased desire to reduce debt. The tax benefits for investors associated with IABs were also removed in 1994, lessening their attractiveness. The appetite for IABs has been maintained, however, due to their excellent liability matching characteristics and, more recently, the 0% inflation "floor" attached to these issues.

Due to increased privatization of a number of previously government-owned assets, the issuance of IABs has been maintained by "structured" issues which finance these assets. A recent trend is for some of those securities to be unrated, as investors learn to become more comfortable with the risk of the underlying cash flows of the particular project.

Exhibit 4: CGL 2005 CIB Historical Real Yields (%)

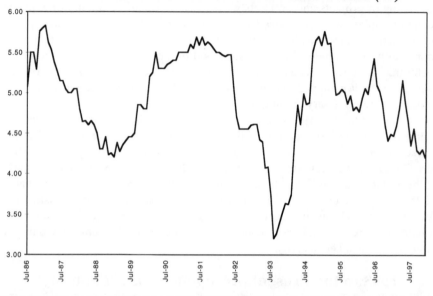

Liquidity in The Commonwealth CIB market has improved considerably in recent years, attracting a much wider range of intermediaries and investors. In addition to the traditional owners such as superannuation funds and insurance companies, new investors include professional fund managers, total return investors, and global funds. The establishment of an inflation-linked swaps market has assisted in attracting more investors and issuers in recent months.

HISTORICAL REAL YIELDS IN AUSTRALIA

Real yields on inflation-linked securities in Australia have been relatively volatile over the past number of years, largely as a result of imbalances in supply and demand (as is often the case with new asset classes). Exhibit 4 shows the real yield on the 2005 Capital Indexed Bond since 1986.

Real yields have moved within a 3.00% band for the last 10 years. In 1993, the inflation-linked market rallied strongly as the asset class was initially established amongst a number of fund managers. Demand far outstripped supply in that year, and real yields fell as low as 3.20% in August 1993. In 1994, the global market selloff caused inflation-linked real yields to rise substantially, almost touching 6.00% in October of that year. Between 1995 and 1997, however, perhaps as a sign of the increased maturity of the market, real yields have returned to their typical trading range of 4.50% to 5.50%, exhibiting the lower volatility that one should expect from this asset class in its mature phase.

METHODS OF ANALYSIS

Modern portfolio theory can assist investors in selecting a portfolio of assets. The basic tenet of modern portfolio theory is that portfolio risk can be reduced by the addition of securities or asset classes whose return patterns are dissimilar to those securities or asset classes already in the portfolio. Conversely, an investor, for a certain level of risk, can achieve a higher portfolio return by diversifying across a large number of securities or asset classes, rather than restricting investments to a few securities or asset classes. Hence the investor who treats inflation-linked securities as a subset of fixed interest bonds may not recognize the potential value of these securities in a portfolio management context, or alternatively overvalue the contribution of conventional fixed interest bonds.

The diversification benefits of inflation-linked securities arise from three factors:

- The return generating fundamentals of inflation-linked securities are unique in that an explicit real yield is grossed up for inflation.
- The inflation driven indexed growth and real yield components give inflation-linked securities both conventional debt and equity type characteristics.
- There is a low correlation of returns with conventional securities and other asset classes.

A fund manager can achieve a more diversified portfolio by including inflation-linked securities in the optimization process, after estimates of return and risk expectations and correlations are taken into account.

The decision to invest or disinvest from the inflation-linked securities asset class is dependent on expected movements in real yields and inflation (which determines expected returns), and the expected returns from other asset classes given an investor's risk/return profile and expected horizon.

There are a number of general "tools" or methods of analysis that have been developed to assist the portfolio manager in the decision making process, both from an asset allocation perspective and within an inflation-linked portfolio. The major methods are discussed in the following section.

Inflation-Linked versus Equities

The *real yield gap* is a useful tool in assessing relative value between equities and inflation-linked securities. This gap represents the risk premium for holding equities over inflation-linked securities less the real dividend growth rate. From another perspective, the equity market represents better value when its real return is high relative to that of inflation-linked bonds, or equivalently the real yield gap is at a high point.

The rationale for its use as a valuation tool arises from fundamental tenets of modern finance theory. Specifically, these are the Constant Dividend Growth Model for equity valuation (which assumes the current dividend grows at a fixed rate in perpetuity) and the Capital Asset Pricing Model for pricing the cost of equity capital.

The real yield gap is defined as:

$$\text{Real equity return} - \text{Real inflation-linked yield} = (K_e - g) - R_t$$

given constant dividend growth.

R_t = long-term real yield
K_e = cost of equity capital
g = constant growth rate
$K_e > g$

Using the CAPM:

$$K_e = (R_m - R_t) - g$$

where R_m is the expected market return.

Thus the real yield gap is equivalent to the differential between the equity market risk premium $(R_m - R_t)$ and the prospective real dividend growth rate (g).

Note that this long-term strategic model is best applied to the core asset allocation process, rather than short-term tactical decisions, which seek to add value through a tactical asset allocation process — looking at factors which may cause the short-term dividend rate to diverge from its long-term trend would need to be considered in such applications. Nevertheless, a low or negative real yield gap must be the result of a reduced equity risk premium and/or the prospect of a sustainable rise in dividend yield growth. At these times, inflation-linked securities may be considered a more attractive asset.

Exhibit 5 shows the real yield gap that has existed since 1986. Interestingly, the time where the real yield gap was most negative was just prior to the stock market crash of 1987.

Exhibit 5: The Real Yield Gap

Exhibit 6: Break-Even Inflation Differential

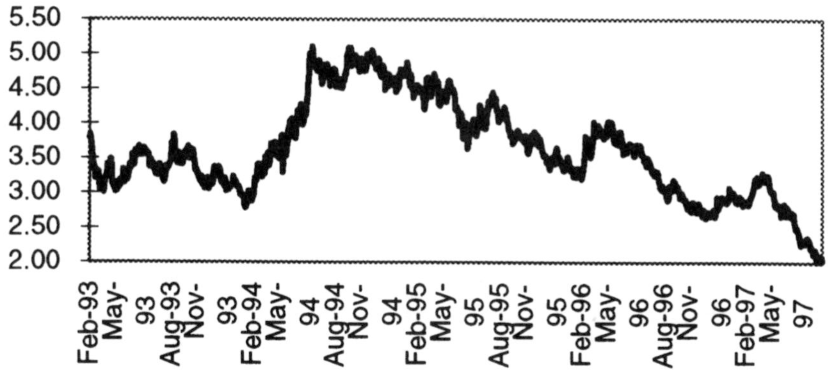

The Break-Even Inflation Differential

The simplest and most-often used (and misused) measure of relative value analysis between inflation-linked securities and fixed interest securities is known as the *break-even inflation (BEI) differential*. This is calculated as the difference between the nominal yield on a long-term fixed interest security such as the 10-year bond, and the real yield on a similar maturity inflation-linked security.

The long-term nominal return on an inflation-linked security is simply the grossed-up return of the long-term rate of inflation over the purchased real yield. This roughly equates to the real yield plus inflation. Hence the current real yield on an inflation-linked security plus a future inflation expectation should roughly equate to the expected return on nominal securities (all other things being equal).

Since the yield on a long-term nominal bond and the real yield on an inflation-linked security are observable factors, the difference between these two yields can serve as an indication of the current market's expectation of the long-term rate of inflation. This is the BEI differential and it is used to estimate the rate of inflation where a buyer is currently indifferent between nominal bonds and inflation-linked bonds (since the expected returns will be similar).

Exhibit 6 shows the BEI differential between the Commonwealth 2005 inflation-linked bond and the 10-year nominal bond for the last five years. Note how the BEI expanded in 1994, reflecting the increase in inflation expectations which accompanied the global bond selloff. The differential has been tightening significantly for most of the period since 1995. This reflects the market's improving inflation expectations over this period and the relative confidence with respect to the Reserve Bank of Australia's ability to maintain underlying inflation within its 2.00% to 3.00% inflation band.

A contraction in the BEI indicator reflects an improvement in inflation expectations, and reflects a rally in long-term nominal bond yields relative to inflation-linked bond yields. On a nominal duration neutral basis, this would represent an outperformance of fixed interest securities over inflation-linked securities. Conversely, a widening in inflation expectations (and the BEI) would reflect a rally in inflation-linked real yields relative to nominal bond yields and hence an outperformance by the inflation-linked asset class.

The capacity to predict successfully the future direction of inflation expectations via the BEI will assist in the choice between fixed interest and inflation-linked securities. However the BEI is an inaccurate and dangerous measure at times for the following reasons:

- The assumption is made that the two types of securities are the same in nature, and that an investor would be indifferent between the two. This is contradictory to the separate asset class argument and is in effect treating inflation-linked securities as if they were a subset of fixed interest.
- BEI is a strategic tool which reflects incongruities in future expected inflation in the long term. As with many indicators, it may stay away from fair value for a long time. "Trading" the BEI for short-term gain may therefore prove fruitless.
- Future inflation is never a constant but generally follows a cyclical path over time. This path is not taken into account in BEI analysis which attempts to approximate an average future inflation rate. The predicted inflation cycle may actually have an effect on the real average future inflation rate.
- It is only a rough estimate of the real "break-even." As noted above, it does not take account of the compounded effect of inflation on the nominal returns from inflation-linked securities.

Horizon Analysis

The above two methods of analysis are essentially long-term in nature, and suggest switches into and out of the asset class with a pay-off which will eventuate over time. However, as we know, long-term fundamentals can be ignored by markets for significant periods of time, and short-term factors can dominate. In particular in Australia, the desire by asset consultants and fund trustees to ensure that outperformance of benchmarks occurs on a quarterly, or even monthly basis, has created a very strong focus on performance of assets in the very short term.

A common practice amongst Australian inflation-linked fund managers in recent years has been to project likely returns on asset classes on a 3- or 6-month horizon. In this instance, in the case of inflation-linked securities, the next two quarters of inflation and the likely short-term movements in real yields are the most important determinants in developing an inflation-linked investment strategy. In this environment, long-term fundamental indicators such as BEI or real yield gaps tend to be ignored until they become too compelling to ignore.

Chapter 14

The Canadian Experience

Karim Basta
First Vice President
Merrill Lynch

Martin Klaponski
Director
Merrill Lynch

INTRODUCTION

Canadian Real-Return Bonds (RRBs) are identical in structure to their U.S. counterparts, inflation-linked bonds. Though the Canadian market is much older, it is smaller in size than the U.S. market. The Government of Canada has begun to regularly auction RRBs quarterly in an attempt to deepen the market and improve its liquidity.

The development of the RRB market in Canada is very much linked to the agreement implemented in early 1991 between the federal government and the Bank of Canada on inflation-control targets. That agreement calls for a 1%-3% target band for core inflation through the end of 1998, and for price stability (the definition for which has not yet been agreed upon) thereafter. The 1%-3% target band was extended through the year 2001 in the February 1998 federal budget.

The development of the RRB market assists the government and the Bank of Canada in successfully meeting those targets in two key aspects. The first is to underpin the credibility of the targets themselves, as the government's costs of both interest and principal are lowered by keeping inflation under control. The second benefit is to monitor the level of inflation expectations in the bond market.

In our discussion of the RRB market in Canada, we will review the size and structure of the market and its trading conventions, as well as its trading history since inception. Finally, by identifying the key forces that drive RRB prices, we will hopefully offer some insight into factors that may affect the index-linked program in the United States.

OVERVIEW OF STRUCTURE

Canada's first RRBs were issued on December 10, 1991. As of this writing, there are now two long-dated issues in the market. The coupon on both issues is 4.25%

payable semiannually. The first issue, maturing in December 2021, has C$5.2 billion outstanding. In 1995, the Bank of Canada surveyed the RRB investors and found that the most interest lay in an even longer maturity issue, so the second RRB, due in December 2026, was issued in December 1995. The 2026 issue has been reopened eight times and has C$4.05 billion outstanding. The Bank of Canada will likely continue to reopen this issue until it is C$5.0+ billion in size to provide for sufficient liquidity before introducing a new maturity.

The bonds provide investors with full inflation protection, compounded and reinvested until maturity, in addition to the fixed coupon of 4.25% per annum. Coupon interest payments are calculated by multiplying one-half of the 4.25% coupon by the original principal and inflation accrual

Investor Profile

The first seven RRB issues up until December 1994 were syndicated deals. Dealer syndicates consisting of 8-10 major Canadian dealers were formed and each dealer was allotted a percentage of bonds to sell. The percentage that each dealer was allotted ranged between 3%-15% and was based on the dealer's expertise in the product and trading volume. There were no exempt lists (a list of customers to which one syndicate member will have exclusive marketing rights) and the dealers were paid 0.50% commission.

Under the syndicated deal program the investor profile included 110 different buyers and approximately 75% of domestic clients had been involved with the product. The 10 largest holders held 50% of the outstanding stock. Of the top 10, seven were either public (government) or private pension funds. There were no foreign buyers that held more than C$30 million bonds.

Since the switch in 1995 from the syndicated commission deals to a Dutch auction process, the investor profile has changed. In November 1997 Merrill Lynch Canada Inc. (MLCI) surveyed the 70 largest domestic bond managers and found that there had been a consolidation, only 60% of domestic managers were either a current holder or had been recently active in RRBs. As well, MLCI estimates that 25%-35% of the existing stock is held by foreigners.

Many of the domestic managers hold the RRBs in an unsegregated bond portfolio. A small number have the ability to segregate the RRBs in a separate asset class. Some large funds have indicated that the conservative nature of the RRB product allows a higher risk profile to be taken in other markets and asset classes.

There is clearly a growing global willingness to issue more inflation linked bonds, as the U.S. Treasury has announced plans to issue a 30-year TIP and the French government is investigating issuing. As the inflation linked bond market grows and makes up a greater portion of G7 debt, there will be more comparison across borders and the universe of potential foreign investors in Canadian RRBs will grow.

Liquidity

The theory behind when-issued (WI) trading is for dealers to find the level at which investor demand can absorb issuer supply. Unfortunately, the small issue size (400-600 million) of the Dutch auctions, a history of auction results either well above or well below the pre-bid auction level and the inability of dealers to bid for more than 25% of the total issue size, regardless of client interest, has left dealers unwilling to trade the product or to develop pre-auction shorts, thereby not contributing to liquidity at a time when liquidity should be at its peak. The experience at MLCI is that the client participation may vary between 0 and 15 clients on the day of the auction. In September 1998, the Bank of Canada is expected to introduce a new bidding process for the 1998-1999 fiscal year making it easier to accommodate client interest and to increase liquidity.

RRBs account for 14% (C\$9.2 billion) of the total C\$65 billion Government of Canada debt greater than 10 years to maturity. As one would expect with a product that many view as a buy and hold instrument, the turnover ratio of RRBs is low when compared to nominal government debt. In the first nine months of 1997 the RRB turnover ratio was 1.5:1 compared to 8.8:1 for the 86% of non RRB long debt. With the relative lack of liquidity, the number of Canadian dealers willing to trade the product has shrunk, with 56% of the market share attributed to the top 3 dealers, as compared to a 33.8% market share by the top 3 dealers in non RRB debt.

REVIEW AND ANALYSIS OF RRB TRADING HISTORY

The trading of the RRBs got off to a rocky start in late 1991 and early 1992 due to the collapse of inflation in Canada (see Exhibits 1 and 2). The effects of recession, and the removal of the effects of the introduction of a 7% Goods and Services Tax from the year-on-year inflation calculation combined to bring Canadian inflation from over 6% in mid-1991 to just under 2% by early 1992. Moreover, as money market yields began to skyrocket in anticipation of the October 1992 referendum on constitutional reform, prices remained depressed until early 1993.

Prices began to rebound sharply in early 1993 as real investor demand for new issues emerged. Canadian RRBs appeared cheap to CPI-linked bonds in other markets (the U.K. and Australia), and real interest rates in Canada were declining across the entire yield curve (reaching a trough in January 1994).

The price collapse that took place in calendar year 1994 was due to two factors. One was the sharp rise in nominal interest rates across the entire maturity spectrum in Canada after the U.S. Federal Reserve first hiked rates in early February. The other was a renewed collapse in CPI inflation as a result of massive government cuts in tobacco taxes. Year-on-year inflation averaged 0.2% in 1994, and was at times negative (see Exhibit 3).

The market never truly recovered from the 1994 collapse until early 1996, as 1995 trading was confined to a fairly narrow range between the 4.5%-5.1% yield levels. Concerns over liquidity and the experiences of 1991-1992 and 1994 weighed on the market as did the fact that real yields on conventional bonds in Canada remained amongst the highest in the world.

Exhibit 1: Canadian Real-Return Bond Price
(Can. Gov't I/L 4.25%, 12/01/2021 to May 1996)
(Can. Gov't I/L 4.25%, 12/01/2026 after May 1996)

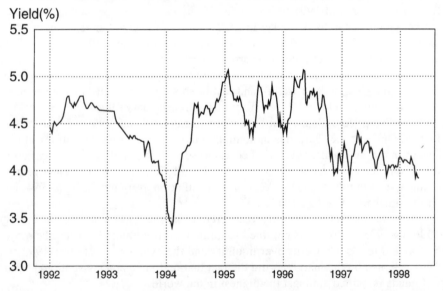

Exhibit 2: Canadian Real-Return Bond Yield
(Can. Gov't I/L 4.25%, 12/01/2021 to May 1996)
(Can. Gov't I/L 4.25%, 12/01/2026 after May 1996)

Exhibit 3: Canadian Consumer Price Inflation

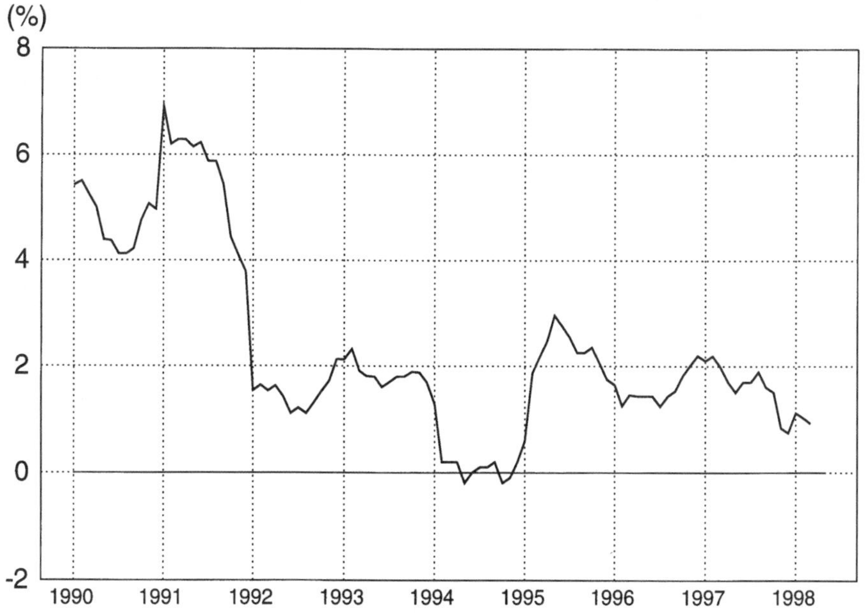

The index-linked sector in Canada posted its best performance since 1993 in 1997 even though the RRB traded at its narrowest spread to conventional 30-year bonds since the 1991 inception date (see Exhibit 4). Both domestic and external forces have been at play behind the sector's steady rise in 1997. Domestically, the sharp decline in short-term rates to their lowest level since the 1950s was of enormous importance. RRBs have had a good historical correlation to 3-month rates, and for the first time since their inception, dealers had been able to earn a steady positive cash flow carry on RRBs (see Exhibit 5). Second, real and nominal rates on conventional long-bonds have fallen to all-time lows as the risk premium on Canadian long-term rates has fallen rapidly in response to improving government finances and reduced political risk. RRBs have also had a good correlation to the nominal and real interest rate levels of conventional 30-year government bonds (see Exhibit 6).

Externally, the May 1997 announcement by the U.S. Treasury that it would initiate its own index-linked bond program provided an enormous catalyst for the market. Though Canada's fundamentals had already begun to improve, concerns over liquidity continued to hamper the market. The prospect of a liquid U.S. program with real yields generally considered to be in the 3.0%-3.25% area, and with the natural comparison of Canada-U.S spreads, the Canadian market was quickly perceived to be undervalued.

Exhibit 4: Canadian Inflation Expectations
(Yield Spread between Canadian 30-Year Conventional and Real-Return Bonds)

Exhibit 5: Yields of Canadian Real-Return Bonds versus Canadian 3-Month T-Bills

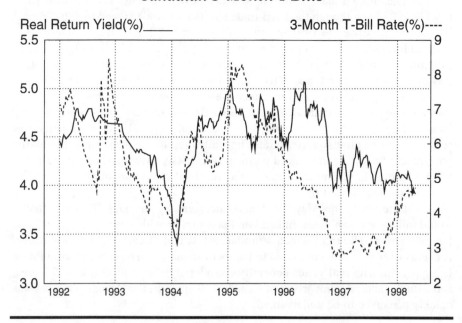

Exhibit 6: Yields of Canadian Real-Return Bonds versus Canadian 30-Year Nominal and Real Yields

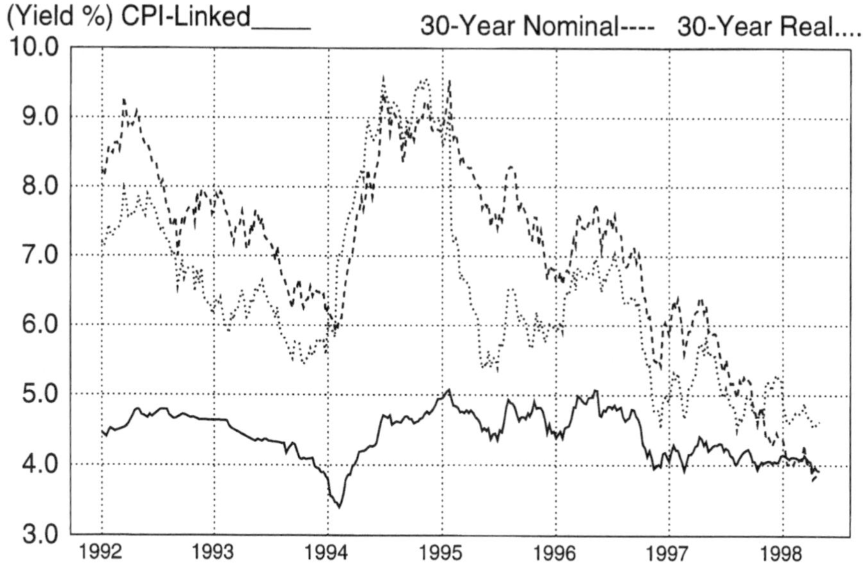

(Yield %) CPI-Linked_____   30-Year Nominal----   30-Year Real....

Historical Valuation of RRBs

How does a 4.25% annual real yield compare to historical real yields on stocks, bond, and Treasury bills? If one were to look at Canadian capital markets history from 1926-1990, 4.25% real yields would have outperformed Treasury bills and long bonds, but underperformed stocks. But a more appropriate gauge would be to compare a 4.25% real yield during different eras in this history of the capital markets. We thus break that history down into five periods (see Exhibit 7), borrowing a concept devised by Keith Ambachtsheer, author of *The Ambachtsheer Letter*. Those periods are 1928-1940 (Mostly Depression), 1941-1951 (War and Controls), 1952-1965 (Reconstruction and Prosperity), 1966-1981 (Inflation), and 1982-1990 (Return of the Invisible Hand). The period since 1990 has for the most part been characterized by exceptionally low inflation.

The 4.25% real return compares favorably to the returns in the other asset classes during most of these periods, especially those on bonds and T-bills. The notable exceptions were stocks during the high-growth 1941-1951, and 1952-65 periods, and bonds during the 1980s as yields adjusted slowly to the sharp decline in inflation.

On a historical basis, the current real yield guaranteed by Canadian RRBs would seem to warrant their inclusion in a diversified portfolio of financial assets. Their favorable historical comparison to returns on bonds and bills would certainly appear to favor their inclusion in an actively managed fixed-income portfolio.

Exhibit 7: Nominal and Real Returns of Canadian T-Bills, Long-Term Bonds, and the Toronto Stock Exchange

	1926-1990	1928-1940	1941-1951	1952-1965	1966-1981	1982-1990	1991	1992	1993	1994	1995	1996	1997
Real GDP Growth	4.1	1.2	5.0	5.0	4.5	2.9	-1.8	0.8	2.2	4.1	2.4	1.0	3.8
Inflation	3.4	-1.3	5.1	1.4	7.0	5.2	5.6	1.5	1.8	0.2	2.1	1.4	1.7
Nominal Returns													
T-Bill	4.6	1.7	0.5	2.9	7.8	11.0	8.7	6.4	4.8	5.6	7.0	4.7	3.3
Long-Term Bonds	5.2	5.5	2.5	2.9	3.7	15.3	24.0	11.9	21.9	-8.2	25.4	13.0	19.8
Stocks	10.3	-1.2	18.7	11.1	9.4	9.8	7.6	-5.3	27.9	-1.3	12.3	26.4	11.7
Real Returns													
T-Bill	1.2	4.9	-4.5	-0.5	-2.5	9.2	3.1	5.0	3.0	5.4	4.9	3.3	1.6
Long-Term Bonds	1.8	6.8	-2.6	1.5	-3.3	10.1	18.4	10.4	20.1	-8.4	23.3	11.6	18.1
Stocks	6.9	0.1	13.6	9.7	2.4	4.6	2.0	-6.8	26.1	-1.5	1.02	25.0	10.1

Source: 1926-1990: *The Ambachtsheer Letter*, February 5, 1992; 1991-97: Merrill Lynch

Assessment of Value

Since the inception of the RRB market in 1991 there have been a number of clients that have used a dollar spread over the 30-year benchmark bond (the Government of Canada 8% June 1 2023 has been the 30-year benchmark since 1993) as a valuation method. Aside from a brief period of outperformance in 1993, this has been a painful and dubious process to establish value. Inflation has remained low and the real yield on the long conventional bond has fallen from 9% to 5%. Over the years 1995 to 1997 the RRB moved from a dollar relationship where it was trading at a $15 premium to the 30-year benchmark conventional bond to as much as a $30 discount — a $35 underperformance in 2½ years (see Exhibit 8). Nonetheless, a number of domestic clients still follow this valuation method.

A comparison of total return of a variety of Government of Canada maturity bonds is found in Exhibit 9. Since 1995 the average annualized return of the RRB has been 10.1%, similar to that of a 5-year bond. However, the volatility of that total return has been greater than a 30-year bond.

The "cost of inflation protection" premium has been shrinking. (See Exhibit 10.) This has been a global phenomenon, Canadian, U.K., and U.S. inflation linked bonds have all seen their premium erode as inflation in each country has either fallen or due to a prevailing attitude that inflation will stay low or decrease. The RRB inflation premium peaked at close to 500 basis points in 1994 when rates on conventional bonds rose to 9% and inflation plunged to a negative year-on-year reading due to the aforementioned tobacco tax cut. RRBs peaked in yield during this period at 5.1%. Despite the 9% real yields available on long conventional bonds, domestic investors favored RRBs, thereby establishing a ceiling on real rates.

Exhibit 8: Price Spread of Canada 8% Bond Maturing 2023 Over Canada 4.25% Bond Maturing 2021

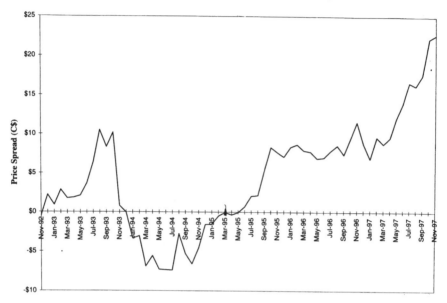

Exhibit 9: Annualized Total Return and Standard Deviation (%)

Time-Period	3 Mo	2 Yr	5 Yr	10 Yr	30 Yr	RRB
				Maturity		
3/95-6/95	8.3	14.5	24.8	26.8	29.4	24.8
6/95-9/95	6.8	7.4	9.2	12.1	13.6	-6.9
9/95-12/95	6.5	14.6	21.5	27.6	36.4	27.5
12/95-3/96	5.6	4.0	-0.9	-8.1	-7.2	-21.9
3/96-6/96	5.0	7.4	7.3	5.7	8.9	11.2
6/96-9/96	4.7	12.8	19.0	20.0	28.1	23.8
9/96-12/96	3.9	12.2	20.1	28.4	38.1	31.6
12/96-3/97	2.9	-2.5	-3.6	3.9	-6.9	-8.5
3/97-6/97	3.2	7.0	12.5	19.4	30.5	9.3
6/97-9/97	3.2	5.9	12.7	24.4	37.3	22.3
9/97-12/97	3.8	1.2	3.8	7.2	20.0	-2.4
Average	4.9	7.7	11.5	15.2	20.7	10.1
Std Dev	1.74	5.51	9.35	11.93	16.88	17.71

Exhibit 10: RRB "Cost of Inflation Protection" Inflation Adjusted Canada 8% Bond Maturing 2023* Minus Canada 4.25% Bond Maturing 2021

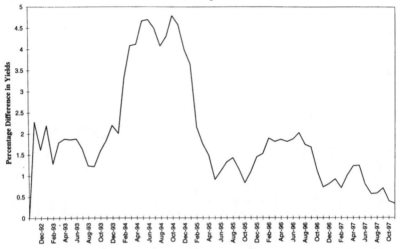

* Nominal yield on Canada 8% maturing 2023 minus CPI year-over-year

LOOKING AHEAD

It was little secret that Canada's real interest rates were the highest of any major country through 1995 in spite of the Bank of Canada's inflation-control objectives largely being met. Policymakers were thus receiving a clear message that markets perceived an inflationary threat from the size of public-sector deficits, political risk, and/or the decline in the Canadian dollar from since late-1991 to early 1995.

At this stage, with the positive outlook for Canada's economic fundamentals there should be good support for RRBs. The federal government has eliminated net new borrowing requirements as of the 1997-98 fiscal year (ending March 31), and seven of Canada's ten provinces have posted a budget surplus since 1985. Moreover, it is commonly perceived that major political risk is well behind the market for some time.

The result of this fundamental picture is that Canada's real and nominal interest rates are moving closer to the G-7 norm. Nominal short-term rates have been lower than those in the United States for over a year and real long-term rates (on conventionals) have been declining for most of the year but still remain more than 50 basis points above real yields in long Treasuries, a spread we see narrowing.

Spreads to comparable index-linked gilts have moved from historical lows (see Exhibit 11) to historical wides. The Canadian dollar's undervaluation against both the U.S. dollar and U.K. sterling on a purchasing power parity basis should make the Canadian sector a good long-term performer against either market (see

Exhibit 12). While total returns for the RRB have not been as good as long conventional bonds, the shrinking inflation premium, the inflation rate close to the low end of the Bank of Canada's 1-3% target band, and the growing international market in both issuers and investors bodes well for the future returns and liquidity of RRBs.

With lower government-financing finally "crowding-in" private investment (dollar corporate issuance shattered all records in 1997), the economy may be set to leave the low-growth years of the 1990s behind it. It remains to be seen whether or not inflation will remain dormant as well.

Exhibit 11: Canadian/U.K. Index-Linked Yield Spread

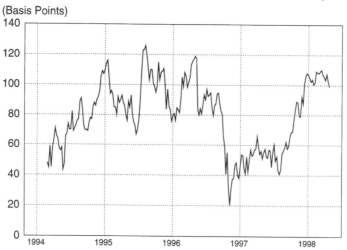

Exhibit 12: Purchasing Power Parity versus the U.S. Dollar

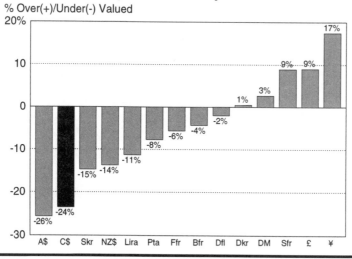

Chapter 15

The U.S. Experience

Roger L. Anderson
Deputy Assistant Secretary
(Federal Finance)
U.S. Department of the Treasury

INTRODUCTION

The introduction of inflation-indexed securities by the U.S. Treasury came after years of research on potential market acceptance. At various times since at least as far back as the 1940s, Treasury had considered issuing indexed securities. Prior to 1996, however, Treasury was unable to conclude that issuing indexed securities would lower its borrowing costs.

In 1993, Treasury began to reevaluate its debt issuance program thoroughly. One result was that Treasury decided to shorten the average maturity of its debt in order to reduce the amount paid to investors to compensate for the risk of unexpected changes in either the real rate of return or the rate of inflation. This compensation, known as the risk premium, is thought to be higher in longer-term securities, because such securities are subject to larger percentage fluctuations in price. Selling fewer long-term securities therefore reduces the amount of the risk premia paid.

The decision to issue indexed Treasuries was also an effort to reduce the risk premium — in this case to capture all of the inflation risk premium.

There were many arguments in favor of issuing indexed Treasuries, but the *sine qua non* was the expectation of reduced interest costs. Among the additional reasons mentioned by Secretary Rubin and Deputy Secretary Summers at the time the decision was announced were: (1) that indexed securities would provide investors, particularly less sophisticated investors, with an instrument that would protect their savings against the ravages of inflation, with the expectation that a more attractive savings instrument might facilitate an increase in the national savings rate; (2) that indexed Treasuries would impose self-discipline on the government, because the government's costs would increase with inflation; and (3) that a market for indexed securities could provide valuable information on inflationary expectations to monetary policy makers.

Given that the cost issue was critical, why was Treasury able to conclude in 1996 that issuing indexed securities could save it money, when it had never been able to reach that conclusion before?

One reason was simply the success that other countries that had issued indexed securities, the U.K., Canada, and Australia, for example, had had in reducing debt service costs. Secondly, Treasury concluded that changes in the financial marketplace improved the likelihood of investor acceptance of indexed securities. There were two such changes, one on the retail side and the other on the institutional side.

On the retail side, the growth of defined contribution pension plans, both absolutely and as a percentage of total pension plan assets, means that more and more individuals are responsible for the financial security of their retirements. These individuals do not have all the time or tools of institutional portfolio managers and do not have the luxury of diversifying risk over numerous beneficiaries. As a result, these plans tend to be invested more conservatively than are defined benefit plans. Treasury believes that indexed securities, by protecting the purchasing power of a retirement plan, could, over time, be attractive to such investors.

On the institutional side, portfolio diversification theory has become more widely used. The essence of the efficient frontier is choosing an appropriate balance in a portfolio between expected risk and expected reward. An investment is not judged solely by whether its expected return is greater or less than that of an alternative investment, but whether its overall effect on a portfolio, from a risk/ reward standpoint, is positive.

The reduction of risk has value, because it can allow a portfolio manager to invest more aggressively with another part of a portfolio. An indexed security can be viewed as being similar to insurance, in that it protects one against a risk, at a slight cost. Few people, for example, ever complain of losing money on life insurance, just because they live to pay another year's premiums.

Over the long term, Treasury expects to capture the inflation risk premium, in essence charging investors for Treasury's bearing the inflation risk, instead of paying investors to do so. Treasury further expects that capturing the inflation risk premium will save it money in the long run, because Treasury can bear the inflation risk more efficiently than can any investor. This is because (1) Treasury's revenues are correlated with inflation and (2) Treasury can spread the risk across a broader universe and over a much longer time period than can any investor. It has also been argued that the correlation of Treasury's revenues with inflation means that indexed Treasuries eliminate inflation risk entirely.

Treasury also expects to reduce its costs by broadening the market for Treasuries and appealing to investors with different goals and needs.

For all these benefits to occur, it is necessary to have an instrument that is broadly accepted by the market. At the time Treasury decided to issue indexed securities, few people in the United States had any experience with indexed securities or had thought much about how indexed securities should be designed to have the broadest market appeal. The structures that had been issued by the U.K., Canada, and Australia were obvious models, but Australia had issued at least three different structures, and the structures in each of the countries differ to some degree. Treasury received substantial assistance from officials in the U.K. and

Canada about how and why those countries had designed their indexed securities the way they had and what they had learned from their experiences.

Treasury also reached out to market participants, both dealers and investors, in a three-step process to ask them what kind of design would have the most appeal. The first step, in May 1996, was the publication of an *Advanced Notice of Proposed Rulemaking*, in which Treasury asked market participants for suggestions.[1] Treasury received more than 50 comment letters in response. The second step was the publication of a *Notice of Proposed Rulemaking*, in which Treasury announced the proposed details for its indexed securities and asked for comments.[2] Treasury received eight letters in response to this *Notice*. Finally, Treasury published the final structure for its indexed securities on January 6, 1997.[3] This process was extremely valuable to Treasury.

TERMS AND CONDITIONS

Treasury made many decisions in designing its indexed securities. First, it structured the securities so that the principal adjusts daily with inflation and a fixed rate of interest is paid semiannually on the adjusted principal. That means that payments of both principal and interest are adjusted for inflation. This structure is similar to that of U.K. and Canadian indexed securities and to one of the Australian structures. Most commentators recommended this structure as providing the purest form of inflation protection and as being the easiest for intermediaries to reengineer. Second, Treasury chose the Consumer Price Index for All Urban Consumers ("CPI-U") as the measure of inflation. Most commentators recommended the CPI-U because it is the broadest and best known index, it is published monthly, and it is not subject to retroactive revision. Third, Treasury decided to begin with a 10-year indexed note, believing it to have the broadest market appeal, and to fill out an indexed yield curve subsequently with issues of 5- and 30-year securities. Fourth, Treasury provided that, in the event of deflation, an indexed Treasury at maturity will never be worth less than its principal amount at issuance.

There are two other design aspects of indexed Treasuries that deserve additional discussion. The first is the tax treatment. For most taxable investors, the annual inflation adjustment to the principal of the securities is treated as ordinary interest income, taxable in the year of accrual, despite the fact that it is not paid until maturity. Some market participants expressed concern that the tax treatment could deter certain investors, particularly retail investors, from buying indexed securities.

The tax treatment was determined, however, by well established principles of tax law applicable to discount debt instruments. The tax treatment high-

---

[1] 61 Fed. Reg. 25164 (May 20, 1996).
[2] 61 Fed. Reg. 50923 (September 27, 1996).
[3] 62 Fed. Reg. 846 (January 6, 1997).

lights the fact that the Internal Revenue Code taxes inflation, but that basic feature of the Code could not be changed just for indexed securities.

On the other hand, the tax treatment also highlights the fact that the Code allows deductions for inflation. There is some indication that the tax treatment of indexed gilts in the U.K., where the inflation uplift is not taxed and, until recently, not deductible, has deterred issuance of indexed securities by taxable issuers. Allowing deductibility of the inflation adjustment in the U.S. should allow for the quicker development of a U.S. corporate inflation-indexed market. This view has been borne out by the more than $2 billion of indexed securities issued soon after the debut of indexed Treasuries.

The second design aspect worth discussing is what is referred to as "Index Contingencies." The terms of indexed securities in the U.K., Canada, and Australia all have some form of protection for the integrity of the index by which inflation is measured. Accordingly, the Treasury in September 1996 proposed some investor protection against possible discontinuance or substantial alteration of the CPI-U.

In December 1996, however, the Advisory Commission to Study the Consumer Price Index (the "Boskin Commission"), which had been appointed by the Senate Finance Committee, issued its report, which focussed market participants' attention on the possibility of the CPI being revised downwards. In response, in publishing the final details of indexed securities, Treasury clarified the protective language to provide:

> If, while an inflation-indexed security is outstanding, the applicable CPI is: (1) discontinued, (2) in the judgment of the Secretary, fundamentally altered in a manner materially adverse to the interests of an investor in the security, or (3) in the judgment of the Secretary, altered by legislation or Executive Order in a manner materially adverse to the interests of an investor in the security, Treasury, after consulting with the Bureau of Labor Statistics, or any successor agency, will substitute an appropriate alternative index.

Treasury explained that:

> A change to the CPI would be considered fundamental if it affected the character of the CPI. Technical changes made by the Bureau of Labor Statistics (BLS) to the CPI to improve its accuracy as a measure of the cost of living would not be considered fundamental changes. Technical changes include, but are not limited to, changes in: (1) The specific items (*e.g.*, apples or major appliances) to be priced for the index; (2) the way individual price quotations are aggregated to construct component price indices for these items (aggregation of item sub-strata); (3) the method for combining these component price indices to obtain

the comprehensive, all-items CPI (aggregation of item strata); and (4) the procedures for incorporating new goods into the index and making adjustments for quality changes to existing goods....

The ... Boskin Commission made a number or recommendations to improve the calculation of changes in the cost of living. Some of these recommendations were directed to BLS and were designed to improve the calculation of the monthly CPI. These recommendations, if and to the extent implemented by BLS, would constitute technical changes rather than fundamental changes.[4]

Ever since the CPI was introduced in 1917, BLS has been trying to improve the way it collects and calculates data. Treasury does not want to interfere with or impede those efforts, so it has provided that any technical, professional changes to the CPI will be incorporated into the calculation of the return on indexed Treasuries. Such changes are, in effect, the market's risk. The risk of political changes, however, should not be the market's risk, but should be, and is, borne by the government.

INVESTOR EDUCATION

After deciding the terms and conditions, Treasury faced a major marketing challenge, because it was in an unusual situation. Typically, new financial products are underwritten in negotiated transactions, and the underwriter's sales and marketing staffs contact investors, organize road shows, and assume the marketing responsibilities. The underwriter puts in the effort, because it knows it will get compensated by selling the securities. Treasury, however, does not use negotiated underwritings. Accordingly, not all dealers have put significant research or marketing effort into indexed securities. Treasury had to do much of its own marketing, going around the country speaking to different groups of investors to educate them about the new securities.

EXPERIENCE

Through July 1998, Treasury has conducted seven auctions of indexed securities, in which it has sold $55 billion of 5-, 10-, and 30-year indexed securities to the public, and more than $2.5 billion to the System Open Market Account of the Federal Reserve. The auctions have all attracted substantial interest, with bid-to-cover ratios in each of the auctions exceeding average cover ratios for auctions of fixed rate notes of comparable maturities.

---

[4] *Id.* at 849.

Exhibit 1: Distribution of Competitive Auction Awards of Treasury Notes

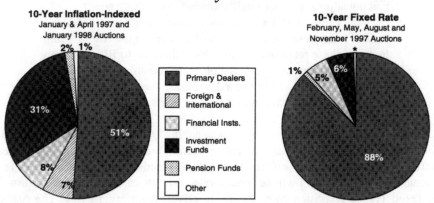

Note: Investment funds include investment managers, mutual funds, and hedge funds. Financial insts. include nonprimary dealers, depository insts., insurance cos., and financial cos. Other includes individuals and nonfinancial cos.

* Less than 0.5%

Source: Department of the Treasury, Office of Market Finance.

Trading volume in the securities though, as measured by GOVPX, has been slight. Most dealers report, however, that most of the indexed securities volume goes through Cantor, Fitzgerald, which is not picked up by GOVPX. The majority of the activity that has been reported has occurred during the when-issued periods just before and after the auctions.

Most portfolio strategists have concluded that indexed securities are a separate asset class from fixed rate Treasuries. The auction results and the trading history show that, in addition, the market for indexed Treasuries is different from the conventional Treasury market. Through the first seven auctions, customer bids have accounted for a much higher proportion of successful bids than is the average in fixed rate auctions. For example, Exhibit 1 shows that, in the three auctions of 10-year indexed notes, primary dealers took only 51% of the securities awarded, as opposed to 88% in the four fixed rate 10-year note auctions conducted in 1997. In the two 5-year indexed note auctions, primary dealers took only 57% of the securities awarded, compared to 68% in the 12 auctions of 5-year fixed rate notes from September 1996 through August 1997. In the April auction of 30-year indexed bonds, primary dealers received only 43% of the bonds awarded compared to 70% of the bonds awarded in the 20 auctions of fixed rate bonds conducted from May 1991 through November 1997. In contrast, the participation by banks, pension funds, investment funds, and private international investors in the indexed auctions has been much greater than in the fixed rate auctions.

This information leads to four tentative conclusions. First, much of the interest in indexed securities seems to be customer-driven, rather than dealer-driven. Second, the increase in customer bids means that Treasury has, in some degree, succeeded in broadening the market for Treasury securities generally. Third, some dealers have found the customer interest and are submitting the customer bids. Other firms have not found the business. Fourth, for dealers, the market for indexed Treasuries may be more sales staff-driven than trader-driven.

In 1997, indexed Treasuries underperformed fixed rate Treasuries, largely because inflation for the period has been substantially below expectations. While there is not yet enough data to draw firm conclusions, the comparison of prices in Exhibit 2 over the period shows no correlation between fixed rate and indexed Treasuries and shows that prices of fixed rate Treasuries have been three to four times as volatile as prices of indexed Treasuries. The lack of correlation and the reduced risk are exactly what the theories forecast, but they are also the reasons that traders have found it hard to work with indexed Treasuries. These securities, however, are different from what government bond traders are used to. Some have adjusted; some have not.

The data support the conclusion that indexed securities are a separate asset class, useful for portfolio diversification. Treasury is not trying to sell indexed securities as an alternative to fixed rate securities, but as an alternative to other forms of inflation protection. For example, since their introduction, indexed Treasuries have substantially outperformed gold. While, again, the data are limited, Exhibit 3 also shows that, over the period, prices of indexed Treasuries have been only 4% as volatile as gold prices.

Since the Treasury first auctioned indexed securities, there have been more than 20 issues of indexed securities by other issuers, including agencies, corporations, and municipal entities, totaling more than $2 billion. Most of that issuance occurred in the first few months after the first Treasury issuance. In addition, most of that issuance had a different structure than do indexed Treasuries, in that most pay the inflation adjustment currently, rather than at maturity. Reportedly, that structure was required by investors who did not want their nominal credit exposure to a nonsovereign issuer to accrete automatically.

Most, if not all, of the follow-on issuers have swapped out of their inflation liabilities. That means that a derivatives market in indexed products has begun to develop, because those issuers were able to swap out of the inflation risk and because the swaps dealers were able to reengineer the Treasury indexed securities into a current pay structure.

LIQUIDITY

As mentioned, trading volume in indexed Treasuries is less than in fixed rate Treasuries. While indexed securities have had substantial appeal directly to investors, liquidity is still important, because even investors who plan to hold securities need to know they can sell them if they need to.

Exhibit 2: Comparison of Prices for IINs and Fixed-Rate Notes
Prices for 10-Year 3⅜% IIN and 10-Year 6¼% Fixed-Rate Note*
Daily Data: Beginning 2/18/97

* Real Price for inflation-indexed note. Correlation: 29% STD IIN/STD Nominal = 0.32.

Prices for 5-Year 3⅝% IIN and 5-Year 6¼% Fixed-Rate Note*
Daily Data: Beginning 7/10/97

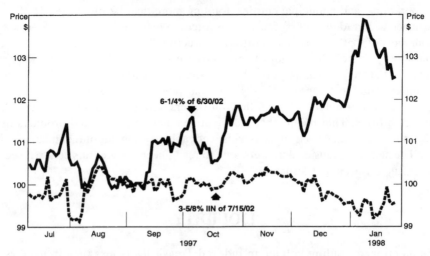

* Real Price for inflation-indexed note. Correlation: -9% STD IIN/STD Nominal = 0.26.
Source: Department of the Treasury, Office of Market Finance.

Exhibit 3: Prices for 10-Year 3⅜% IIN versus Spot Gold
Daily Data: Beginning 2/6/97

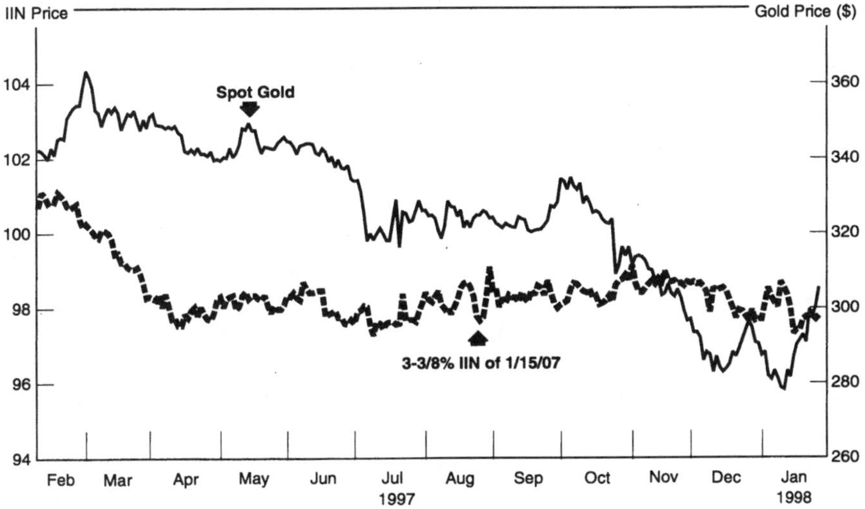

Real price for inflation-indexed note. Correlation: 34% STD IIN/STD Gold = 0.04
Source: Department of the Treasury, Office of Market Finance.

When Treasury began to design its indexed securities, the poor liquidity in other countries that had issued indexed securities was a cause for concern. Treasury accordingly put substantial effort into trying to ensure adequate liquidity, including trying to design an instrument that would appeal to the broadest range of investors, educating as many investors as possible about indexed securities, talking to the futures exchanges about derivatives contracts, and selling issues that were large enough for liquidity.

After 18 months, indexed Treasuries are not as liquid as fixed rate Treasury securities are, but Treasury never expected them to be that liquid. To some extent, indexed Treasuries are disadvantaged by being compared to fixed rate Treasuries, which have the largest, most developed, most liquid and most efficient market in the world. The indexed market is still in early stages of development, and, viewed from that perspective, liquidity is satisfactory. Liquidity in indexed Treasuries is also better than the liquidity in indexed securities issued by other countries.

Further, both trading volume and bid-asked spreads appear to be comparable to those of the most recent off-the-run fixed rate Treasuries. That seems appropriate, because indexed securities and off-the-run Treasuries are more investment vehicles, while on-the-run fixed rate Treasuries are more financing vehicles.

For Treasury, the most telling number is not trading volume, but the bid-asked spread, because that is basically the market's indication of confidence in being able to buy or sell when there is a need. And that spread has been lower than in other countries.

The U.S. market has several advantages that help liquidity. First, there are more participants in the market. Second, there is a better developed infrastructure, meaning a better developed repurchase agreement market, a better developed STRIPS market, and a better developed government derivatives market. Third, the Chicago Board of Trade has listed futures contracts on indexed Treasuries that should, over time, help liquidity. As the indexed market continues to develop, liquidity should continue to improve.

FUTURE DEVELOPMENTS

The Treasury has always viewed the development of the indexed market as a long-term project, and Treasury has made a long-term commitment to its continuing development. Treasury has expanded the yield curve by issuing 30-year indexed bonds. Treasury has committed to making indexed securities a substantial portion of its debt portfolio. It has not yet established a target, but hopes to do so by the end of 1998. The relevant calculation is probably not the percentage of Treasury's total debt represented by indexed securities, but the percentage of annual coupon issuance. In 1997, indexed Treasuries represented about 6% of new coupon issuance. Treasury has also said that, by the end of 1998, it will establish a regular schedule for issuing indexed securities of different maturities.

Inflation-indexed Treasuries have been eligible for the Treasury STRIPS program since their first issuance, but the interest components of stripped indexed Treasuries that have the same payment dates are not yet fungible for reconstitution purposes. Treasury published a proposal to permit fungibility of indexed interest STRIPS,[5] and, after receiving one comment, adopted the proposed rule. The change involves breaking the $1,000 minimum denomination for interest STRIPS and calculating stripped components down to the penny. To accommodate concerns about the time required to adjust some dealers' systems to handle pennies, the rule change will not become effective until March 31, 1999.

Treasury is looking for even bigger developments to come from the market. Some mutual funds specializing in indexed securities have already started. As the retail sector gets more interested in indexed securities, especially through retirement plans, this area can be expected to grow. Other anticipated retail products include indexed annuities and indexed insurance policies. The derivatives market will be crucial to these developments. Over time, as more opportunities develop to trade among different indexed instruments, the CBOT futures contracts on indexed Treasuries should also become more active.

As liquidity improves, there should be more arbitrage among indexed securities of different countries. To the extent currency exchange rates reflect different inflation outlooks between countries, indexed securities have a partial currency hedge built into them, and the market has not yet learned enough about the relationship between exchange rates and prices on indexed securities.

---

[5] 62 Fed. Reg. 64528 (December 8, 1997).

The development of the indexed securities market is a long-term process, and nobody can foresee clearly all that will result. Treasury is satisfied with the development of the indexed market to date and continues to be committed to the full scale development of the market. Given that indexed securities have under-performed fixed rate securities since January 1997, as both inflation and inflation expectations have fallen, Treasury considers the acceptance that indexed securities have had to date in such an environment to be encouraging.

Chapter 16

The French Experience

Ciaran O'Hagan
Vice President
CIC

INTRODUCTION

France looks set to enter a new page in its financial history by issuing an inflation indexed bond in 1998. Indeed, France is no stranger to indexation: bonds have been indexed on gold over the past 50 years, with ultimately painful consequences for the State coffers. However, lessons have been learnt. In the past 15 years, France has substantially reformed its debt, aiming to become the most investor friendly bond market in Europe with large, liquid issues, and simple and transparent debt issuance procedures.

The new inflation indexed bond(s) are all the more significant as this will be the first issuance of such a structure in the euro zone. They are likely to become a benchmark, like other French government bonds, and set should the standard for other sovereign, banking or corporate issuers in the euro zone.

HISTORY — LESSONS TO LEARN

Here's a summary of the lessons learned by the French government since 1952.

1952

A government had just fallen because of its proposals to hike taxes and France was reeling after another explosive devaluation. Pinay, a businessman, was elected to head a new government — a motley coalition of interests on a mainly pro-business Liberal economic program. Pinay — President and finance minister rolled into one — had the stroke of genius to pull in finance by calling a tax amnesty, and providing a tax free savings vehicle where taxpayers could lodge their funds. The Pinay bond was born.

Pinay was clear why he did it.

> The State has to prove it is an honest borrower who will guarantee lenders that their loan will keep its value. That is why I decided that this bond should be indexed on gold. And why pay a coupon of 3.5% while yields were 7% or 8% at the time? I said

229

to the experts: let us keep things simple; you are going to issue a loan at 7% and then apply an income tax; that means you will take away around half. Let's be simple: let's give a smaller coupon and take nothing afterwards. Psychologically, that is important and it avoids the cost of controls.[1]

The Pinay bond was initially a 60-year callable issue indexed on the price of a gold coin on the Paris Bourse, in addition to paying a nominal coupon of 3.5%. Capital was guaranteed and indexed on gold (but not the coupon payments), and this indexation kicked in above a price of FRF40 (FRF30 at the time of issuance). The French Trésor reserved a call, but this was on different tranches worked by lottery, "tirage," until 2012. It was a complicated call that was to prove most costly 15 years later.

The advertising slogan of the Pinay bond was "Gold that pays interest." The bond met Pinay's optimism (he had hired a leading advertising executive of the time just to make sure). The initial issue size was FRF 428 billion, large at the time. Moreover, it hauled in 34 tons of gold — real gold that was hidden in the mattresses, a prime objective as well. In the two years afterwards, however, the loan was to prove a disappointment. The price of gold was falling (see Exhibit 1) with the Consumer Price Index even turning negative. Meanwhile, the government went so far as to admonish companies at the time for not seeking enough capital through indexed bonds.

Exhibit 1: Gold Price and CPI, 1948-1973

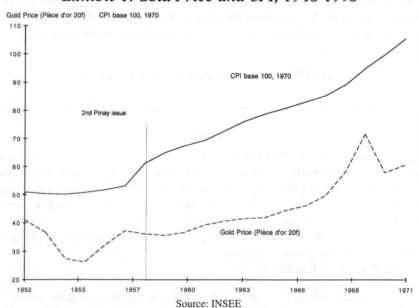

Source: INSEE

---

[1] Translated from Sylvie Guillaume, *Antoine Pinay ou la Confiance en Politique* (Fondation National de Sciences Politiques, 1984), p. 78.

1958

The U.S. economy had gone into recession, the Algerian crisis was unfolding while the French economy was going through another inflationary crisis. The franc was in free fall but exchange controls were trying to mask it. De Gaulle was elected as head of a crisis government and called Pinay back as finance minister. Pinay's policy response at the time was to cut inflation by indexing or regulating prices. And it worked. For example, the wholesale price index essentially was stable for the six months following the election. On June 17, 1958, just days after the election, the Pinay bond was re-launched. Similar tax advantages were granted — a tax amnesty on foreign cash holdings in addition to lifting inheritance and income taxes (with conditions). This issue found more popular support — even if its size was slightly smaller than the 1952 issue. For example, compared to the Pinay bond six years earlier, this reissue obtained a much higher proportion of subscriptions coming from investor cash or dormant gold holdings (another 34 tons unearthed), rather than from the transfer of previous fixed rate bond holdings.

As disinflation progressed, the disapproval of public servants increased, leading to the forbidding of new indexed loans on prices or wages (there were several costly loans issued by public and private companies). An ordinance was published prohibiting "mechanisms of indexation based only on goods or services prices, having no direct relation to economic activity" (ordinance February 4, 1959).

From 1958 to 1963, the lack of new indexed issues contributed to pushing up the prices of indexed issues, some 50% beyond the cost of living (itself up 23% over this period). Gold never really outperformed CPI in the following years, until the 1970s when the yield of the Pinay bond fell close to zero (fixed rate bonds were generally paying around 7% in the 1960s while the Pinay yielded around 2%). See Exhibit 2. What had really made the Pinay issue so attractive — and dear — was that interest payments and redemption were net of income taxes, and, in particular, inheritance tax. This progressively captured the imagination of taxpayers, as they sought a means of divesting their wealth to their families. The effect on public finances was to be dramatic in terms of the opportunity cost of lost revenue. This was perhaps the major legacy of the Pinay bond, in diverting wealth away from the French State. And this led to the effective death of the Pinay bond in 1973, although its successor was to prove a much greater burden on public finances.

1973

The *Giscard bond* was launched in 1973. It was designed to attract investors away from the Pinay bond, killing the exoneration on inheritance tax. This was proving to be a very heavy burden on public finances at the time. Gold indexation was no longer in favor, but was kept as the only means to entice a large enough number of investors out of the Pinay bond. The Giscard bond paid a 7% coupon, not enough to attract investors at the time without indexing the coupon as well as principal on gold (the Lingot). The initial outstanding of the Giscard bond was FRF 6.5 billion ($1.5 billion).

Exhibit 2: Pinay Bond — Yield History

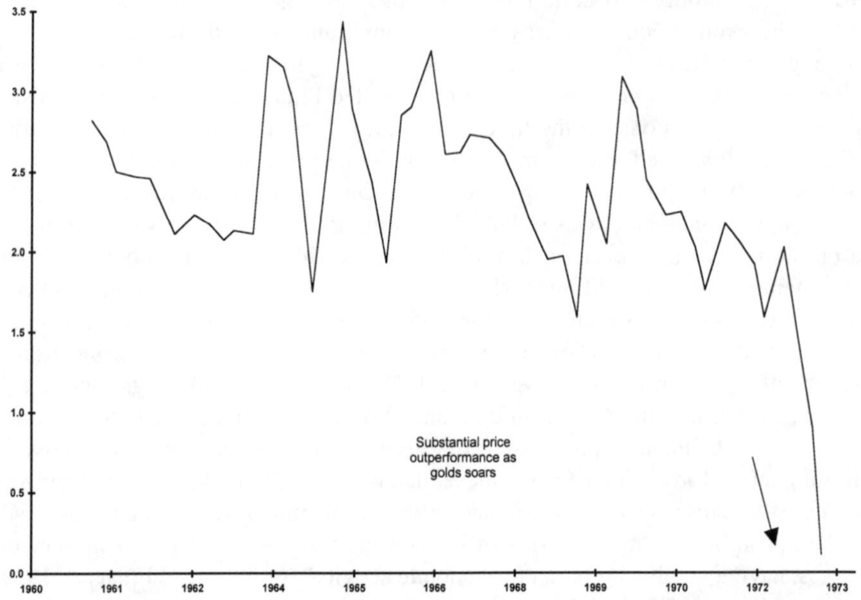

Substantial price
outperformance as
golds soars

However, in the aftermath of the Jamaica accord in 1976, the stage was set for an explosion in the price of gold in the late 1970s (see Exhibit 3). Coupon payments were almost multiplied by three. In 1987/1988, the Trésor redeemed the Giscard bond for close to 10 times the initial issuance amount (while prices had risen just over 2.5 times). In 1987, the government of the time was embarked on a program of privatization, allowing the cost of the Giscard bond to be swallowed without too much obvious pain. But the French State had paid dearly. It had indexed on a price it had no control over, a resource that was extraneous to French economic performance. This was the painful lesson learned, and in this context, it is difficult to see France issuing indexed bonds again based on the inflation rates of other economies.

1987

The current OAT primary dealer system was established (Obligations Assimilables de Trésor). This set a clear break with previous practices. Simplicity, transparency, efficiency, liquidity, and internationalization have become key. The French Treasury in the past 15 years has considerably streamlined its issuance, creating the large and liquid market of French Treasuries, OATs. Since then, France has been innovative in terms of creating repos, strips, and floaters (known as OAT TEC, similar to U.S. Treasury CMTs). This innovation has set the pace for Europe as a whole. It is all the more strategic now, coming before the foundation of the new European currency, the euro, in January 1999.

Exhibit 3: Gold Price (Lingot) and CPI, Base 100 = 1970

Source: INSEE

The two key mistakes of the 1950s-1970s were distortive taxes and indexation on a variable that could bear little relation to French tax revenues. We are very unlikely to see a repetition of such errors in today's increasingly competitive and global markets. Certainly, there remain parallels between today and the history of the Pinay bond. Today, French life insurance investments still provide a means of substantially avoiding inheritance taxes, while they also benefit from lower tax rates than most other savings vehicles. Variable-rate bonds — such as the new indexed bond — benefit from favorable treatment as there are fewer regulatory constraints on buying and selling them, and so this is a factor that could contribute to their dearness in the euro zone.

TODAY

There will be new issuance of indexed bonds by the French Treasury in 1998, as well as public agencies and corporates. The French Treasury appears to be motivated by two main factors. The first motivation is to enhance the reputation of French bonds as the benchmark reference for European bond issuance. The second motivation is to diversify away from fixed rate issuance and reduce the cost of servicing.

Simplicity and transparency have been key in establishing the reputation of OATs. These principles are also likely to inspire the new inflation indexed OATs, which will have characteristics similar to the U.S. TIPS.

What is less obvious — especially with the dissolution of the French franc within the euro — is the choice of the underlying index. The control of inflation will be the responsibility of the European Central Bank in Frankfurt from 1999. French GDP will not amount to even a quarter of GDP within the euro zone (and will likely diminish in time as other countries join the euro).

The French Treasury is indexing the new indexed bonds on French CPI (less tobacco taxes). Some thought was given to this choice. There are now European inflation indexes published by Eurostat, the statistics body of the European Commission (the public service of the European Union). These cover all 11 States of the European Union that will be in the first wave of European Monetary Union in 1999. What is foreseeable is that the definition of the index for OATs may evolve to a more general index (many years further on, but even that does not appear likely). An evolution in the index will always be theoretically possible as the French Treasury no longer publishes a prospectus for its bonds (unlike in the case of the Giscard bond, whose prospectus was followed to the letter).

In practice, however, the French Treasury would appear to have little choice other than using one of the existing French inflation indexes. This would also appear to be in the interests of the French Treasury, as its revenues will track a domestic index better.

In the longer term, the nature of investor demand will be important too in determining the underlying index. It is always likely that a French investor with French liabilities would prefer French CPI. However, international investors may prefer the lower volatility of a more diversified euro-wide index. One good reason why the volatility would be lower is that tax changes would typically be smoothed out. However, a hike or cut in the French value added tax would impact directly the index. The management of a wider index by an independent institution such as the future European Central Bank would reduce the impact of local administrative once-off decisions.

WHAT WILL THE MARKET LOOK LIKE?

The best clue as to what the market for inflation indexed bonds is going to look like comes from OAT TEC floaters (Constant Maturity bonds). OAT TECs were issued in April 1996 for the first time. Inflation indexed bonds may well repeat the same patterns.

Dear Bonds

The TEC bonds were issued close to fair value in 1996 but gradually became more expensive afterwards. The TECs continue to maintain a substantial premium to fair value despite investors expectations alternating between periods of curve flattening and steepening in Europe since 1996. Investors in the two years since then have clearly been looking to add floating rate instruments to their over-whelmingly fixed rate bond portfolios. This is especially true if their liabilities are not fixed rate, or if accounting regulations encourage them to buy floating-rate bonds. Typically, this is the case of one of the largest group of investors in Europe, French life insurers (who have been investing almost euro100 billion new cash alone in each of the past few years). Their flexibility is very limited in taking profits on fixed rate bonds, whereas the same restrictions do note apply to variable rate bonds (and inflation indexed ones should fall into this category). Inflation indexed bonds should interest them not just for the diversification of risk, but also to enhance the liquidity of their portfolios.

New Indexes

The TECs are currently indexed off OATs, and nothing suggests this is likely to change. However, the TEC family of indexes is managed by the CNO (Comité de Normalisation Obligataire, an agency founded by an association of French banks). And it might be possible to envisage TEC style issuance — whether OAT or another issuer — indexed on bonds of other sovereigns in the euro zone.

New Markets

A number of banking and corporate names have issued TEC-type bonds as a spread over OAT TEC. The TEC bonds gave rise to new derivatives markets — swaps as well as investor structures. Inflation indexed OATs should give rise to similar markets.

One of the biggest issuers of inflation indexed bonds could be the CADES. This is a closed end French Social Security fund managed directly by the French Treasury,[2] and is one of the largest and most prestigious public agencies in Europe. Its receipts are indexed on French income tax revenues, and indexation would appear to be an excellent hedge for its liabilities.

The Macroeconomic Heritage

Fixed rate bond yields as well as inflation are close to their 50 year lows (see Exhibit 4).

Several factors suggest inflation in the euro zone will indeed remain low:

- High public budget deficits, just below the Maastricht ceiling (the level specified in the treaty agreeing to the European Monetary Union), suggest-ing the risk of fiscal induced inflation is small.

---

[2] See www.cades.fr.

Exhibit 4: French CPI and Long Bond Yield (%)

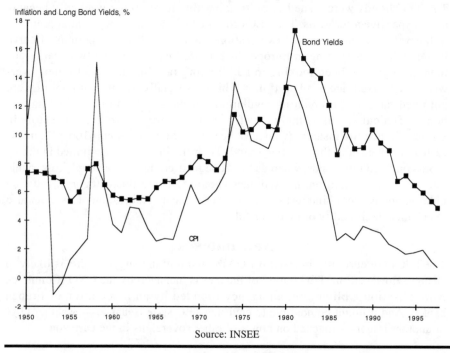

Source: INSEE

- High taxes on goods and services, approaching 20%, with the longer term risk being that competitive pressures between States lead to cuts.
- Structural rigidities (labor immobility, non-competitive markets, etc.) contributing to low growth.
- A capital account surplus, resulting in a high savings ratio and ample funds for investment.
- A legacy of hard nosed European central bankers, particularly from Frankfurt, whose prime occupation is combating inflation.

These factors are likely to be priced into inflation indexed OATs from the inception of trading. Yields are likely to be the lowest of any world market. Paradoxically, this just might suggest that inflation indexed OATs might give the most leverage if ever there is a world-wide correction in inflationary expectations.

Section IV:

Issuers

Chapter 17

Arguments for Issuing Linkers

William T. Lloyd
Head of Market Strategy & Credit Research
Barclays Capital

INTRODUCTION

At a time of relatively low inflation, some investors are questioning why they should buy inflation protected bonds, and simultaneously some potential issuers are asking why they should issue inflation-linked bonds ("linkers") when it seems that inflation can only increase. More than 20 countries currently have inflation-linked securities outstanding, and that number is expected to grow. The reasons for issuing inflation-linked bonds are compelling, and as the market develops a better understanding of this relatively new asset class interest in inflation-linked securities will flourish. This chapter presents the benefits of issuing inflation-linked bonds and also discusses the issues that need to be resolved prior to a government's issuance of the securities.

MOTIVATION FOR ISSUING INFLATION-LINKED BONDS

There are a number of reasons why countries should issue securities linked to the rate of inflation. The rationale most frequently cited for issuing inflation-linked bonds is that it will enable the country's treasury to reduce its overall cost of funds. The factors that lead to the reduction in the overall cost of funds are (1) expanding the traditional investor base; (2) saving the risk premium that would otherwise be paid to buyers of fixed-rate securities; and, (3) rewarding the government for prudent policy management. Additionally, by issuing inflation-linked securities the government is providing individuals and other risk averse investors with a low-risk instrument that provides a rate of return above the inflation rate — a real return. The establishment of an inflation-linked bond market can also result in the development of new financial markets. And, finally, there are some additional benefits to countries participating in EMU.

Expanding the Traditional Investor Base
As we all know, if the supply of a product is unchanged and the demand increases then the price should increase. Applying this lesson to the bond market, the

The author would like to thank Mark Capleton and Henry Willmore for their invaluable contributions.

increase in the price means a reduction in the yield, and thus a reduction in the issuer's cost of funds. This is precisely why expanding the investor base for treasury debt can help to reduce the overall funding cost.

A large percentage of the investing public is risk averse, and therefore is unlikely to purchase long maturity bonds having significant market exposure. Inflation-linked bonds offer long maturity funding for the issuer without the associated interest rate risk for the investor. For hedging purposes many bond dealers and investors have attempted to label inflation-linked bonds with a duration, but they have been unsuccessful. Inflation-linked bonds truly represent a new asset class, and as more investors become comfortable with this notion the demand for the product will grow.

One concern of many individual investors is that they will earn a return below the inflation rate — in real terms their savings will be worth less in the future than it is today. This brings us to another benefit of issuing inflation-linked securities: providing the individual investor with a low risk means of earning a return above the inflation rate. Investors who hold the inflation-linked bonds to maturity will earn a return greater than the inflation rate. Therefore, while expanding the market the government is also providing investors with an attractive asset.

The introduction of inflation-linked securities also provides investors with an opportunity to take a view on the rate of inflation while earning a positive real return. Prior to the introduction of linkers, investors who expected an increase in the inflation rate would purchase floating-rate securities, which may produce a return below the rate of inflation. Linkers are particularly attractive when short-term interest rates are low relative to the inflation rate.

The Risk Premium

Another potential source of savings for governments issuing inflation-linked securities is the capture of the risk premium. This concept is more fully developed in Chapter 11, but it is an important reason why governments issue inflation-linked bonds, and therefore it is important we mention the topic here. The easiest way to understand the value of the risk premium is to examine the components of yield for a fixed-rate security. In general, the reason for purchasing a fixed-rate security is to earn a return above the expected inflation rate for a given period of time. Therefore yield has three components: (1) the expected inflation rate; (2) the real yield; and (3) the risk premium.

Since the future inflation rate is unknown, investors demand to be paid an uncertainty premium for holding nominal bonds. Therefore the issuer must compensate the investor for this risk. An increase in the yield would reduce the value of the security. Therefore the issuer must pay the investor a risk premium to compensate for this risk. By issuing linkers, governments hope to avoid paying this risk premium.

One of the benefits of inflation-linked securities is that investors should no longer require a risk premium. Were the inflation rate to increase then the security's cash flows would also increase and thus eliminate the need for the risk premium. Therefore the issuer of the inflation-linked security should be able to keep the risk premium that would otherwise be required by the investor.

Rewarding Good Government

Inflation-linked bonds provide a government with a particularly strong incentive to keep inflation rates low. The government issuing inflation-linked securities is in effect taking a view on its ability to influence the inflation rate — if the government is able to reduce the level of inflation then its cost of funding would also decrease. Governments with nominal debt always face a temptation to escape the real burden of their obligations with inflation. Though difficult to identify empirically, there is a sense of "open positive feedback" in issuing linkers: by improving the perception of an anti-inflation commitment, inflationary expectations are reduced. In the United States, the low rate of implied inflation can be seen as a vote of confidence for Fed Chairman Greenspan and the current administration.

Developing New Financial Markets

Another benefit of issuing inflation-linked bonds is the development of new financial markets. Since the first issuance of inflation-linked bonds in the United States, a number of new products have come to market. There have been agency, corporate, and municipal issuance of linkers. Some insurance companies are now offering insurance products that are tied to the rate of inflation, and a derivatives market has also evolved as a result of the Treasury's issuance of notes indexed to the inflation rate. As the real yield curve continues to develop there should be an increase in the number of inflation-linked products that come to market.

Pension Funds

The concept of a pension is ultimately about providing an individual a desired standard of living in retirement. Therefore it is critical to provide a return above the rate of inflation. Inflation indexed bonds are the lowest risk route to meeting that objective. In the U.K., approximately 50% of pension fund weightings of sterling denominated bonds are held in linkers. In the United States, very few liabilities (outside of the Social Security System and public sector pensions) are explicitly linked to the CPI. Nonetheless a number of pension funds have invested in inflation-linked securities and it is expected that this market will grow over time.

European Monetary Union

The 11 countries that are participating in the first round of the European Monetary Union have an additional reason to issue inflation-linked securities: differentiation. With the advent of EMU and a single currency, the Euro, it will be more challenging to attract investors to a specific country's bonds. A bond whose return is linked to the inflation rate of a specific country will provide a means for investors to take a view on that country's economy. This point is in line with that made earlier about expanding the traditional investor market, but it is specific to EMU participants. Furthermore, this would provide investors with the opportunity to take a view on the inflationary impact of EMU.

As of this writing, none of the 11 governments that are expected to be in the first round of EMU have issued inflation-linked securities. It is widely expected that France will issue linkers before the end of the third quarter of 1998, and we suspect at least one more of the 11 will issue inflation-linked bonds by the end of 1999.

ISSUANCE CONSIDERATIONS

The Structure

As with any new product, the issuance of inflation-linked securities requires a fair amount of forethought and planning. Once the decision has been made to issue inflation-linked bonds a number of issues need to be resolved. While a standard structure is beginning to emerge, different countries have developed very different structures. The U.S. structure, the most recent to be unveiled, is very similar to both that of Canada and Sweden, and early discussions lead us to believe the French will adopt a structure substantially similar to that of the United States.

The structure of inflation-linked bonds in Britain is quite different than that of the United States, Canada, or Sweden. The U.K. issues incorporate an 8-month lag, significantly longer than that of the U.S. issues. In January 1998, the Bank of England released a survey addressing the structure of the linkers market. One of the topics of the survey involved the possibility of restructuring the U.K. linkers to look more similar to the U.S. and Canadian linkers markets.

Of the governments that have issued linkers, the U.K. has the largest amount outstanding. After less than 18 months in the market, the United States stands in the number two position. It is widely expected that the United States will surpass the U.K. in terms of linkers issuance before the end of the decade. We expect the U.S. structure, which was based on the Canadian model, will be adopted as the market standard.

Index Selection

Issuers of inflation-linked bonds must also decide how to define inflation. A number of different indices can be used as a proxy for the inflation rate. The United States ultimately selected the non-seasonally adjusted U.S. City Average All Items Consumer Price Index for All Urban Consumers (NSA CPI-U), but the use of other indices as the benchmark for inflation was considered. Most recently, France opted to use the French CPI as the index for its upcoming inflation-linked notes, but the use of a Euro inflation rate was also contemplated. Understandably, the selection of an appropriate inflation benchmark is an important part of the structuring process. As discussed later, the market must be comfortable with the index as an accurate measure of the inflation rate. It is also beneficial if a certain portion of the investment community has a liability similar to the selected index.

One of the issues that has consumed many investors and potential investors in the U.S. market is the calculation of the Consumer Price Index (CPI). The Boskin Commission, a blue ribbon panel established by the U.S. Congress to evaluate the construction of the CPI, released its report in late 1996, shortly prior to the initial auction of U.S. inflation-linked notes. The Commission estimated that the CPI overstated the actual rate of inflation by approximately 1.1%. The Commission found that there were a number of biases in the calculation and made a number of recommendations regarding the computation of the CPI. The findings of the Commission created concern among many potential purchasers of the Treasury's soon-to-be issued inflation-linked notes.

Prior to the initial auction, the market's fears were assuaged to some degree by statements from the U.S. Treasury. Changes have been made to CPI since the first issuance of inflation-linked notes, but these changes were not a result of any legislative action. The Bureau of Labor Statistics (BLS) periodically recalibrates CPI to take into account changes in the economy. Changes to CPI have already shaved approximately 0.4% off the inflation index, and changes that are to be incorporated during 1998 and 1999 are expected to reduce the inflation benchmark by an additional 0.3%. One of the pending changes is the method used to calculate the CPI. Presently, the BLS uses an arithmetic mean to calculate the rate, but beginning in 1999 the BLS will use a geometric mean for certain subcomponents. This change should account for approximately 0.2% of the reduction that will take hold in 1999.

It is this last change which appears to most infuriate holders of inflation-linked securities. While the market understands that the government must make adjustments to the CPI from time-to-time, it is more difficult to accept a change in methodology that will clearly have a negative impact on the calculation of the inflation rate. In fact, some owners of inflation-linked notes believe they should be compensated for the change in methodology.

Similar grumbling can be heard from investors down under. In late 1997, both the governments of Australia and New Zealand decided to remove the mortgage interest charges from the calculation of CPI. The housing component will be removed from the Australian CPI in 1998, and from the New Zealand index in 1999. During the mid-1990s the fall in the mortgage interest costs helped to reduce the CPI and therefore reduce the return on linkers. As of this writing, inflation is low in Australia, and investors are upset because they rode the housing-led fall in inflation down and will not be the beneficiary of an increase in mortgage interest changes once inflation comes back.

In each of the above situations the investors in inflation-linked bonds believed they were being negatively impacted by governmental decisions. In the United States a number of government payments are based on the level of CPI, and therefore the government has an incentive to keep the inflation rate measure as low as possible.

Taxability

One of the issues that governments have wrestled with regarding the issuance of linkers is whether to make the interest on these securities taxable or tax-exempt. The United States, the most recent member of the club, opted for the taxable route. The interest paid and interest accrued are taxable income. Many market participants believe the decision to tax accrued interest limits the market potential for inflation-linked bonds. The concern is that individual investors will not purchase the securities due to the phantom tax issue — a holder must pay taxes on income that has been accrued but not yet received. We believe this concern is overstated, as much of the retirement investing in the United States is done via special accounts, such as individual retirement accounts (IRA) and 401(k) plans. Securities held in these accounts are not subject to taxation until the funds are withdrawn. Furthermore, individual investors have been very active in the Treasury STRIPS market. Owners of STRIPS face a similar, in fact more severe, tax issue and this has not deterred the success of STRIPS with individual investors.

The Bank of England and the British government took a different tack. In the U.K. the aim is to tax only the real return. Therefore investors are allowed to offset the inflation escalation of principal against their income tax bill each year. Private investors are not liable for paying taxes on the capital appreciation. While this tax feature has helped to make the linkers very popular with individual investors, it is believed that this special tax treatment has also hindered the development of a non-government market for inflation-linked securities.

Distribution

Another decision that needs to be made by the issuing government is the best method to distribute the inflation-linked securities. In the United States, the Treasury conducts quarterly Dutch auctions as its means of selling the notes. Traditional 2- and 5-year U.S. Treasury notes are also sold via a Dutch auction, whereas 3-, 10-, and 30-year notes are distributed through a traditional auction. Australia, Canada, and New Zealand also distribute their inflation-linked securities via auctions.

The U.K. currently uses a "tap" system to issue inflation-linked gilts, but the expectation is the authorities will move to an auction system in the near future. In each fiscal year's financing remit, U.K. authorities set a target for gross gilt sales based upon a budget deficit forecast. Within that figure, a target proportion of funding do be done in linkers is set (20% for the 1997/98 year). A tap is announced in a given gilt in a given size for sale at a fixed price. Bids are invited on a first come, first served basis until the tap is completed. The authorities reserve the right to adjust the price according to market conditions. Participation in the tap is limited to gilt-edged market makers (primary dealers). Individual investors in the U.K. can purchase inflation-linked securities at the post office — much the way individuals in the United States can purchase savings bonds at local banks.

Sweden employs an "open tap" system where it is continuously buying and selling securities in the market, often to facilitate swaps from one maturity to another.

Another way to distribute inflation-linked securities, especially in the early stages, is via a selling group. Fannie Mae, a U.S. government sponsored enterprise, is employing this technique for distributing its Benchmark (traditional) Note program.

Education

Educating investors and the public about inflation-linked bonds is a vital part of the process to having a successful linkers program. For many individual investors the relationship between yield and price on a fixed-rate bond can seem to be counter intuitive. Inflation-linked bonds are more complicated than nominal bonds and therefore require additional hand holding. In order to attract investors to this new asset class, investors need to understand how the security works. One of the reasons that investors in the U.K. have been involved with U.S. linkers is that U.K. investors understand the market. Inflation-linked bonds will become more popular in the United States as investors develop a better understanding of the asset class. The issuing government need not shoulder the full responsibility for educating investors. In fact, the country's primary dealers should play a large role in the education process through research reports and other publications.

Market Experience

If a picture is worth a thousand words then Exhibits 1 to 5 provide a powerful argument for the issuance of inflation-linked securities. In each of the five countries, the inflation rate, as measured by CPI (RPI in the U.K.), is lower today than when linkers were first issued. While we are not claiming that the issuance of inflation-linked bonds is the cure for inflation, it is an interesting coincidence.

The U.S. linkers market is in its infancy, but we are convinced the market will expand for inflation-linked securities as investors develop a better understanding of this unique asset class — neither stock not bond. We do not credit the emergence of the Treasury Inflation Indexed Securities with the fall in the U.S. inflation rate, but the government, and therefore the taxpayers, are being rewarded for the low rate of inflation.

CONCLUSION

The U.S. Treasury's issuance of inflation-linked securities in early 1997 drew a great deal of attention in the international bond markets, but the United States was far from the first to issue linkers. Long before the U.S. issued inflation-linked bonds a number of other countries, including the United Kingdom, Sweden, Australia, and Canada, to name a few, reached the conclusion that the issuance of inflation-linked securities made good sense. More than 20 nations have issued inflation-linked securities, and several more are expected to issue them in the near future. The governmental issuance of inflation-linked securities represents a win-win situation for the issuer and the investor: we expect the number of governments issuing linkers will continue to grow.

Exhibit 1: United States

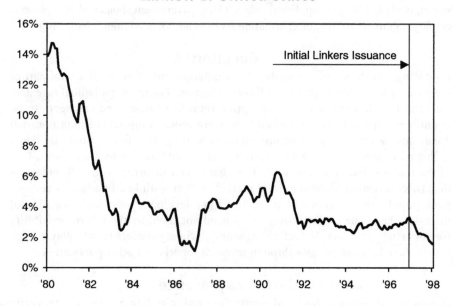

Exhibit 2: United Kingdom

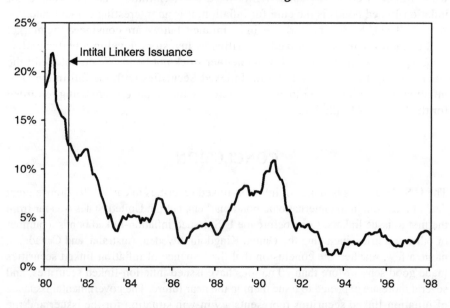

Exhibit 3: Sweden

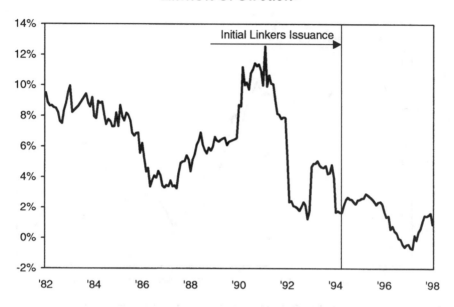

Exhibit 4: Canada

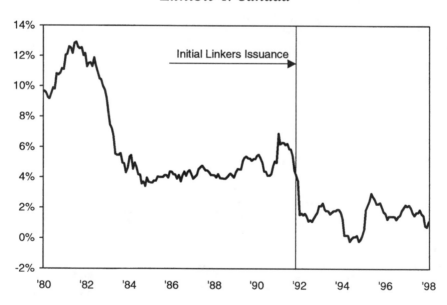

Exhibit 5: Australia

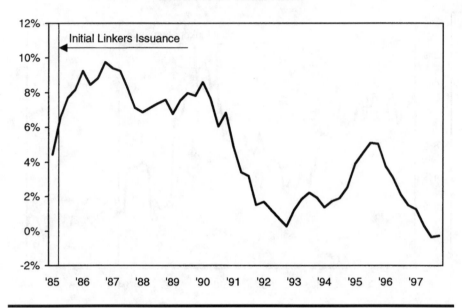

Chapter 18

Corporate and Agency Inflation-Linked Securities

Andrew Rosen
Analyst
Salomon Smith Barney

Michael Schumacher
Director
Salomon Smith Barney

John Casaudoumecq
Managing Director
Salomon Smith Barney

INTRODUCTION

The U.S. Treasury Department's auction of its first Treasury Inflation Protection Securities (TIPS) in January 1997 catalyzed a flurry of inflation-linked agency and corporate issuance. Although as of this writing issuance of inflation-linked bonds has subsided, many investors now view inflation-linked securities as a distinct asset class, and believe the sector is here to stay.

MARKET OVERVIEW

In addition to the U.S. Treasury, entities as diverse as federal agencies, commercial banks, investment banks, and corporate finance subsidiaries have issued inflation-linked securities. Exhibit 1 lists the dollar denominated inflation-linked issues in the United States through March 1997. Each issue to-date has been investment grade. Although demand for inflation-linked securities could still grow, so far secondary trading has been light, and issuance has ebbed. With the Treasury announcing that it intends to issue 2-, 5-, 10-, and 30-year TIPS, liquidity and market awareness should grow and additional issues are a possibility.

249

Exhibit 1: Dollar Denominated Inflation-Linked Issues

Issuer	Sector	Coupon	Issue Date	Term (years)	Size ($ millions)
Anchor Savings	Bank	CPI+3.00	Aug-88	20.0	20
Federal Farm Credit	Agency	CPI+3.00	Feb-97	5.0	100
Federal Home Loan Bank	Agency	CPI+3.15	Feb-97	5.0	300
Federal Home Loan Bank	Agency	CPI+3.37	Feb-97	10.0	100
Fannie Mae	Agency	CPI+3.14	Mar-97	5.0	100
J.P. Morgan & Company	Bank	CPI+4.00	Feb-97	15.0	200
Korea Development Bank	Bank	CPI+3.40	Mar-97	5.0	300
Merrill Lynch & Co.	Investment Bank	CPI+3.00	Mar-97	5.0	25
NationsBank Corp.	Bank	CPI+3.25	Feb-97	5.0	100
Salomon Inc.	Investment Bank	3.65	Feb-97	5.0	450
Sallie Mae	Agency	CPI+2.90	Feb-97	3.0	200
Toyota Motor Credit Corp.	Finance Co.	CPI+3.20	Feb-97	5.0	100
Tennessee Valley Authority	Agency	3.375	Feb-97	9.9	300

STRUCTURES

Inflation-linked bonds are essentially long-term debentures whose coupon varies with the inflation rate. Typically, the inflation rate is measured by changes in the Consumer Price Index (CPI). Inflation-linked corporate bonds have been issued in two structures: non-accreting and accreting. In the *non-accreting structure*, the investor receives a floating-rate coupon equal to a spread plus the change in the CPI. Coupons are generally paid semiannually. The non-accreting structure was utilized by nine issuers in February and March of 1997. The U.S. Treasury's TIPS program uses an accreting structure.

In an *accreting structure*, coupon payments are determined by multiplying the inflation-adjusted principal by the fixed-rate coupon. Thus, the real purchasing value of the principal is unchanged throughout the life of the bond. When the bond matures, the increased nominal value, adjusted by the change in the CPI, is paid out to the bondholder. The return of the full original principal is generally guaranteed even if a deflationary environment exists during the life of the bond. However, the notional balance used to compute interest payments could fall below the original balance in a deflationary environment.

The U.S. CPI has numerous subindices. The CPI component used for all inflation-linked issues thus far is the CPI-U (U.S. City Average All Items Consumer Price Index for All Urban Consumers) for the third preceding calendar month.

CPI SWAPS

In a CPI swap, one counterparty receives trailing CPI plus a spread while the other counterparty receives either a fixed rate or a floating rate (typically 3-month LIBOR). The spread on the CPI leg of the swap can be quoted either as a fixed amount (e.g., CPI + 4.00%), or a spread to the yield of the nearest TIPS issue. The swap can be structured as either accreting or non-accreting. As with most over-the-counter derivative products, the swap can be customized, and the specific terms are negotiated between the two counterparties.

The CPI swap market remains is in its infancy but is likely to grow as the Treasury expands its TIPS auction schedule. As the market matures, dealers will have more securities with which to hedge their CPI exposure. This will likely increase liquidity for both CPI swaps and bonds.

ISSUER STRATEGIES

A corporation may choose to issue CPI-linked bonds for a variety of reasons. Inflation-linked bonds provide a natural hedge against earnings volatility for corporations whose earnings are positively correlated with inflation. The earnings of pharmaceutical, aerospace, and natural resource companies fit these criteria and give companies concentrated in these sectors a natural incentive to enter the CPI-linked bond market.

Inflation-linked debt may also provide cheaper funding than a comparable fixed-rate or LIBOR-based issue. A corporation can use CPI swaps effectively to convert inflation-linked debt either to fixed-rate or floating-rate non-inflation-linked debt. In Exhibit 2, a company issues inflation-linked debt, then enters into a swap in which it receives CPI plus a spread and pays a fixed rate. The effective fixed rate the issuer pays is Fixed rate$_1$ + Spread$_1$ − Spread$_2$. If the issuer's inflation-linked debt is well received by the market, Fixed rate$_1$ could be lower than the rate at which the issuer could issue comparable fixed-rate debt, and inflation-linked debt could be the most efficient funding choice. Similarly, in Exhibit 3 the issuer enters into a CPI versus LIBOR swap. In this example, CPI-linked debt is attractive if LIBOR + Spread$_1$ − Spread$_2$ is below the issuer's typical floating-rate funding cost. Each of the corporate issuers in early 1997 achieved attractive floating-rate funding by entering into a swap similar to the one outlined in Exhibit 3.

Exhibit 2: Inflation-Linked Debt Plus CPI versus Fixed-Rate Swap

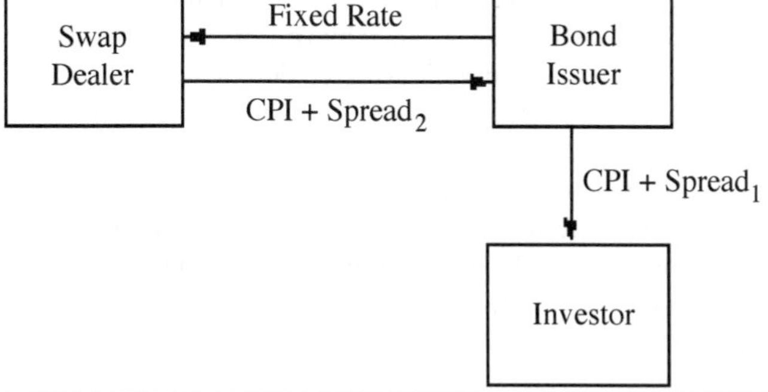

Exhibit 3: Inflation-Linked Debt Plus CPI versus LIBOR Swap

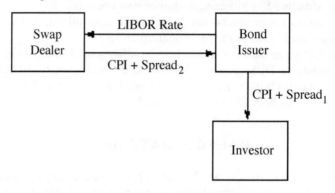

Exhibit 4: Inflation-Linked Debt Plus Fixed-Rate versus CPI Swap

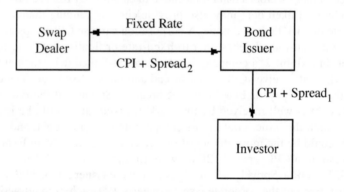

An issuer may find inflation-linked bonds attractive if it believes inflation will be lower than the market's expectation. For example, in Exhibit 4 the issuer combines inflation-linked debt with a swap in which it pays a fixed rate and receives CPI plus a spread. The issuer's swapped funding cost is Fixed rate + $Spread_1$ − $Spread_2$. If the realized CPI is below the market's forecast as implied by CPI swap spreads, then the issuer can achieve low cost funding.

Finally, issuers can use inflation-linked debt to secure long-term floating-rate funding. Floating-rate issuance in the U.S. bond market is concentrated in maturities up to five years. However, in the inflation-linked sector, long maturity floaters have been accepted by the market. Therefore, a corporation can realize the benefits of floating-rate debt but with the extended maturities not available from traditional floating-rate issuance. Furthermore, the corporation can use a CPI swap to eliminate the inflation exposure while maintaining the floating-rate nature of the liability.

INTEREST RATE RISK

Inflation-linked securities have somewhat different risk characteristics than typical fixed income products. The nominal yield of a security equals the sum of its real yield, the expected inflation rate, and the product of the real yield and the expected inflation rate.[1] If expected inflation is low, the nominal yield is approximately equal to the real yield plus the expected inflation rate. Prices and durations of securities such as non inflation-linked Treasury and corporate bonds are determined by nominal yields.

However, by definition, inflation-linked securities are effectively protected from changes in inflation. Therefore, real, not nominal, interest rates affect the prices of CPI-linked bonds. Thus, since CPI-linked bonds' yields are measured in real terms, their yields are quite low. For instance, as of March 11, 1998, the nominal yield of the on-the-run 10-year Treasury note was 5.63%, while the 10-year TIPS yielded approximately 3.70%. Because CPI-linked bonds have low real yields, they have long durations with respect to changes in real rates. However, since CPI-linked bonds are unaffected by inflation, their durations with respect to nominal interest rates are lower than those of their non-inflation-linked cousins. Consequently, hedge ratios of non-inflation-linked bonds versus comparable maturity inflation-linked bonds are typically well below 1.0.

INVESTORS

The primary buyers of the original bonds included mutual funds, pension funds, and, to a lesser extent, insurance companies. Pension funds are a natural buyer of accreting notes as they do not need to pay taxes on the increase in principal. Individual investors do not have this advantage and may find the lack of current income coupled with the increased short-term tax liability undesirable. The bonds are lightly traded in the secondary market and it is believed that most of the issues reside with the initial purchasers.

CONCLUSION

As with many new asset classes, the inflation-protected bond market is marked by illiquidity and sporadic issuance. Nonetheless, the U.S. Treasury is likely to expand TIPS auctions at the expense of traditional bullets, and the inflation-protected asset class is likely to move forward. Furthermore, inflation-protected bonds

---

[1] To see this:

$$(1 + Y_n) = (1 + Y_r) \times (1 + I)$$
$$(1 + Y_n) = 1 + Y_r + I + Y_r \times I$$
$$Y_n = Y_r + I + Y_r \times I$$

are a valuable tool in gauging the market's inflation expectations and the credibility of government fiscal and monetary policy. Inflation-linked bonds in foreign markets, including the United Kingdom and Canada, have come to be viewed as a distinct asset class. As the U.S. inflation-linked bond market matures, U.S. investors may increasingly share the view that inflation-linked assets truly are unique.

Section V:

Investors

Chapter 19

The Individual Investor and Inflation-Indexed Bonds: Tax Issues and Retirement Planning

Christopher F. Kinney
Manager
Brown Brothers Harriman & Co.

INTRODUCTION

After debating the merits of issuing inflation-indexed bonds several times in the past, the U.S. Treasury decided to begin issuing Treasury Inflation-Indexed Securities (TIIS) on a regular basis starting in early 1997. The Treasury highlighted two central benefits of TIIS: they would save the taxpayer money and they would be a good investment for the individual. This chapter explores how an individual investor should approach investments in this new asset class by examining tax and retirement planning issues. It concludes with a prescription for inclusion in the asset mix of investments designed to secure a targeted level of real (i.e., adjusted for inflation) retirement income.

NEW ASSET FOR INFLATION PROTECTION

TIIS are truly an outstanding addition to the array of financial instruments available to the individual investor. Unlike other financial assets, TIIS are by definition perfectly correlated with consumer price inflation because of the inflation adjustment to principal. In fact, over the last 50 years, inflation's correlation with stocks (−0.28), intermediate Treasury bonds (0.05), and Treasury bills (0.69) has left a gaping hole to be filled by a true inflation hedge. Other generally accepted hedging vehicles have their weaknesses. Gold has been a weak hedge against inflation, though it also serves as a hedge against unexpected political instability as well as country-specific inflation. Additionally, since gold pays no dividends, its long-run

The author wishes to thank Dr. Nicolo Goodrich Torre and Dr. Mark J. Ferrari of BARRA for their assistance.

expected real return is zero. Real estate has liquidity and leverage drawbacks and requires its own set of business analyses. With TIIS, however, the individual investor now has contractual assurance that the U.S. Treasury will guarantee purchasing power from the consequences of unpredictable events.

Since it is becoming increasingly evident that many conventional inflation indices overstate the true rate of price changes, it might be argued that with recorded inflation rates of less than 2%, we have effectively attained price stability for the first time in decades. An examination of rolling 5-year inflation over the last 50 years and its effect on the returns of stocks, bonds, and bills, however, is a sober reminder of the dangers of complacency. History suggests that reversals of favorable inflationary environments should be expected, and prudence dictates that the individual investor protect against unanticipated inflation.

Exhibit 1: Consumer Price Index — Rolling 5-Year Periods: 1947-1997

Source: Ibbottson Associates and BBH & Co.

Exhibit 2: Rolling 5-Year Real Returns: 1947-1997

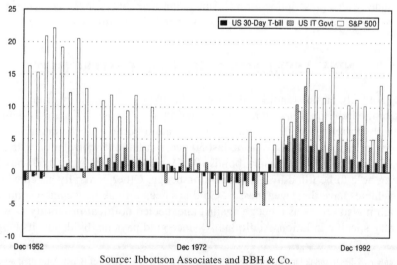

Source: Ibbottson Associates and BBH & Co.

Exhibit 3: Nominal versus Real Returns
Annualized Returns 1947-1997

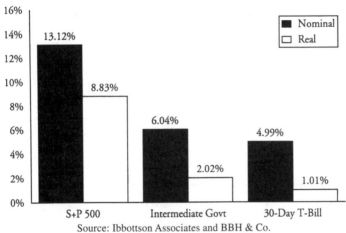

Source: Ibbottson Associates and BBH & Co.

Exhibit 4: The Efficient Frontier

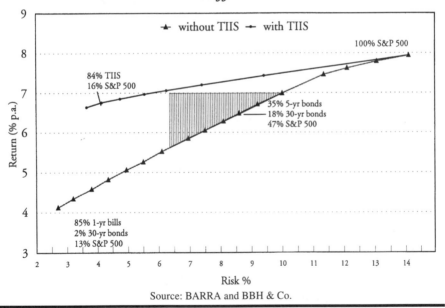

Source: BARRA and BBH & Co.

Conceptually, then, the individual investor's asset allocation would be improved with the addition of the inflation protection afforded by TIIS. The following exhibit illustrates the potential benefits provided by the inclusion of TIIS in a portfolio of stocks, bonds, and bills: TIIS improve portfolio returns for a given level of risk and reduce risk for a targeted level of return.

Exhibit 5: After-Tax Real Return
After-Tax 10-Year Horizon Real Return on TIIS (Real Coupon 3.50%)

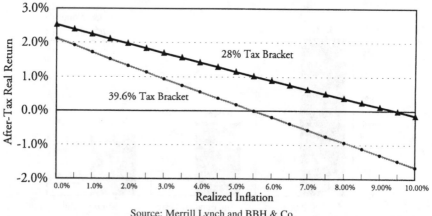

Source: Merrill Lynch and BBH & Co.

TAXES IMPAIR THE PROTECTION

Given the potential value of TIIS as a distinct asset class to complement an individual investor's traditional financial assets, the question becomes how best to incorporate them. Unfortunately, like non-indexed bonds, TIIS are taxed on inflation and this reduces the inflation protection for the taxable individual investor, as can be seen in Exhibit 5. In this example, the individual investor in the highest tax bracket will begin to have a negative after-tax real return on a 10-year TIIS with a 3.5% real coupon if inflation rises above 5.5%.

The key here is that the inflation adjustment to the principal of the TIIS is taxable as if it was a zero-coupon bond. That is, the individual is taxed assuming that the inflation compensation was paid as income each year, although the accretion to principal is not actually received until the bond matures.

Hence, the tax effect prevents the individual investor from achieving complete inflation protection, and, in fact, a higher inflation rate will result in a lower after-tax return. Let us assume, for example, that an individual in the 39.6% bracket receives a real yield of 3.5% and inflation is 2.0%. The combined nominal yield of 5.5% would generate taxes of 2.18% (5.5% × 0.396) and an after-tax nominal yield of 3.32% (5.5% × (1 − 0.396)). But the after-tax real yield is only 1.32% (3.32% − 2.0% inflation) and the effective tax rate on the real yield is 62.2% (2.18% ÷ 3.5%, or actual tax ÷ real yield).

Should inflation jump to 5.5%, this same investor would have a real after-tax yield that is negative and would have an investment with negative cash flow. The taxes on the combined nominal yield of 9% (3.5% real and 5.5% inflation) would be 3.56% which would result in an after-tax nominal yield of 5.44%, which in turn is less than inflation at 5.5%.

Exhibit 6: Tax-Deferred Real Return

Tax-Deferred 10-Year Horizon Real Return on TIIS (Real Coupon 3.50%)

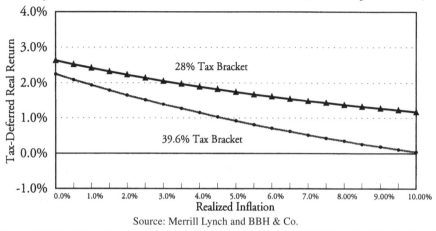

Source: Merrill Lynch and BBH & Co.

RETIREMENT PLANNING WITH TIIS
IN A TAX DEFERRED VEHICLE

The fact that the tax code penalizes the inflation-adjusted cash flow is a compelling reason for the taxable investor to shelter TIIS investments in a tax-deferred environment such as a 401(k) defined contribution retirement plan. The advantages are depicted in Exhibit 6. Here the individual investor in the highest bracket can withstand inflation rising to 10% before the tax-deferred real return becomes negative.

What are some of the variables one should consider after making the decision to place TIIS in a tax-deferred retirement plan? Specifically, given that they will play a unique role in preserving purchasing power, what percentage of the assets should they represent as one invests for retirement, and how should that percentage change as one approaches retirement? To help frame the issues and approach an answer, we use a model that incorporates essential variables for a hypothetical individual. The solutions that result suggest those combinations of stocks, bills, and TIIS, changing through time, that best accomplish the objective of achieving a targeted level of real retirement income.

The subject individual in our model saves at a constant $5,000 annual rate. All income earned prior to retirement is re-invested. After retirement, investment income and principal are spent at a rate appropriate to the investor's wealth and life expectancy. In this base case example, the minimum constant-dollar income needed to ensure the desired lifestyle is $10,000, and life expectancy is 80 years. Parameters for stocks (S&P 500) and bills (30-day) were taken from the 1953-to-present period. The TIIS has a 30-year maturity and is modeled from inflation-linked bonds available in the United Kingdom, and from recent experience in the

United States. TIIS substitute for the conventional bonds that are included in traditional asset allocations, because, in addition to their inflation protection, they offer essentially the same expected return with considerably less volatility.

Suggested Allocations to TIIS

Exhibits 7 to 15 display the changing asset mixes for an individual through time. These result from the use of a dynamic optimization that considers multiple investment horizons simultaneously. Each asset in the exhibits is not to be seen as an overlay, but rather as a percentage of the total. The asset mixes are best in the sense that changing them will not increase the annual income without increasing its variability, and that the balance chosen between increased income and reduced variability is appropriate for an investor with a moderate sensitivity to risk. As can be seen, solutions vary considerably with the commencement of savings (30, 35, and 40) and retirement (55, 60, and 65).

What is at play throughout the analysis is the trade-off between the desire for greater wealth and the fear of falling below the minimum acceptable real income requirement. For example, the individual represented in Exhibit 15, who has the longest period of investing (from age 30 to normal retirement at age 65), is the most motivated by the desire to increase wealth and the least fearful of failing to have the minimum real income in retirement. Here the allocation to stocks is large for the longest period, and because this individual is likely to accumulate the most wealth, there will be a correspondingly reduced need to protect it to ensure the minimum real income in the normal retirement period. This individual's confidence should also be enhanced by the likelihood that the salary from which benefits will be based is staying even with inflation until normal retirement age.

Exhibit 7: Retirement Planning and Asset Allocation
Age 40, Retire 55

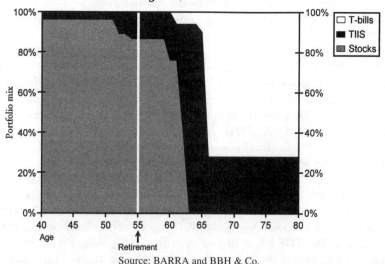

Source: BARRA and BBH & Co.

Exhibit 8: Retirement Planning and Asset Allocation
Age 40, Retire 60

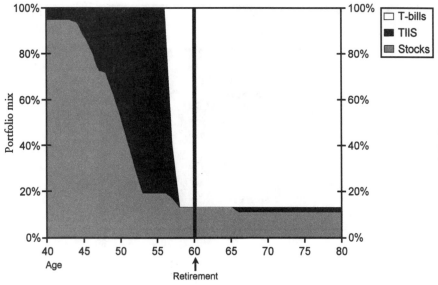

Source: BARRA and BBH & Co.

Exhibit 9: Retirement Planning and Asset Allocation
Age 40, Retire 65

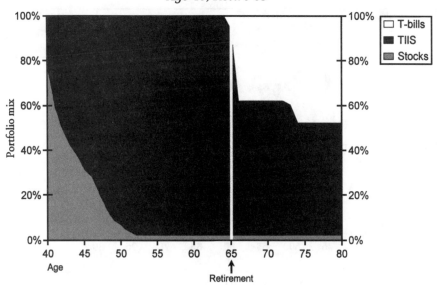

Source: BARRA and BBH & Co.

Exhibit 10: Retirement Planning and Asset Allocation
Age 35, Retire 55

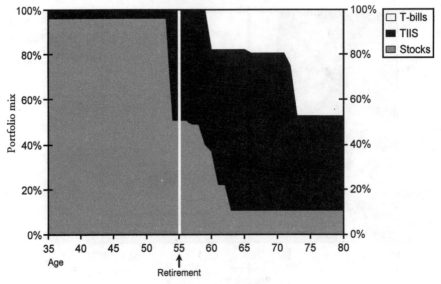

Source: BARRA and BBH & Co.

Exhibit 11: Retirement Planning and Asset Allocation
Age 35, Retire 60

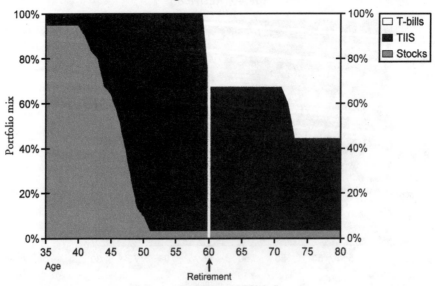

Source: BARRA and BBH & Co.

Exhibit 12: Retirement Planning and Asset Allocation
Age 35, Retire 65

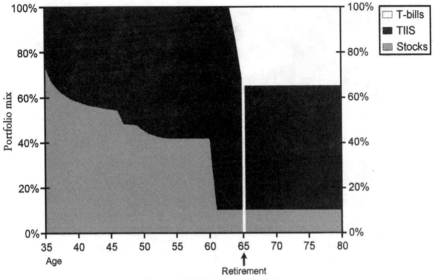

Source: BARRA and BBH & Co.

Exhibit 13: Retirement Planning and Asset Allocation
Age 30, Retire 55

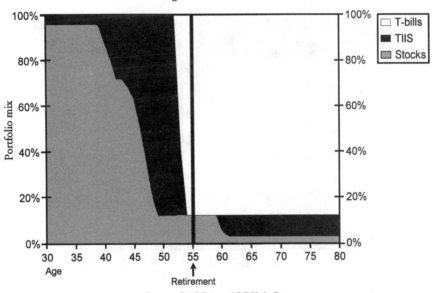

Source: BARRA and BBH & Co.

Exhibit 14: Retirement Planning and Asset Allocation
Age 30, Retire 60

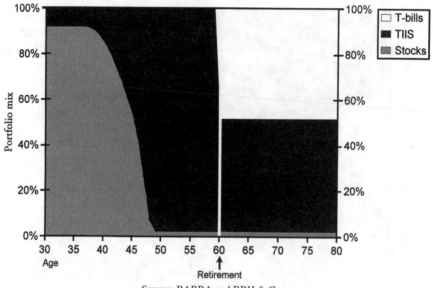

Source: BARRA and BBH & Co.

Exhibit 15: Retirement Planning and Asset Allocation
Age 30, Retire 65

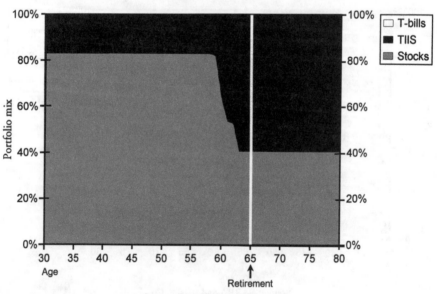

Source: BARRA and BBH & Co.

In contrast, the individuals represented in Exhibits 7, 10, and 13 are more motivated by a fear of falling below the targeted real return since theirs is the longest retirement. While they are initially aggressive during the relatively short savings period by having a large allocation to stocks, risk is abruptly curtailed as soon as their fear is assuaged. At that point, the dominant motivation is to preserve the real purchasing power of the assets that must provide for the longest period of retirement, and large allocations to TIIS and to bills are made.

Individuals represented in Exhibits 9 and 12 might be considered more typical. Having delayed the commencement of saving for retirement, there is somewhat less opportunity to build enough wealth to maintain the confident asset mix held by the individual represented in Exhibit 15. These individuals will be inclined to gradually pare back the allocation to stocks to reduce the volatility of their total portfolio. On the other hand, because of the more normal length of retirement and the relatively long period of savings which precedes it, the risk that the minimum real income might not be achieved is of less concern for these investors than it is for those represented in Exhibits 7, 10, and 13 who retire early. Hence, the shift into TIIS and bills for these individuals, while important, is not as abrupt.

These exhibits suggest other perspectives on the role that TIIS might play in retirement planning and asset allocation. One is that if the main objective for an individual is early retirement, the earlier the savings commences, the earlier a significant allocation to TIIS is called for (Exhibit 13). Conversely, if the objective is to postpone retirement to age 65, the later the savings commences, the earlier a significant allocation to TIIS is suggested (Exhibit 9). Another insight that could be drawn is that if the objective is to start saving early for retirement, TIIS play a more significant role as retirement approaches if early retirement is taken (Exhibits 13 and 14) than if retirement is postponed (Exhibit 15). On the other hand, if the objective is to wait to save for retirement, TIIS play a greater early role the later retirement is taken (Exhibits 7, 8, and 9).

The Logic of a Mutual Fund

The individual investor planning for retirement, then, will have varying and often substantial needs for allocating assets to TIIS. As with other investments in a defined contribution plan such as a 401(k), the mutual fund vehicle offers many benefits. Perhaps chief among them is exposure to professional investment management techniques designed to improve returns over those that could be achieved by a "buy and hold" strategy. These would include duration management to take advantage of general movements in interest rates, yield curve management to capture often significant reshapings of the yield curve, and varying exposure to different domestic issues, as well as hedged or unhedged foreign real return issues as they become relatively attractive.

Chapter 20

Inflation Indexed Products for Stable Value Funds

David B. LeRoux, FSA, CFA
Senior Vice President
Jackson National Life Insurance Company

Victor A. Gallo, FSA, CFA
Vice President
Jackson National Life Insurance Company

INTRODUCTION

While there has been considerable discussion of the potential use of inflation-linked products in stable value funds, few actual purchases have taken place. In this chapter we first examine the suitability of such products for stable value funds. We then go on to discuss a methodology for determining an appropriate allocation. Finally, some practical considerations in obtaining inflation indexed exposure in a stable value fund are presented.

SUITABILITY FOR STABLE VALUE FUNDS

Stable value investing evolved through time primarily in the free market environment of participants selecting investment options which suited their needs. As such, it does not come with the clearly specified boundaries of most other asset classes. To say a particular investment "fits" in a stable value fund ultimately depends on whether it is consistent with participant expectations when they allocate their funds to the stable value option of their plan.

While this is subjective, we believe that there are two criteria which most clearly embody participant expectations and which can be used to evaluate the suitability of products and investment strategies. First, the value of participant accounts allocated to this option should be strictly increasing. Second, the actual

Much of this chapter is excerpted from articles published in the September 1997 and December 1997 issues of *Stable Times*, a publication of the Stable Value Investment Association. Such material is included with permission.

participant return for any reasonably long holding period should be significantly higher than that available from money market funds.

Based on the first criterion, an inflation indexed bond held at market is not a good fit. The price of the 10-year Treasury inflation indexed bond, for example, is quite sensitive to changes in real rates, and can go down in value. In fact, during a 2-month period shortly after the initial issue in February 1997, the bond dropped in price by about 3%. For this reason, stable value funds investing in inflation indexed bonds will likely choose to hold them at book value by obtaining some form of benefit responsive protection. This protection may come in the form of a synthetic wrap, or it may be part of the product itself (such as an inflation-indexed GIC), allowing participant withdrawals at book value.

Assuming the product is held at book, then it will satisfy the first criterion. Even during a period of deflation, the Treasury bond guarantees a final principal payment at least as large as the initial principal, resulting in a nominal return of at least the real rate. Stable value funds will likely require this feature in any potential inflation indexed product. By holding the product at book value, the positive return is earned throughout the product's life and contributes well to the continuously increasing feature participants value so highly.

Regarding the second criterion, there is ample historic evidence that the real returns offered by current inflation indexed products are significantly higher than the real returns of money market funds, and comparable to the real returns of nominal bonds. For example, Exhibit 1 shows the excess of bond yields over the CPI for nominal bonds in consecutive 10-year periods over the last 30 years. The excess yields are for 3-month Treasury bills and for 3- and 5-year Treasury notes.

The excess yields of Treasury bills, which are comparable to the real returns of money market funds, look quite small compared to the real returns in the range of 3.50% to 3.75% recently offered by both the 5- and 10-year Treasury inflation indexed bonds. It seems clear that inflation indexed bonds meet the second criterion, perhaps as much as the nominal coupon instruments that are the mainstay of stable value funds.

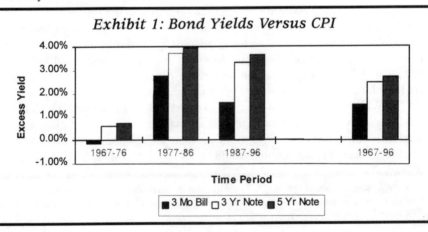

Exhibit 1: Bond Yields Versus CPI

Of course, higher real returns than shown above could have been achieved by investing in sectors other than Treasuries. However, the same is true in the inflation indexed market where significantly higher real rates may be obtained when credit or call spreads are added.

HOW MUCH OF A GOOD THING?

Once a plan sponsor or stable value manager becomes convinced of the suitability of inflation indexed products, the next question is "how much"? One technique commonly used by investment professionals faced with an asset allocation problem is "mean/variance optimization." This technique seeks to find the mix of allowable assets offering the highest expected return for a given level of risk, where risk is defined as the volatility, or standard deviation, of total return of the portfolio on a market value basis. We would argue that this is an appropriate risk measure from the fund manager's perspective for a stable value fund held at book value, since any market value underperformance is eventually passed through to participants. In addition, this risk measure assesses the likelihood that the market value of the underlying assets will diverge from the book value, creating participant equity issues and withdrawal risk.

The assumptions needed to perform a mean/variance optimization are the expected returns, standard deviations, and correlations of the asset classes under consideration. A thorough asset allocation analysis for a stable value fund would likely include many fixed income asset classes with varying credit risk, duration, convexity, etc. As a simple example, let's consider a three asset class model consisting of cash, nominal coupon bonds, and inflation indexed bonds (IIB). This illustration is based on the following assumptions.

	Expected Return	Standard Deviation	Correlations Cash	Bond	IIB
Cash	5.0%	0.5%	1.0		
Bonds	6.0%	3.5%	0.1	1.0	
IIB	5.8%	2.0%	0.1	0.2	1.0

For Cash and Bonds, these assumptions are consistent with the actual total return performance of these asset classes over the five years 1993-1997, and they approximate yields as of the date of this analysis. Since there is not much historical data for inflation indexed bonds, these assumptions must be based on other considerations, such as historical CPI data, current real rates offered by these bonds, performance of inflation indexed bonds in other countries, etc. Using an expected return for IIB equal to that of Bonds seems reasonable considering the relative real return results of these two asset classes described above. To be conservative in determining an allocation to IIB, we have arbitrarily reduced this to a return 20 basis points below that of the Bond asset class. This reduction may also be thought to represent the inflation risk premium that nominal bonds theoretically pay to compensate investors for the risk of inflation.

Exhibit 2: Allocation Among Cash, Bond, and IIB to Optimize Return per Unit of Risk

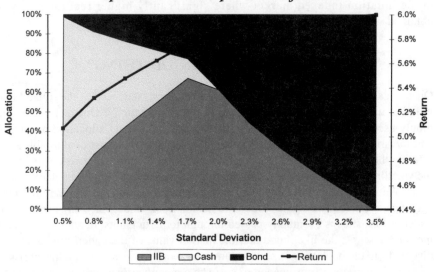

The standard deviation for IIB depends upon the volatility of the CPI, the volatility of real rates, and the "real duration" of the IIB. Since real rates are likely to be much more stable than nominal rates, it makes sense that the standard deviation assumption for IIB be lower than that for Bonds. To date, the price volatility of the 10-year inflation indexed Treasury has been about half that of 10-year nominal bonds. The assumption above is likely a high estimate for the volatility of the 5-year inflation indexed Treasury issued around the time of this analysis.

Another important assumption for this analysis is the correlation of the Bond and IIB returns, for which, again, there is little historical data in the United States. It is clear that these two asset classes do not move in tandem, since an unexpected increase in inflation will cause an increase in returns for IIB and a decrease in returns for Bonds, at least in the short run. The assumption shown in the table is close to the actual correlation between nominal Treasury bonds and the inflation indexed Treasury since it was issued.

Once you accept the assumptions, and the underlying assumptions of modern portfolio theory, the rest is just math. For each level of risk tolerance (expressed in terms of standard deviation of return for the overall portfolio) there is a mix of these asset classes that will produce the highest expected return. For these assumptions, the results are shown in Exhibit 2.

Even using assumptions which should lead to a low weighting, the model gives a sizable allocation to inflation indexed bonds. Without inflation indexed products, the stable value manager's primary method of reducing risk is by shortening duration, or in this simplified example, by holding more cash. By introducing an asset class which is not highly correlated with nominal coupon instruments, the stable value manager has a new way to reduce risk. Alternatively, the manager can keep overall risk at the same level and boost return by allocating a portion of the portfolio to inflation indexed products and taking slightly higher risks in the areas of credit, duration, and convexity. In either case, the resulting portfolio is more efficient through better diversification of risks.

This type of analysis is not highly dependent upon the exact assumptions chosen. For any set of assumptions where IIB has an expected return premium over cash and only a moderate correlation to Bonds, the moderate risk portfolios will contain a significant allocation to inflation indexed securities. Why, then, have stable value funds not begun making allocations to these products? It is likely due to the novelty of the asset class and the lack of spread product, rather than to serious differences of opinion on the suitability of inflation indexed products to stable value funds.

INFLATION INDEXED PRODUCT CHOICES

Once a decision is made to allocate a portion of the stable value fund to inflation indexed products, the next question is which vehicle to use. At a high level, the choices are similar to those for nominal rate products: (1) buy a bundled product backed by the credit of an insurance company or other financial institution (i.e., an inflation indexed GIC); (2) create the product synthetically by buying inflation indexed bonds and a benefit responsive wrap; or (3) buy inflation indexed bonds without a wrap and hold them at market. In our opinion, the last option is not a good choice for the same reason as with nominal bonds, i.e., because the market value volatility can be greatly reduced for the small price of a benefit responsive wrap.

The choice between a bundled insurance company product and a synthetic product has all the same considerations as with nominal products, plus some new ones. The primary arguments in favor of a bundled approach are: flexibility in tailoring the product to a plan's particular needs, provision of a credit spread in the real rate, current lack of inflation indexed bond issues, and automatic inclusion of benefit responsiveness. On the other hand, the synthetic approach offers potential for better credit diversification, greater flexibility in adjusting exposure to the inflation indexed sector, and the ability to add value through active management within the inflation indexed sector. Of course, these choices are not mutually exclusive. The current lack of inflation indexed product may argue in favor of using a combination approach.

Actively Managed Synthetic Considerations

The decision to add inflation indexed securities using an active bond manager involves a number of considerations not present with a bundled product or a buy-and-hold synthetic.

One question that arises involves whether inflation indexed securities (IIS) should be managed as a separate portfolio, or simply added to a nominal bond portfolio? The question comes down to whether the investor views the allocation as strategic or tactical.

Managers should be allowed to use IIS tactically (added to nominal portfolios) if they have expertise. Tactical allocation of IIS becomes an "arrow in the manager's quiver." But in addition to tactical allocations implemented by managers, IIS can be used as a dedicated allocation within the asset allocation process, to address structural needs. In particular, IIS provide protection against the structural problem inherent to every stable value fund — the risk of a lagging blended interest rate when market rates rise significantly. To the extent that inflation is positively correlated with nominal interest rates, an allocation to IIS allows the blended rate to better track rising rates. Such structural needs cannot, in general, be addressed through tactical use alone, and call for dedicated allocations. In such a case, it is probably better to manage a separate IIS portfolio.

Active managers must also define a strategy to be used to add value. Given the newness of the market in the United States, are there enough securities to add value by trading within inflation indexed securities?

According to John Brynjolfsson of PIMCO, some value can be added within the government/agency arena alone, mainly through managing inflation and duration exposure. A manager can also make use of a broader universe of tools, including strategies involving inflation-indexed corporates, foreign bonds (perhaps hedged), and futures (backed by cash if wanting to avoid leverage).

Designing a benchmark for a portfolio which includes inflation indexed securities is an important consideration that must be addressed when deciding to allow a manager to use IIS in the portfolio. Obviously, if IIS is used in a purely tactical manner, then the benchmark need not necessarily include any IIS itself. For structural allocations to IIS, however, there are at least two possible approaches. One approach is to create a custom hybrid benchmark by blending an inflation-linked benchmark with a traditional benchmark in weights derived from the asset allocation analysis. The account's performance as a whole (that is change in market value) can then be compared to the hybrid index performance, as a whole. Alternately, the asset classes can be managed and monitored completely separately.

Setting Duration Constraints

When dealing with nominal instruments, duration is a useful tool in measuring the price sensitivity with respect to changes in nominal interest rates. With inflation indexed products, duration usually refers to the sensitivity of the price to changes in real interest rates. Real interest rates tend to be much more stable over time than nominal interest rates, so inflation indexed products will have significantly less price volatility than nominal bonds of the same duration.

Exhibit 3: U.S. Treasury Bond Comparison

	5-Year		10-Year	
	Nominal	Inflation Indexed	Nominal	Inflation Indexed
Duration[a]	4.0	4.2	6.9	7.7
Price Volatility[b]	0.23%	0.10%	0.37%	0.17%
Correlation[c]		20%		54%

[a] Modified duration for nominal bonds and real duration for inflation indexed bonds.
[b] Standard deviation of daily percentage price change through 10/22/97.
[c] Correlation coefficient of nominal and inflation indexed daily percentage price changes.

To illustrate this point, consider Exhibit 3 which shows two inflation indexed bonds issued by the U.S. Treasury (one 10-year bond and one 5-year bond) compared to nominal Treasury bonds. This exhibit compares the daily price volatility of each of the inflation indexed bonds with the next-issued nominal bond with the same maturity. Notice that even though the durations of the inflation indexed bonds are somewhat longer (due to lower coupons), the actual price volatility is less than one-half that of the nominal bond. Furthermore, the price volatility has not been highly correlated with changes in nominal interest rates.

Based on these considerations, a plan should have greater tolerance for real duration of inflation indexed products than it does for nominal duration. Other factors to consider in selecting a real duration target include real rate differences for different maturities (i.e., the real term structure) and views about future inflation prospects. As of this writing, the real rates offered for the 5- and 10-year inflation indexed Treasuries have been quite close to each other, indicating a flat real term structure. The real rates offered by products with a credit component are generally more upward-sloping.

Selecting Payout Patterns

Inflation indexed Treasuries pay coupons of the real rate and accrue the inflation component by increasing the principal. This payout pattern, which is called the "Canadian" structure, is also used by some corporate and agency issues. Other issues use a "current pay" structure, under which both the real return and the inflation return are paid in semiannually coupons, leaving the principal amount constant. Inflation indexed GICs are available with either of these payout patterns, or any other pattern a plan may choose (e.g., a compound, or zero-coupon, structure which pays everything at maturity). An actively managed portfolio of inflation indexed securities also allows for flexibility in design of the payout pattern. Regardless of the payout pattern selected, the participant accounts should be credited with both the real and inflation returns.

Considerations which affect the choice of a payout pattern include: the liquidity needs of the stable value fund, the desired future allocation levels to the inflation indexed sector, the real duration target, and relative value comparisons among instruments with different payout patterns.

Crediting Rate Formula

There are several product design possibilities with an inflation indexed GIC, and it is too early to say whether one approach will become dominant. One possibility is to define the crediting rate for each period as a fixed real rate plus a recent past measure of inflation. For example, the contract could credit a real rate of 3.50% plus the annualized rate of inflation based on the last six months of published CPI data. All benefit responsive withdrawals and maturities would be paid at book value, and no adjustment would be made if inflation during the period turns out different than the past inflation assumed in the crediting rate. This approach has the advantage of simplicity and a crediting rate which is known prior to each reset period. It has the disadvantage of high volatility in the crediting rate due to fluctuations in the CPI, which may be a problem if a significant portion of the stable value fund is based on this formula.

To overcome the rate volatility problem, a "smoothed" crediting rate technique may be used. A wide variety of smoothing formulas are possible, but they generally will look similar to the renewal rate formulas with synthetic GICs. The renewal rate will be determined periodically to be equal to the real rate plus an estimate for inflation, and the result will be adjusted to amortize any gains or losses from past inaccuracies of the inflation estimate. Because the inflation estimation errors will be corrected in the renewal rate calculation, a more stable, long-term estimate may be used for the inflation rate, resulting in a more stable crediting rate. As with the prior structure, insurance companies should be willing to offer this on a non-experience rated basis with respect to benefit responsive withdrawals.

To illustrate these two approaches, consider the crediting rates that would have emerged under two, hypothetical inflation-indexed GICs begun in 1970. One GIC credits actual inflation plus a real rate, and the other uses a smoothing formula, as follows:

$$\text{Rate} = (IC/A)^{1/d} \times (1 + g) - 1$$

where

IC = the value of the contract had actual inflation been used in crediting interest instead of a smoothed interest rate

A = the actual value of the contract, using the smoothed rate

d = the remaining, real duration of the contract (although any period shorter than this can be arbitrarily used for these purposes)

g = some assumed rate of total yield (real plus inflation) over the remaining life of the contract. For instance, one may assume that future inflation will equal the prior 12 months of actual inflation.

Exhibit 4 illustrates the effectiveness of the smoothing technique. Both contracts provide the same return over the period, they just credit that return in a different pattern.

Exhibit 4: Crediting Actual versus Smoothed Inflation

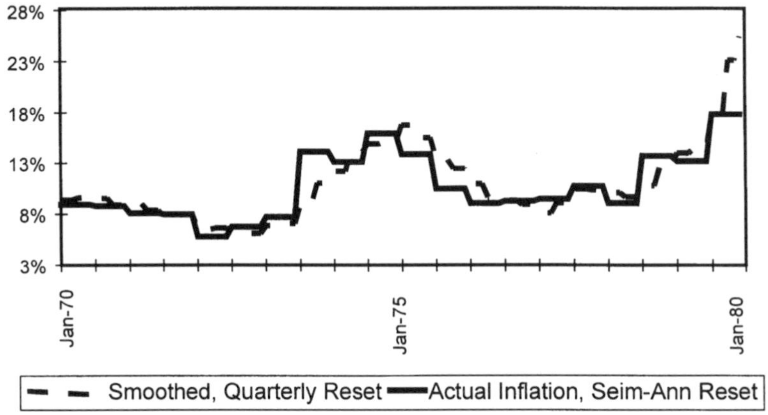

| — — Smoothed, Quarterly Reset ——Actual Inflation, Seim-Ann Reset |

The benefit responsive wraps for synthetic products will likely use the "smoothed" crediting rate approach described above. For a buy-and-hold synthetic, the gains/losses may be amortized over the remaining real duration of the assets to ensure convergence of book and market values. For an actively managed synthetic, the smoothing period is somewhat arbitrary prior to the termination phase. If the inflation indexed securities are held as part of a largely nominal bond portfolio which is benchmarked against a nominal bond index, the duration of the benchmark index is probably a suitable amortization period.

An important consideration for both issuers and purchasers of benefit responsive inflation indexed products is that the risk of benefit responsive withdrawals should be significantly lower than with nominal rate products. Issuers charge for benefit responsive risk because they believe that participants will find other investment alternatives more attractive if interest rates move up to a point where a plan's blended rate lags prevailing market rates. If this were to occur, issuers would suffer losses on nominal rate products (traditional GICs and synthetic wraps). However, if there is a low correlation between nominal rates and real rates, issuers might be almost as likely to find themselves in a gain position in this scenario with inflation indexed GICs and wraps. The result should be greater willingness of issuers to assume the benefit responsive risk and to do so on a non-experience rated basis. On the other hand, plan sponsors should also be more willing to self-insure this risk via experience rating.

CONCLUSION

Theoretical asset allocation arguments strongly suggest including inflation indexed products within a stable value fund. There are no serious practical problems in doing this. The largest obstacles seem to be in getting decision-makers comfortable with this new asset class.

Chapter 21

Inflation Protection Bonds and Endowment or Foundation Investment Policy

William A. Schneider, CIMA
Managing Director
DiMeo, Schneider & Associates, L.L.C.

INTRODUCTION

Treasury Inflation Protection Securities (TIPS) and other types of inflation protection bonds (IPBs) represent a new asset class. While these instruments are relatively new instruments in the United States, other governments have utilized them for years. As of this writing, the U.S. Treasury Department has auctioned 5-year, 10-year, and 30-year TIPS. They are issued with a stated *real* rate of return. Every six months the bond's principal amount is adjusted based on changes in the Consumer Price Index (CPI). The semiannual interest payment is calculated by multiplying the new principal amount by one-half the stated rate. Several corporations have issued IPBs. The advantage to the issuer is lower interest expense. The advantage to the purchaser of IPBs is a positive rate of return even in periods of rising inflation. The purchaser should also enjoy less price volatility.

IPBs have special applications for endowment and foundation funds. In this chapter, I will offer a brief examination of the unique characteristics of endowments and foundations, asset allocation (particularly the essential inputs), nominal bonds, IPBs, and risks inherent in their analysis.

ENDOWMENTS AND FOUNDATIONS

Endowment and foundation funds share many characteristics with other institutional pools of money (defined benefit pension plans, defined contribution retirement plans, insurance company reserves, etc.). However, there are some crucial differences. The first difference is that there is generally a spending requirement. To preserve the tax-exempt status of the fund, at least 5% of the assets must be paid out per year.

279

The second difference is that the investment committee that oversees such a fund is typically a volunteer group. The members are usually intelligent people, often highly respected in their particular field. But the financial understanding of the group may be very uneven. There is often a tendency toward an overly conservative investment posture. (It's human nature to regret a loss more than a missed opportunity for an equal gain).

One particularly problematic tendency is that of categorizing return into "income" and "capital gains." The idea that "we can only spend income" is inherently flawed. In times of low interest rates, this posture forces the fund into a large percentage of debt instruments, virtually assuring that there won't be enough growth to stay ahead of inflation.

A more savvy approach is the *total return concept*. Return is return regardless of the source. This is important in that stocks have produced a far greater total return than bonds although less *income*. For example, according to Ibbotson Associates, the growth of a $1,000 investment in cash, bonds, stocks, and small stocks over the 1946-1996 period was $10,425, $16,760, $302,190, and $670,172, respectively.

ASSET ALLOCATION

Once an investment committee adopts the total return concept, it has begun to solve the problem. However, the question is not which is the highest returning asset class, but rather how can we mix various types of investments to achieve the best blend of risk and return? Fortunately, modern portfolio theory includes very specific asset allocation techniques. Since capital market returns fall into (relatively) normal distributions, one can use mean/variance analysis to devise optimal allocations. (There are other approaches including downside risk analysis that produce somewhat different outputs.)

Computer programs called optimizers calculate efficient allocations, i.e. the mix with the highest expected return at each risk level. *A word of caution*: Optimizers are forecasting tools. And, to paraphrase Yogi Berra, "Forecasting can be hazardous, especially if it involves the future."

These programs use three inputs in order to calculate the *efficient frontier*. An example of an efficient frontier is presented later in this chapter. The inputs are the *expected return* for each asset class, the *volatility* of each class (as measured by the standard deviation of the returns), and the *correlation coefficients* among the various asset classes. The first challenge is to come up with reasonable estimates for these inputs.

Correlation coefficients measure the interaction between assets. Correlations tend to be relatively stable over time. The volatility of each particular asset class is perhaps a little less stable; that is, there tends to be periods of greater and lesser volatility of returns. Expected return, however, is the wild card. Returns vary enormously from period to period. For example, in the 1970s large company stocks returned an average of 5.9% per year; in the 1980s they averaged 17.5% per year.[1]

If the estimated inputs are off, the optimizer becomes an "error maximizer." The classic rookie mistake is to blindly accept recent market results as inputs for the optimization process. If one uses real (after inflation) numbers the problem is minimized somewhat. We will discuss the estimates we've utilized.

The input with the greatest effect on the optimization process is correlation. Non-positive correlating assets reduce portfolio volatility. That is, if a portfolio contains two asset classes and one zigs when the other zags (negative correlation), you'll enjoy the best of all worlds: the blended return of both and little overall volatility. In the real world there are very few asset classes which are negatively correlated. The task is to find those classes that have *low* correlation with each other.

This brings us to the question of why bonds should be part of a diversified portfolio at all. Since 1926, intermediate U.S Government bonds have produced an anemic 2.4% per year over inflation. That includes the 1980s when those bonds produced 6.49% per year above inflation! In fact, in many of the decades since the 1920s, bonds have produced negative real returns![2] So why would a rational investor include such securities in a portfolio?

The answer is that the bonds are included because of their diversification effect. Their relatively low correlation with stocks dampens the inherent volatility of an all-stock portfolio. If one could find another asset class with even lower correlation with stocks and that also happened to produce positive returns above inflation, one would be able to derive optimal portfolios with higher expected real returns at almost every risk level.

NOMINAL BONDS

Traditional, or *nominal*, bonds promise to pay a stated rate of interest and to repay the lender's principal at maturity. When a bond's yield is initially set, that rate is comprised of several components. One can think of the basic component as the current inflation rate. The second building block is a real return above the current inflation rate. But since inflation rates can change over time, there is also a third component of the nominal rate, an *inflation risk premium*. This component compensates the investor for the uncertainty of future inflation. When interest rates rise in the market place, the value of existing bonds falls.

TIPS and other IPSs, however, promise to pay a stated rate of return above inflation. The principal value of such bonds and the interest income are both adjusted upward based on changes in the Consumer Price Index (CPI). There is no inflation risk component built into the bond's yield. If *real* yields rise in the market place, existing TIPS will fall in price. However, *nominal* interest rates

[1] Ibbotson Associates, *Stocks, Bonds, Bills, and Inflation 1997 Yearbook*
[2] *Ibid*

often rise because of increasing inflation or inflationary expectations. Real yields have been relatively stable. It is probable that in periods of rising inflation, TIPS and other IPBs would experience little price fluctuation.

THE BOTTOM LINE

To produce an after-inflation optimization utilizing IPBs as an asset class, we made the assumptions shown in Exhibit 1. Real returns, standard deviations, and correlation coefficients for stocks, nominal bonds, and Treasury-bills were derived from long-term historical numbers. The real return for IPBs was assumed to be 3% (below the current real rate of approximately 3.5%). Volatility was assumed to lie midway between intermediate government bonds' and Treasury bills' historic numbers. Since their return fluctuation should not be driven by either increasing inflation or increasing inflationary expectations, we assume zero correlation to nominal bonds. For the same reason and because of their low expected volatility, we also assume zero correlation with stocks. These, of course, are crucial assumptions.

Exhibits 2 and 3 show the comparison between an optimized portfolio utilizing nominal bonds (labeled current portfolio) and a portfolio including IPBs (5.95% *real* return versus 5.16%). The result is higher expected return at the same risk level.

Exhibit 1: Assumption for After-Inflation Optimization

Forecasts				Correlations			
	Asset	Real Return	Std.Dev.	1	2	3	4
1	Intermediate Bonds	2.3%	3.5%	1			
2	IPBs	3.0%	2.8%	0	1		
3	T-Bills	0.7%	2.1%	0.74	0	1	
4	Large Stocks	9.4%	10.2%	0.19	0	0.11	1

Exhibit 2: Graph of Asset Allocation Analysis
Return versus Risk (Standard Deviation)

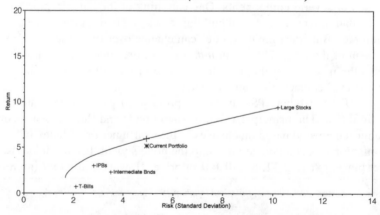

Exhibit 3: Asset Allocation Analysis Table

	Percent of Portfolio	
	Current Portfolio	IPB Portfolio
Return	5.16%	5.95%
Risk	4.95%	4.94%
R-Squared	90.92%	99.41%
Tracking Error	5.97%	5.86%
Intermediate Bonds	59.74%	0.00%
IPBs	0.00%	53.93%
T-Bills	0.00%	0.00%
Large Stocks	40.26%	46.07%

Of course, the major risk in the above analysis is that the estimates for IPBs are in error. Since these are relatively new securities, we do not have the wealth of historic data on which to rely. If such bonds turn out to have greater volatility than estimated, the relative advantage may be less.

CONCLUSION

Endowment and foundation funds face a variety of challenges. Typically there is a 5% spending requirement. That is an ongoing real liability; over time the fund must increase nominal spending in order to stay even with inflation. In addition, such funds tend toward a conservative investment posture. Inflation protection bonds may prove to be a valuable tool to help fund trustees face these challenges.

Chapter 22

Foundation Applications

Alan Heuberger
Investment Analyst
W.H. Gates Foundation

INTRODUCTION

The charitable foundation, as an entity, serves a very important social role in the United States and the world. From these foundations, billions of dollars are given each year to organizations and individuals to support some segment of society: everything from funding art museums to furthering education to feeding the hungry. Because of this, the importance of foundations is clearly evident. The foundation's monetary assets are entrusted to the foundation managers and trustees, whose main function is to direct the responsible distribution of these funds. Although the investment function is often secondary, it is probably the most important aspect of ensuring a foundation's long-term viability. This viability can be threatened by, among other things, overspending, poor returns, and inflation.

This chapter seeks to provide insight into the investment management of these eleemosynary foundations and to explain why Treasury Inflation Protection Securities (TIPS) fit into this investment framework. Foundations have some peculiar characteristics and constraints that make them different from other investment funds, and these will be outlined. It is not the case that TIPS belong in every foundation portfolio, but in general a good argument can be made for including these securities.

THE FOUNDATION AS AN INVESTMENT VEHICLE

On the surface, foundations are as diverse as the people who run them, each with its own goals and objectives, reflecting their management's differing philosophies on how best to allocate monies between consumption (in this case gifting and operating budgets) and reinvestment. However, the universal problem is apparent: take a (usually) fixed pool of capital and provide current income while preserving or growing the principal base. In other words, provide funds for perpetual operations.[1] Sounds simple enough, but in practice and at certain times in history, this

---

[1] This is not to say foundations are required to last forever. Some foundations are set up for special purposes and may only exist for short periods of time. Also, it can be argued that accelerated giving programs provide just as much benefit as their perpetual brethren.

task has proven all too difficult. For example, Exhibit 1 shows the value of $1,000,000 invested during the 10-year period from 1973 through 1982. In nominal terms the composite doubled over the period, but in real terms the assets lost over 10% of their original value. What makes this charge even more interesting and challenging are several characteristics that, when taken together, make foundations a somewhat unique animal in the financial kingdom.

The 5% Disbursement Requirement

Foundations face a federally mandated minimum payout ratio of 5% of asset value, less certain expenses. For the investment staff, this furnishes a concrete baseline for returns: provide a total return of at least 5%. But since we live in the real world, this means a *real* total return of 5%. By producing this level of real return, the foundation succeeds in meeting its disbursement requirements while maintaining the real value of the asset base from which future distributions will be made.

Taxation

For all practical purposes, as it relates to the investment management function, foundations are tax exempt. (There is a small excise tax imposed by the Internal Revenue Service of 2% of investment income, which shrinks to 1% when certain qualifying disbursements are made. There are also some penalty taxes that result if the 5% payout is not met.) With this in mind, TIPS present no possibility of negative cash flow to a foundation portfolio.

Exhibit 1: Value of $1,000,000 Invested in a Composite of Stocks and Bonds, (1973-1982)

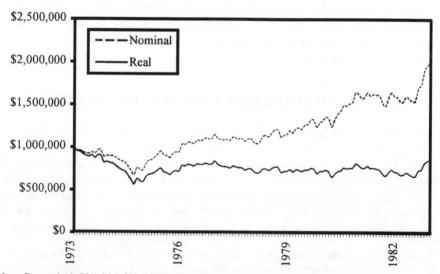

Note: Composite is 70% S&P 500, 30% Lehman Brothers Government/Corporate.

Limited Supply of Capital

Once a founding donor has gifted assets to his or her established foundation, that is usually the only infusion of capital that the fund will ever see. From then on, the management is, so to speak, "on their own." This is quite unlike pension funds or endowments that are often compared to foundations because of their non-profit, tax-exempt structures. In the case of a pension fund, the sponsoring institution can support the fund with fresh resources should there be a shortfall. For endowments, donations and capital campaigns typically provide, at the very least, a somewhat predictable source of cash. This is in contrast to the mature foundation (one in which the major donor has gifted all earmarked assets), which has nothing to lean back on but its own reserve of capital.

Self-Imposed Guidelines

Whether there is one trustee or an entire board, these are the people who oversee all aspects of the foundation's operations. From an investment standpoint, they typically will set guidelines on investment returns and impose restrictions on asset classes or particular issuers. Examples could range from the imposition of a restriction on owning so-called "sin" stocks to the determination of maximum equity exposure to the direction of program related investments. Derivatives, venture investing, and real estate are often addressed as well. Because of their hedging and diversification properties, more and more boards allow these investments, but this has not always been the case.

TIPS IN THE FOUNDATION FRAMEWORK

It is essential for portfolio managers and administrators alike to understand the somewhat unique nature of the foundation structure that is outlined above. It is not that the characteristics are hard to understand; rather, it is simply that in practice it is hard to unite all parties in a symbiotic way. Donor staff wants higher returns so they can give away more; trustees want more control and impose restrictions on certain investments; and the portfolio managers want *and* need to maintain the real asset base over time. The latter point is the most important, because the failure to do this endangers the existence of the foundation itself. The following will focus on this point in the framework of the foundation setting.

To state the obvious, TIPS work well in preserving a foundation's capital base against the specter of inflation. In fact, the securities ensure an absolute level of return after inflation, making them the best inflation hedge around. It is important to emphasize the word "hedge," because this is really what the securities are meant to do. They will not grow a portfolio over time like equities, but they will also not face negative real returns during periods of rising inflation. Other real assets, such as real estate and gold, have been promoted as inflation hedges, but as Exhibit 2 shows, only real estate is somewhat correlated with changes in the price level during the period shown. Therefore, if foundations currently hold these other real assets for the stated purpose of inflation hedging, then TIPS may well be a perfect addition or substitute to their current allocations. Granted these other asset classes may have higher historical returns, but they also have greater risk. Thus it becomes a standard asset allocation exercise, in relation to a foundation's goals, as to how much and what type of risk a portfolio should take. It seems prudent in most cases to eliminate some inflation risk and thereby make an allocation to TIPS in the portfolio, especially if assets that purport to do the same are already present.

Many foundations face real liabilities as a part of their disbursement requirements, so TIPS are an obvious complement to matching these outflows. For example, a grantee may receive a yearly donation that rises and falls over time with the level of prices. For the foundation making such payments, the use of TIPS would be an easy way to match liabilities and assets going forward. With respect to this real liability, the portfolio would be immunized against changes in the price level. It should be noted that different institutions may be exposed to different aspects of changing prices (e.g. prices for energy, services, transportation, etc.). As the asset class gains attention, more issuers will seek to place these securities with investors, and may even customize the indices used for the inflation component. The advent of these inflation protection securities, along with the forthcoming 30-year TIPS issuance, will allow managers more flexibility in matching real liabilities with an appreciating real asset.

For whatever reason, inflation hedging or real liabilities may not apply to a particular foundation, but TIPS will always present possibilities for opportunistic investment. In a disinflationary environment, TIPS will perform poorly compared to nominal Treasuries. That said, it is also during these periods when TIPS (or in other words, inflation hedging) can become relatively cheaper. So while inflation may not be worrisome as of this writing, over a long time period (25+ years) the likelihood of an inflationary episode occurring may be greater than what the markets are pricing in.[2] It is during the times when assets or asset classes have fallen out of favor that investors can often find bargains, either for a shorter-term relative value trade or for a longer-term hedging play. After all, at some price TIPS will make sense for any investor and knowing the benefits of using these securities will help the investor know where their threshold price is. Markets are dynamic; even if TIPS do not make sense currently, there is always the chance they may at some point down the road.

Exhibit 2: Correlation Based on Quarterly Returns
1981 through First Quarter, 1997

	Real Estate	Farmland	Russell 3000	Gold	Bonds
CPI	0.17	0.25	−0.26	−0.16	−0.35

Source: Frank Russell Company, Lehman Brothers, NCREIF

[2] A look at break-even inflation rates is an easy way to determine what level of inflation the market is pricing in. If the break-even is too low in relation to an investor's forward projection of inflation, then the securities are relatively cheap to their nominal counterparts. It is also useful to track the break-even level from a historical perspective to see how inflation expectations have changed relative to where they are at present.

As a final point on TIPS and their use in foundation portfolios, it is often the case that whenever a foundation is dealing in a new or exotic asset class, there is usually a board of trustees to contend with. Whereas certain types of derivatives and commodities might not be allowed in the portfolio, TIPS, albeit a "new" instrument, are still Treasury obligations and as such fit neatly into most current guidelines. This also makes them easy to explain and even easier to justify: if the "end" is to hedge inflation, then this is the best "means" around.

SUMMARY

Inflation, or simply the possibility of it occurring, is a big risk to any pool of investment assets. To a foundation, with its somewhat quirky elements, the risks are even greater. If not properly hedged, inflation can eat away at the investment base, reducing the real value of the assets, thereby reducing the giving potential of the entity and harming the beneficiaries who depend on foundations for funding. From a portfolio manager's perspective, and more importantly from society's standpoint, this is not a good outcome. It is difficult to know how much inflation protection foundations need. In an inflationary period the answer is probably, "There is never enough protection," but contrast that to today's disinflationary environment where one might hear the apathetic, "Why worry about it?", and it is easy to see how fickle investors can be over time. The true answer lies somewhere in between, and for this reason attention should be given to this emerging asset class and the uses it has in a portfolio. Like any other security or asset class, TIPS should be viewed as another important tool in the investor's toolbox, an indispensable one when considering foundations.

Index

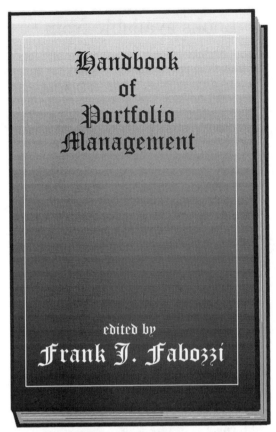

HANDBOOK OF PORTFOLIO MANAGEMENT
Frank J. Fabozzi, Editor
1998 Hardcover $89

Books available from
Frank J. Fabozzi Associates

Fixed Income Securities, Analysis, and Portfolio Management

Book	Price	QTY	Sub Total
Bond Portfolio Management	$65.00		
Fixed Income Securities	$65.00		
Managing Fixed Income Portfolios	$75.00		
Valuation of Fixed Income Securities and Derivatives 3rd. Ed.	$60.00		
Selected Topics in Bond Portfolio Management	$45.00		
Advanced Fixed Income Analytics	$65.00		
Treasury Securities and Derivatives	$53.00		
Managing MBS Portfolios	$60.00		
Corporate Bonds: Structures & Analysis	$65.00		
Collateralized Mortgage Obligations: Structures and Analysis	$50.00		
The Handbook of Corporate Debt Instruments	$87.00		
Handbook of Structured Finance Products	$95.00		
Asset-Backed Securities	$75.00		
The Handbook of Commercial Mortgage-Backed Securities – 2nd Ed.	$95.00		
Trends In Commercial Mortgage-Backed Securities	$85.00		
Handbook of Nonagency Mortgage-Backed Securities	$95.00		
Basics of Mortgage-Backed Securities	$42.00		
Advances in the Valuation & Mgmt. of Mortgage-Backed Securities	$65.00		
Valuation of Interest-Sensitive Financial Instruments	$55.00		
Perspectives on International Fixed Income Investing	$60.00		
Handbook of Emerging Fixed Income and Currency Markets	$75.00		
The Handbook of Stable Value Investments	$95.00		
Inflation Protection Bonds	$42.00		
Bank Loans: Secondary Market and Portfolio Management	$69.00		

Equity and Fixed Income

Book	Price	QTY	Sub Total
Handbook of Portfolio Management	$89.00		
Analysis of Financial Statements	$55.00		
Introduction to Quantitative Methods For Investment Managers	$58.00		

Risk Management and Derivatives

Book	Price	QTY	Sub Total
Measuring and Controlling Interest Rate Risk	$55.00		
Dictionary of Financial Risk Management	$45.00		
Risk Management: Framework, Methods, and Practice	$90.00		
Perspectives on Interest Rate Risk Management for Money Managers and Traders	$60.00		
Essays In Derivatives	$42.00		

Equity Portfolio Management

Book	Price	QTY	Sub Total
Active Equity Portfolio Management	$70.00		
Applied Equity Valuation	$65.00		
Handbook of Equity Style Management – Second Edition	$65.00		
Foundations of Economic Value-Added	$49.00		
Selected Topics in Equity Portfolio Management	$45.00		
Professional Perspectives on Indexing	$75.00		
Equity Management	TBA		
Investing By the Numbers	$58.00		

Other investment topics

Book	Price	QTY	Sub Total
Modeling the Market: New Theories and Techniques	$55.00		
Securities Lending and Repurchase Agreements	$85.00		
Pension Fund Investment Management – Second Edition	$95.00		
Credit Union Investment Management	$55.00		
Investment Management for Insurers	$125.00		
Perspectives on Investment Management of Public Pension Funds	$65.00		
The Use of Derivatives in Tax Planning	$150.00		
Issuer Perspectives on Securitization	$60.00		

Other Books Distributed By Frank J. Fabozzi Associates

Book	Price	QTY	Sub Total
The Handbook of Fixed Income Securities – 5th Ed. (Irwin, 1997)	$95.00		
Fixed Income Mathematics 3rd. Ed. (Irwin, 1996)	$60.00		
The Handbook of Mortgage-Backed Securities 4th Ed. (Irwin, 1996)	$85.00		
Advanced Fixed Income Portfolio Management (Probus, 1994)	$65.00		
Active Total Return Mgmt. of Fixed Income Portfolios (Irwin, 1995)	$65.00		
Handbook of Fixed Income Options – Revised Ed. (Probus, 1995)	$65.00		
Handbook of Asset/Liability Management – Revised Ed. (Irwin, 1996)	$75.00		

Totals:

Shipping Charge*:
(Domestic orders, $4 for the first book, $1 each additional)

Total:

To order: please check the books you would like to order, fill out the form below, and send along with check to Frank J. Fabozzi Associates, 858 Tower View Circle, New Hope, PA 18938.

Name:
Company:
Address:

City:
State:
Zip:
Phone:
FAX:
Email:

MAKE CHECK PAYABLE TO: FRANK J. FABOZZI.   Sorry, no credit card sales.
All foreign orders must be paid by check in US funds, drawn on US banks. *International or bulk orders please call for shipping estimate: (215) 598-8930 Visit our WW Web site: www.frankfabozzi.com